May God Rich y
You Always !

Thank you for your Support !

my little piece
of sunshine

Angela Will

ANGELA WILLS

my little piece of sunshine

Bryanna Faith's Story

TATE PUBLISHING
AND **ENTERPRISES**, LLC

Published by Tate Publishing & Enterprises, LLC
127 E. Trade Center Terrace | Mustang, Oklahoma 73064 USA
1.888.361.9473 | www.tatepublishing.com

Tate Publishing is committed to excellence in the publishing industry. The company reflects the philosophy established by the founders, based on Psalm 68:11,
"The Lord gave the word and great was the company of those who published it."

Book design copyright © 2013 by Tate Publishing, LLC. All rights reserved.
Cover design by Rodrigo Adolfo
Interior design by Joana Quilantang

Published in the United States of America
ISBN: 978-1-62746-829-9
1. Biography & Autobiography / General
2. Biography & Autobiography / Personal Memoirs
13.09.13

Dedication

This book is dedicated in loving memory of Bryanna Faith Draper, my deceased daughter, and all of the other children who have suffered abuse from hands that should have loved. May God keep them safe in his arms.

Acknowledgments

First of all, I would like to thank God for helping me to get through the tragic loss of my daughter. Without his love and guidance, I would not be here today. There were times that I thought he had deserted me only later to discover that he was carrying me. Second, I would like to personally thank the following people for their contributions, support, wisdom, and friendship. Without the following people, my book would never have been possible.

My mom and dad, Kay and Wayne Wills; my grandparents, Pauline Wills, Earl Wills, and Herman Graybeal; my sister, Anna; my brother, Andy; my sister-in-law, Lisa; my brother-in-law, Kenny; the detectives for their kind persistence; the district attorney and assistant district attorneys for their unfailing pursuit of justice; the pathologist for completing such a difficult task with the utmost professionalism; my pastor and his wife for their undying faith; my counselors throughout the years for their always sympathetic ears; the employees of the CAC for their encouragement; the judge for his fairness; my deceased lawyer for his often tested patience with me; my current two lawyers that helped me through a most difficult day in court recently; several aunts and uncles, Linda, Lisa, Patty, Kenny, Shelby, Gary, Tim, Randy, Jo Ann; and many close and wonderful friends who have stuck with me through thick and thin: Teresa Smith, Janet and Keith Meadows, Arlene Payne, Michelle Hensley, Beatrice Vanhorn, Maggie Potter, Debbie Davis, Susan Barnett, Terry Harris and many other friends—too many to mention.

I would also like to thank Tate Publishing for giving me the opportunity to share my story. I am unknown author and they took a chance on me. A special thanks to Noel Thrasher and

Rachael Sweeden for their patience in answering all of my questions as I struggled through a new and unfamiliar process. A special thanks to Tyler Worsham, my editor, for helping polish my work and decide on the title. And also many thanks to Kristine Sims my project manager.

Contents

Preface

The contents of this story are based on a real life experience. I have detailed everything to the best of my memory and knowledge and will attest to the factual truth contained in the following pages. However, all of the names have been changed or masked except the actual perpetrator and the victim in order to protect the innocent.

All court proceedings were reproduced in an abbreviated form using the actual court transcripts. At times, repetitious material was eliminated and interactions were summarized; therefore the court scenes are not a verbatim account, but nothing was changed so drastically as to alter the content of the litigations.

Introduction

On June 2, 2000, my only baby girl mysteriously died. With every shovel full of dirt that covered her, my hopes and dreams for the future were buried. Her death caused a huge void in my life. Never really knowing grief, I was now consumed by dreadful sorrow. I cried to God, "Why me?" He promised to not place more upon us than we can endure, but the pain was unbearable. What horrible thing could I have done to be punished so severely? I often wondered. Almost a year would pass before any of my questions were answered, and the revelations were the beginning of a completely new nightmare.

Bryanna Faith suffered a horrible death of child abuse from her father, and I lived and slept with him for almost a year after the violence started, not knowing what he had done. He weaved a careful web of deceit to hide his crime from everyone. Why did he do it? The answer to that question still eludes me. All I know is that God has protected me throughout this tragedy and that Bryanna is safe in his arms. She will never know pain again, and someday, we will be together for eternity.

The Beginning

To everyone's surprise, I entered the world on the same day as my father, only twenty-two years later. My dad always proudly said that I was the best birthday present that he ever received. Fortunately, God blessed me with a wonderful, loving family. My mother did not work outside the home; she spent her days as a busy full-time mom. My father worked with my grandfather and uncle in a small family-owned car body repair shop. When I was four-years-old, my mother gave birth to my younger brother, and many years later, when I was fifteen years old, she gave me a baby sister. I can remember looking at her for the first time in the hospital and thinking that I wanted to be a mom someday.

I always performed well in school and maintained excellent grades, but I was extremely shy and and had very few friends. Never exactly fitting in with the popular crowd caused me to have very low self confidence. As a matter of fact, I was so timid that I could barely talk or maintain eye contact with strangers. My shyness and the cruelty of fellow classmates crippled my self-esteem. Naturally, all young girls dream of falling in love and getting married, but that became a fantasy for me that would never come true.

At age seventeen, a senior in high school, I had never been on a single date and remained very shy. My grandparents had moved into a subdivision about five minutes from our house. My grandmother and her friend in the new neighborhood had been scheming for some time to match make me with her son, Daniel. Together, they planned for me to be Daniel's date for his work-related Christmas banquet. I had only seen him once briefly several years ago and could not even remember what he looked like. A few days before the party, we talked on the phone for a few minutes to make arrangements for him to pick me up. He had a wonderfully deep voice and told me that he had seen my picture and thought that I was very pretty. Hearing a comment like that from someone other than my family boosted my self esteem. It was so exciting to finally be going on my first date.

Daniel arrived to my house at six in the evening on December 10, 1988. I had been shopping for the special occasion and bought a fancy black velvet party dress with a big bow in the back. Daniel was a few inches taller than me and clean shaven with dark hair and light crystal blue eyes. He looked very handsome in his black suit and red tie. After he introduced himself to my parents and promised to have me home by ten, we walked nervously to his car—a brand new, gorgeous, bright blue Mustang that sported all kinds of impressive state-of-the-art equipment including a premium sound system. He asked me if I liked the classic rock group Boston. I barely knew who they were so he played some of their music as we drove to the party.

The Christmas banquet was held at a classy restaurant in a town about thirty minutes away. The drive gave us a little time to get to know each other. He told me that he preferred to be called Danny. He had graduated from college the previous year with a manufacturing engineering degree and had been working for a brick company for about eight months. My mind quickly calculated that he was probably quite a bit older than me, but I didn't ask. His two favorite hobbies were ship modeling and looking through the telescope at the stars.

The restaurant was elaborately decorated. The tables were adorned with lacy white tablecloths and napkins made of silk with a full setting of silverware. Which fork do you use for each dish? I wondered. I feared that I would look foolish fumbling with all those utensils. Drinks were served in tall long stem glasses. The waiters were dressed in black tuxedos with bow ties. The glass chandeliers that hung from the ceiling were dimmed to a low romantic light setting making the decorative candles cast glaring shadows upon the porcelain plates and everyone's faces. I tried to unfold my napkin and place it in my lap daintily, but I was so nervous and shy, I was sure that I looked like a klutz instead. In the center of the table sat elegant swirled orange and red port wine cheese balls surrounded by a variety of delicate crackers.

Clueless about how to order, I opened the leather bound menu and found it filled with unfamiliar, expensive dishes. Danny recommended the orange roughy, pan blackened. I whispered to him, "What is pan blackened?" He replied that it meant "spicy." Since I loved spicy food, I ordered the orange roughy, and it proved to be absolutely delicious. While we waited for dessert to be served, I went to the restroom with the girlfriend of Danny's associate supervisor. In the bathroom, she asked me how long Danny and I had been dating, and I told her "not very long." That was as honest as I could be without admitting that we were on our very first date, and I was far too embarrassed to do that. When we returned to the table, I enjoyed a fluffy chocolate silk treat—Mississippi Mud Pie. The whole banquet seemed like a fairy tale to me at age seventeen.

On the return trip, we had a little more time to talk. Danny asked if he could hold my hand. I reluctantly reached my hand across the console. He commented, "Your hands are so small," but in reality his hand was so big that it engulfed my tiny fingers. I finally mustered the courage to ask his age. He said he was twenty-four, much older than I had thought he would be. I secretly worried how my parents would feel about our age difference if he wanted to date me again. He walked me to the door, promised to call me, gave me my first kiss lightly on the lips, and was gone. I felt beautiful for the first time in my life. Afterwards, it seemed like the entire evening had been a dream. I feared that I would never hear from him again, but in my heart, I hoped otherwise.

The following week, I waited impatiently for Danny to call me. By midweek, I had heard nothing from him and decided that, like Cinderella, I had experienced one glorious evening and that was all. My grandmother visited our house on Thursday after her weekly errands. I overheard her whispering something to my mother. Assuming that it involved Danny, I demanded to know what they were saying. Reluctantly, my grandmother confessed that Danny had been convicted with driving under the influence (DUI) the previous June, and his driver's license was revoked until June of the next year. He was too embarrassed to tell me about it. If we went out again, I would have to do the driving. I resolved right then that was the end of any potential relationship between us. Even if he called me, I knew that my parents would never permit me see him with that type of conviction, nor would they allow me to drive his car. Besides, I was a pitiful driver. It had taken me two years to gain enough confidence to take the driver's test. If those two factors did not discourage them from allowing me to see him, then the seven years of age difference would definitely do it.

We had only dated one time, but I was so thrilled that anyone would be interested in me that I begged them to let me see him again. They were, of course, very reluctant. When Danny finally called me that same Thursday evening to ask me for a date Saturday night, he confessed about the DUI and revealed that the restrictions on his license only permitted him to drive to work or work-related functions which explained why he was able to drive to the Christmas banquet. If we went out for a date Saturday night, unfortunately, I would have to do all the driving. I told him that I would like to go out Saturday in spite of everything but that I would have to obtain my parents' permission first. He promised to call me the following evening and check on their answer. Meanwhile, I urged my parents to let us go out one more time. Finally, they relented based on the fact that my grandmother had known Danny's mom for a long time. She assured my parents that Danny came from a decent family. He had just become involved with the wrong crowd for a while but had learned a valuable lesson from his mistake. When

Danny called me Friday night, I told him the good news, and he arranged to pick me up at six the following evening. Since our houses were only five minutes apart, he decided to risk the short two mile drive to my house, but then I would have to take the wheel.

At first, I was apprehensive about driving his new blue Mustang, but I quickly grew to love it! Its powerful V8 engine required exercising great caution. Too much pressure on the gas pedal could send us flying into something. On our second date, we ate at Pizza Hut and went to the movies. Danny laughingly told me that Pizza Hut was a "far cry" from the elaborate restaurant last week, but I did not care. I had a wonderful time anyway, and Pizza Hut quickly became our favorite restaurant.

As the weeks passed, we continued to go out on Friday and Saturday nights. I always felt like my parents did not like us dating, but they allowed it. They were strict about how many days we could go out and enforced curfew times of ten or eleven at night. Maybe they secretly hoped that the age difference and all their restrictions would cause us to lose interest in one another. However, all of their stipulations actually had the opposite effect—it increased our desire to be together.

During those first weeks, as Danny and I shared our pasts with each other, I discovered a heartbreaking fact about his childhood. He was born with a serious heart condition called Tetralogy of Fallot. Tetralogy of Fallot was a disease characterized by four critical defects in the heart. To make it simple, the four flaws caused an overall lack of oxygen rich blood circulating in his body. The condition had to be corrected very early in life, or it was fatal. Danny had open heart surgery when he was two-years-old that left him with a long scar down the center of his chest and a scar on his leg where a vein was removed. The disease may be hereditary, but the exact cause remains unknown. Fortunately, Danny lived a relatively normal life in spite of his childhood illness. He was routinely checked by special cardiologists every year to make sure that he was not developing any other problems.

However, Danny's mother fretted about his heart all of the time. She was afraid the he would over exert himself and constantly pampered him. Danny was never allowed to mow the yard. She was extremely worried about his well being when he served his forty-eight hour jail sentence for the DUI. When we started to date, he still lived at home with her and his stepfather. Danny's parents were divorced when he was only a toddler before the open heart surgery. His natural father lived about three hundred miles away. Danny visited with him two or three times per year, but he had not really been an active individual in Danny's life; basically, Danny's stepfather had raised him. A major problem that my parents had with Danny was they thought he was a "momma's boy." They did not believe that he could separate himself enough from his mother's control to have a meaningful, long-term relationship with me. I felt that he wanted to be independent, but that he had suffered setbacks beyond his control such as taking longer to finish his college degree because he worked part-time. As a matter of fact, he seemed very mature to me, much more than all those high school boys that had ignored me throughout the years.

We continued to date during the winter months. He bought me a beautiful fourteen karat gold heart necklace for Valentine's Day and a fourteen karat solid gold chain for my birthday. Danny doted on me right from the very beginning. My self-confidence soared from all of his attention, and I slowly emerged from my timid shell.

One evening after we had been dating for a few months, Danny shared something very personal with me. When he was arrested for the DUI, he was partying with friends, an activity that had become routine for him on the weekends. After the conviction, he vowed to change his delinquent ways. He prayed that God would send someone special into his life to help him become a better person. He truly believed that person was me. Consequentially, in my despair, my mom had advised me to ask God to send me a good man to marry. She said that was what she had done and then she met my dad. Heading her advice, I had prayed for the same thing just a few months prior to the night of our first date. His confession confirmed to me that God had brought us together and no one could part us.

In May 1989, Danny took me to my junior/senior prom. We returned to the elegant restaurant of our first date for the Christmas banquet to enjoy our prom dinner. When we arrived at the event, we danced and danced. Danny still did not have his driver's license back, but for that one night, he risked the repercussions of being caught so that he could properly escort me. Besides, he said, treating me like a queen, "You might mess up your gorgeous dress."

Shortly after prom night, I graduated high school. Danny accompanied me to my commencement ceremony. He quickly became a major figure in all of the significant moments of my life. During the summer break, at my parent's encouragement, I applied at a local fast food restaurant where my aunt worked, and they hired me immediately. I did not really want to work because it infringed upon my already limited time with Danny, but as I experienced the luxury of having my own money, I learned to enjoy it. After his driver's license was reinstated in June of 1989, Danny frequently came to see me on my fifteen minute breaks at work. He must have loved me dearly to drive all the way to town for a mere fifteen stolen minutes.

One day, during that summer, while Danny and I were walking at the park, he confided to me that his job at the brick company might eventually require him to relocate to the other side of the state. I was upset at the very thought that he would desert me, and I blurted out my feelings without thinking. He confessed that he had no intention of leaving me and that if he had to go, he would take me with him. That occasion marked our first real commitment to each other.

That fall, I started college at a very expensive private school. Admittance was based on excellent academic performance. Since I ranked number five in my high school class, I was accepted. My tuition was almost completely covered with scholarships and grants. Life became very hectic as I juggled studying lessons, working part-time, and dating Danny.

⋘

When Danny and I had been dating for two years on December 10, 1990, he surprised me with an engagement ring and officially asked me to marry him. To celebrate, we ate at our favorite restaurant, Pizza Hut. The ring was a three-fourth carat diamond solitaire with a yellow fourteen karat gold band. It was a gorgeous piece of jewelry and looked perfect on my finger. That night, I showed it to my parents. They were, of course, not thrilled about our engagement, but with no plans for marriage in the immediate future, they eventually accepted it. We intended to wait until I finished school to marry unless Danny was transferred to the other side of the state.

In January of the following year, 1991, Danny presented me with some dreadful news. Over the past two years, he had accrued a large amount of credit card debt and had been trying to figure out how to pay it off so he would not have to tell me about it. When I asked him how much debt he owed, he said almost ten thousand dollars. I couldn't believe my ears! My first reaction was to demand to know how he could waste that much money living at home with his mom and stepdad. He explained that some of the money was used to buy my engagement ring and his telescope, but regretfully, the majority of the debt could not be accounted for. He apologized and told me he would understand if I never wanted to see him again. I did not know how to feel. He ultimately decided to use his savings account to pay it off and promised that he would stop all frivolous spending and concentrate on rebuilding us a nest egg. With his savings account depleted, we had no hope of marriage in the near future. I was angry at him for wasting his money, but I loved him so much that I could no longer imagine life without him. In the end, I forgave him, but not without letting him know how his careless actions had hurt me and our future together.

In the spring of that same year, we faced yet another major setback. First of all, Danny was transferred indefinitely to the evening shift supervisor position at the brick company which really interfered with our time together. He could not visit me on my breaks at the fast food restaurant any more, our phone time in the evenings became very limited, and there would be no more Friday night dates. We were only able to see each other on Saturday nights. After I finished my spring semester of college, we decided to go out for a little while on Friday mornings before he went to work. On the first Friday morning date, after we were in the car driving down the road, he said, "I have some very bad news to share with you." My heart sank into my chest. What could it be now? Painfully, he continued, "I have been fired from the brick company." All of our plans for marriage dissolved as he spoke those words. The director had told him that he was not "aggressive" enough to be a supervisor, and they were going to have to let him go. He signed up for unemployment but it was way less than half of his other pay. Danny received a severance check in the amount of two thousand dollars, but that improved his financial situation very little. Not enough time had passed to replenish his lost savings. He submitted multiple job applications over the next six months with no results. It seemed that all obstacles were working together to prevent our marriage.

During that time, I was also struggling with the educational dilemma of deciding on a major. I had always wanted to become a writer but I knew in my heart that it was not a practical career so I thought about becoming a medical technologist. During my first semester, I took calculus. For the first time in my educational history, I found myself completely confused by the new math. Since several more calculus courses were required for a medical technologist degree, I changed my major to psychology. It proved to be very interesting, but I could not determine what type of job I could get with a bachelor's degree in psychology.

A good friend of mine at the college was majoring in Elementary Education so I decided to study Elementary Education with her. I completed my first teaching course during the month of May 1991. I was assigned in a real first grade classroom at the elementary school that I had attended as a child with my first grade teacher. The teaching experience was very enjoyable; however, the manager at the fast food restaurant had worked me too many hours during the past year in spite of my protests. The extra shifts had caused my income to reach a level that excluded me from the government grants that made it possible for me to attend the private college. At that point in time, there was a severe nursing shortage so I decided to transfer to the local university and pursue a career in nursing. However, the multiple changes in my major resulted in it taking me five years to finish my degree instead of four.

As I started nursing school in January of 1992, Danny had still not found a job. He decided to return to school for a degree in medical technology because that was his dad's occupation. Since his unemployment was about to expire, he began working part-time at a local department store which was a big step down from being a supervisor, but it was better than no income at all. He continued to submit applications to various companies during that time with no results until May 1992. A new mail order company was opening in our area. After an extensive interview process, the mail order company hired Danny for a supervisor position. We were both thrilled that he finally had a job equal to his education and abilities, but the job turned out to be anything but wonderful. The work hours became longer and longer until he was working from eight in the morning until about eight or nine at night and sometimes as late as eleven. At least, he had the weekends off, but that also soon changed. Eventually, upper management mandated that he work on every Saturday. Then they discussed requiring Sunday workdays also. They were trying to expedite their opening to the public at the expense of killing their employees. Danny was physically and mentally exhausted from long hours of being on his feet. I was concerned about the effect it was having on his health and heart condition. He was seriously considering quitting the job, but he did not have the opportunity. In the fall of 1992, they called Danny into the office and fired him because his productivity was unacceptable. Again, Danny was told that he was not "aggressive" enough to be a supervisor. In reality, the company had experienced major computer problems. Management was forced to place the blame for their shortcomings somewhere so they chose the supervisor. Danny was actually more relieved than upset when he was terminated.

Unemployed again, Danny did some soul searching and decided that he was not management material after those two terrible job experiences. He was actually the meekest, mildest person I had ever known and really did not have the commandeering personality of a supervisor. I had never even heard him raise his voice. Knowing that, I advised him to consider returning to school and obtaining a healthcare degree. With his tender heart and easy going manner, I was sure that he would excel in the medical field; plus, the healthcare market overall was experiencing a shortage of personnel. After reviewing his options, he found radiology to be interesting. At the university, he could obtain a degree as a radiologic technologist (someone who actually performs the x-rays) in two years. When he applied for the fall semester of 1993, he was admitted. Then fate finally smiled on him with a fortunate occurrence. He was able to work at the electric company while he completed his radiologic technologist degree. It was a decent paying job that he had when he was in college the first time, and it very easily integrated with a busy life of school. As Danny worked toward becoming a Radiologic Technologist, I survived the last semesters of nursing school. The word "survive" was putting it mildly. The hours were long and grueling, filled with classes, labs, and clinical time in the surrounding area hospitals.

But In May of 1994, my efforts were rewarded with a B.S. in Nursing. I graduated with honors and a 3.7/4.0 GPA. During my last year in nursing school, I quit the fast food restaurant and began working for a small home health agency as a sitter with a lady that had Alzheimer's Disease.

While I was finishing nursing school, the health care market drastically changed from high demand to being flooded with registered nurses, and it was almost impossible to secure a full-time position. I signed up to take the state exam to obtain my nursing license that summer. Within a week, my results arrived in the mail revealing that I had passed the test and could now practice as a Registered Nurse. However, there were no available jobs. As I talked with several fellow students, I discovered that most of us found that, after all those years of hard work, we were virtually unemployable. Several of my fellow classmates moved out of the area to secure positions. I did not want to relocate and leave Danny behind so I continued to work for the home health agency on a per diem basis, doing staff relief at various hospitals throughout the region. The agency mainly placed me at South Memorial Hospital. The work was very unpredictable and often on short notice with no benefits whatsoever, but it provided income until September 1994 when I finally obtained a registry position at the large local medical center across town from South Memorial Hospital. That job generally gave me full-time work, but the hours were not guaranteed, and it had no benefits either. I continued to work at the large local medical center until eventually, through persistence, I was able to secure a full time position at South Memorial in the intensive care unit.

While I was working diligently to obtain a full-time job, Danny graduated from Radiologic Technologist School the fol lowing spring of 1995. By the time Danny had graduated, the radiologic technologist job market was as crowded as nursing, maybe worse. After months of an exhaustive job search, a small rural hospital about sixty miles away from our home offered him a position where he would work Friday evening and sixteen hour shifts on Saturday and Sunday and receive full-time benefits. The hours were terrible but he gratefully took the vacancy anyway.

After we both secured full-time employment, we decided to take the next step and prepare for marriage. Since the rural hospital was about sixty miles away from where we currently lived with our parents, we decided to rent an apartment located about half way between our jobs. We announced to everyone that the wedding would be in September 1995. My parents were not pleased at first, but as time passed and we planned for the ceremony, they gradually accepted it and even became happy for us. Slowly, they were beginning to think of Danny as a son.

Marriage

After a very extensive courtship of almost seven years, Danny and I were finally united in holy matrimony on September 9, 1995 by our beloved pastor at our small home church. My parents said that we could have either a fancy wedding or the money that they would spend on it. We chose to have a small ceremony and use the money to start our new life together.

Danny wore a black suit, white shirt, and red necktie. I dressed in a quaint but attractive *new* white wedding gown. It scalloped around the bottom hem landing right below the knees in the front and almost brushed the floor in the back. The neckline was modest, and the gathered sleeves rested at mid-arm. The back of the gown was decorated with a large white bow. I wore a pearl choker necklace and matching earrings both *old* and *borrowed* from my mother. My *blue* garter remained hidden beneath my dress throughout the entire ceremony. I carried a bouquet of red and white roses that I had made myself.

We decided not to have any attendants except my little sister as the flower girl. Danny did not have a best man because his brother was stationed in the navy in Hawaii leaving him unable to attend our wedding. In the absence of his brother, Danny really did not have any other close friends to ask. Under those circumstances, I choose not to have a maid of honor as well. My brother played the piano music for our wedding.

At the reception, we had finger food trays and a three tier white wedding cake decorated with red roses. I had chosen my favorite color, red, for our theme. A coworker of Danny's at the electric company took photographs for us. He did an excellent job and gave the pictures to us as a wedding gift. Danny's father had a video camera and recorded the entire ceremony and reception for us. Of course, at the end, they battered us with bird seed

as we climbed into a car covered with shaving cream and stream-
ers. We set off on our honeymoon to Atlanta, Georgia, where we
spent three days touring Six Flags, the zoo, and Stone Mountain.

On our wedding night, Danny made a promise to me: "I want
us to never let the sun set on our anger. If we do argue, we should
always make up before we go to bed at night." I vowed to honor
that commitment. Danny truly believed that never going to bed
mad would keep us happily together forever, and I totally agreed.

When we returned from our honeymoon, we moved into
our small apartment. Geographically, the apartment was almost
exactly half-way between our jobs leaving us both with about
a thirty minute drive to work. Danny really enjoyed being an
x-ray technician and helping people. After his two past job
experiences, I was pleased that he was finally experiencing some
satisfaction from his career. He was also very well liked by all
of his coworkers. After working at the small rural hospital for
only a few months, Danny was able to change into a Monday
through Friday dayshift position. My hours continued to fluctu-
ate between dayshift and nightshift with about every other weekend off. Basically, our free time together was limited to some
evenings and every other weekend.

A few weeks after we were married, we began to think about
getting a pet. However, living in an apartment restricted our
choices. One day, we went to a nearby pet store just to look. They
had an open wooden box display in the middle of the store of
hand-fed cocktail birds. One of the birds climbed onto my hand
and refused to get back on his perch. He had a mixture of grey
and yellow feathers that was striking. Each time I tried to leave
the store, he squawked at me when I reached for the door. I went
back to him several times. He willingly climbed back onto my
hand where he seemed to enjoy picking at the stone in my diamond engagement ring with his beak. I was not sure that I wanted
a bird. I had two pet birds as a child, and I remembered my mom
fussing all the time about how messy they were. However, that

bird was determined to go home with us. I wanted to think about it for a few days, but Danny really wanted to buy him right then. He said, "What if we come back tomorrow and he is gone?" The bird was kind of cute. In the end, I relented, and we expanded our family that day.

We named him Spike because he had a small tuft of feathers on the top of his head that resembled a "spike." He did turn out to be a very messy little creature scattering his birdseed all over the floor and constantly shedding feathers. I had to vacuum around his cage every two or three days. His untidiness caused me to dislike him; however, Danny adored him. Spike would bend his head down and allow Danny to scratch it. Many times, I wanted to give him away, but Danny would not hear of it. I even told Danny that I thought I was allergic to Spike, but he disagreed. Spike became "his pet," and I tolerated him only because I loved Danny.

Since we had signed a year contract to live in the apartment, the following spring of 1996, we began to consider buying a house. We spent many days driving around looking at homes for sale. Finally from a newspaper advertisement, we accidentally discovered a newly constructed neighborhood about two miles from our apartment. There, we found a perfect ranch style house to buy. It had three bedrooms, two full bathrooms, a living room, an eat-in kitchen, and a full unfinished basement with a two car drive under garage. The siding was grey accented with burgundy shutters. After taking my parents and Danny's mom and stepfather to look at it, we signed a purchaser's contract and invested five hundred dollars of earnest money toward the house.

While we waited for our loan approval, I began to pack our belongings at the apartment. One day, while I was empting Danny's top dresser drawer, I found a credit card bill for eight thousand dollars. It took me several minutes to finally realize that he had again created a huge amount of credit card debt without my knowledge. Evidently, he had not kept the promise he made five years ago to stop all frivolous spending. I was furious at him for deceiving me like that especially since we had agreed to buy a new house. Eight thousand dollars was a significant amount of debt to hide from me. As his girlfriend, I could see why his financial situation might not be my business, but since I was now his wife, he was obligated to tell me about his bills. I searched under our bed to see if I could find anything else. I pulled out several boxes of modeling equipment and model kits that I did not know he had.

That evening when he came home from work, I confronted him with the bill. He explained that some of the money was spent on things for our apartment, but once again, he had nothing to show for the large amount of missing money. I contemplated how we would manage a house payment with the unanticipated extra debt. He confessed to me that he had an impulse control problem with spending. We decided that it might be best if he destroyed all of his credit cards and let me manage the finances. We proceeded to combine our checking and savings accounts. I used my assets for the down payment and closing costs on our new home. Danny did not have any money to contribute at all; he had never replenished it from his last episode with credit card debt. I applied for a low interest credit card and moved Danny's enormous debt to a lower percentage rate. The interest rate was so high on the present card that he was making no progress in decreasing the principle owed since he was only making the minimum monthly payment; thus, I began the arduous task of paying bills and managing money for us.

We decided to place ourselves on a strict budget, limiting our expenditures to only the necessities so that the rest of our income would go toward eliminating Danny's debt. We both knew that I had a good business head on my shoulders and could straighten out his pitiful financial situation. Danny did not mind me controlling all of our money. He knew he had a problem with spending and he really wanted to overcome it. It was just fortunate that

I had been saving my money since graduation from college, or we would not have been able to afford the down payment and closing costs on the house.

A few days after I found the credit card statement, I dropped my engagement ring on the floor, and it rolled underneath the couch. In a panic, reaching under the couch to find my ring, my hand brushed across something bulky and strange. I pulled the unfamiliar object out from under the couch, and to my surprise, it was a pouch of chewing tobacco.

I asked Danny, "Is this yours?" He shamefully hung his head and nodded. I could not help but be angry again that he had hid something else from me. "Why couldn't you just tell me that you chewed tobacco?"

He replied, "I was too embarrassed about it. I did not want anyone to know, not even you."

"What else are you hiding from me?" I asked furiously.

He adamantly denied having any other secrets; yet, I still remained skeptical for a long time. I kept waiting to find something else he had hidden from me, but from that day forward as far as I knew, he was honest with me about everything. It would be a long time before he deceived me again, and those two instances were very mild in comparison to what the future would hold.

※

During the days that followed, we organized our belongings in our new home. We planted several flower gardens outside. We worked hard, but life was very good. We were so happy and content during those early years.

Since we now had our own home with a decent sized backyard, on our first anniversary, I told Danny that I really wanted a dog. He took me to the pound to search for a dog. We chose a young beagle mix pup to adopt. Her coat was a blend of brown and white, and she was medium built. A worker at the pound estimated that she was probably about a year old, which meant that she was born around the time that we were married. Her age would always match the number of years that we were married. Since she was an anniversary present, I named her Annie.

⟪⟪⟪

As time passed, I became tired of my long drive to work. South Memorial Hospital was an unstable for-profit hospital. We were constantly hearing rumors of closure and bankruptcy. If the census dropped in the hospital, nurses were asked to stay at home without pay which was in a sense a mini layoff. South Memorial Hospital also did not offer a lot of educational opportunities to its employees. I really wanted to take the critical care class required for working in an intensive care unit, but South Memorial Hospital could only afford to send one nurse at a time. Several coworkers were ahead of me on the waiting list to attend. Due to these factors, I began to actively seek employment at a larger closer facility, First Street Hospital. The market was still flooded with nurses making it very difficult to secure a better position. I made repeated phone calls and visits to the nurse manager over the cardiac unit at First Street Hospital to inquire about vacancies. After almost a year of perseverance, she finally called and offered me a position.

I started working in the cardiac unit at First Street Hospital in April of 1997. While working at South Memorial, I cared for a variety of critically ill patients, but my true interest was always in cardiac nursing because of Danny's heart condition. My devotion to Danny caused me to specialize in heart patients so that I could take better care of him now and especially if he should develop any medical problems in the future.

⟪⟪⟪

Eventually, Danny's boss started twelve hour dayshifts at the small rural hospital. Danny volunteered to do them so that we could have the same days off each week. When I started working at First Street Hospital, I did not entirely quit South Memorial Hospital. I remained on their registry so that I could work extra days there occasionally to finish paying off Danny's credit card debt. That additional income helped to almost completely eliminate the eight thousand dollar debt. After it was paid off, we decided to trade Danny's mustang for a brand new maroon Ford truck for him to drive.

The following year, since our financial situation was improving, Danny and I decided to take the vacation of a lifetime. Danny's brother was still stationed in Hawaii. Danny's mom and stepdad had already visited them twice and told stories of how beautiful it was. Somehow, we were both able to get two weeks of vacation from work during the same time period. A local travel agency provided us with two airline tickets at very good rate. To avoid major hotel expenses, we stayed with his brother and family. It turned out to be an adventure every step of the way starting with flying on an airplane for the first time in our lives.

We arrived in Honolulu, Hawaii, late on a Wednesday night in the middle of April 1998. The following two weeks were filled with so many exciting experiences. Danny's brother and sister-in-law had two little boys and a brand new addition to the family, a six-month-old baby girl. Danny and I both enjoyed playing with her. While visiting with them, we privately expressed our desire to each other to have a little girl one day.

During the first few days, we toured the island of Oahu where his brother lived. There, we visited the Arizona Memorial, The Valley of the Kings, the Punch Bowl, and many other fascinating places. The Pacific Ocean was a beautiful shade of blue that stretched all the way into the horizon. The following week, Danny and I traveled to the Big Island of Hawaii and stayed overnight so we could see Mount Kilawau (the only active volcano in the

Hawaiian Islands) in the dark, but first Danny wanted to go to South Point so we could say that we had been to the southernmost tip of our country together. The landscape to South Point was dry, arid, and barren resembling a vast wasteland. No civilization was present, only some large windmills, used for electric power. Except for a few other parked rental cars that looked very similar to ours, and a couple of fishermen, the place was deserted. South Point rested at the edge of the ocean, but it was not a beach at all. The island ended in huge, high cliffs that rose several feet above the water, very different than how I imagined it would be.

After standing at the very edge of the United States together, we headed toward the main attraction of the Big Island, Mount Kilawau. The entrance to Mount Kilawau National Park was several miles up the side of mountain. It was late afternoon by the time we arrived but thankfully, we still had several hours of daylight left. An eleven mile road, Crater Rim Drive, circled the top of the volcano. We drove around it two times, stopping to see the various attractions along the way. The entire top of the volcano was covered in black dried lava with signs stuck in it stating the date of the eruptions.

That evening, we had reservations to dine at the restaurant that rested at the peak of the mountain. From the large viewing window of the restaurant, we watched the steaming Kilauea Caldera while we ate. After dark, we drove down a twenty mile long twisting road to the edge of the island. The road ended abruptly due to a river of dried black lava across it. We parked at the dead end and walked on a cliff of rocks until we could see in the far distance the bright red lava as it poured into the ocean. With only the scant glowing of a flashlight, it was pitch black dark. I could hear the ocean crashing onto the rocks beside me as I walked but I could not see it. I was very scared knowing that one tiny step in the wrong direction could land you directly off the side of the cliff. I clung to Danny's arm in fear all the way. Danny was fascinated by how vividly all of the stars were illuminated because the sky was so dark. He said he wished he could bring his telescope out there for a night of observation.

Our last full day of vacation in Hawaii was my birthday. Danny planned a very special date for us at the Polynesian Cultural Center. During the day, we walked through various native villages watching shows about each of the seven Polynesian Islands. At dusk, we ate at the Alii Luau, feasting on authentic Hawaiian foods such as roasted pig, chicken long rice, poi, and purple taro rolls.

At tables surrounding the Luau area, crafters sat weaving long coconut leaves into elegant hats, baskets, and headbands. I commented several times on how beautiful they were. During dinner, Danny pretended to go to the restroom but instead returned with a braided headband decorated with purple orchids. He placed it on my head to wear during the rest of the Luau so that I would feel like a princess on my birthday.

When we returned home from our splendid vacation, Danny and I switched from twelve hour dayshifts to twelve hour nightshifts. His credit card debt was gone, but we faced yet another unexpected financial hardship. The lawyer that did the closing of our house figured our taxes wrong. He based them on the house resting on a vacant lot. The mistake went undetected for two years until our mortgage was sold to another company. One day shortly after we returned from Hawaii, we received a letter in the mail that stated our house payment was going to be raised by one hundred and fifty dollars a month for the next year. The increase would compensate for the back taxes that we owed as well as future taxes for that year. Since they were originally done wrong, our house payment would always be higher. Even though Danny's debt was gone, we were destined to have very little spare money for at least another year. The main reason that we changed to nightshift was for the extra cash from shift differential to make the increased house payment.

The switch to nightshift required some modifications on our parts. We found it difficult to sleep during the daytime hours due to the light and noise. Since we made the change in the spring of the year, we had to deal with lawn mower sounds. I began to run a humidifier which did a wonderful job masking the annoying commotions going on outside our window. I found that the humidified air also helped my sinuses and allergies. After getting used to that steady humming noise, I discovered that I could not sleep without it whether it was during night or day. In spite of the adjustments that we had to make, it was a very pleasant time period in our marriage, spending all of our days off together.

Danny and I, basically, had a very harmonious relationship with each other. We rarely spoke a cross word. Since Danny frowned upon my outings with friends, I spent almost all of my free time with him. Danny had acquaintances at work, but he never went out with any friends while we were married. His complete social life involved only me. One of our favorite things to do was watch movies. Danny bought and installed a theater surround sound system to make that activity even more enjoyable for us. Danny did not believe in skimping on stereo equipment (or a lot of other things for that matter). He always wanted the best available product offered on the market which was usually the most expensive as well. That was probably another reason he accumulated so much credit card debt.

I can only recall a rare few characteristics about Danny that even irritated me. One of them was his love for heavy metal music. I enjoyed listening to rock music, but some albums that he liked disturbed me. He purchased very hard death metal music like Pantera. He let me listen to some of it, but quite frankly, it just sounded like noise and gave me a headache. I enjoyed music lyrics because they are like poetry, so incomprehensible screaming held little meaning for me. He also bought some Rob Zombie and Marylin Manson. Their CDs depicted distressing images in the artwork and explicit lyrics. When I expressed concern to

Danny about some of his music choices, he insisted that music did not possess people or cause them to commit horrible actions. He thought that the publicity about it was ridiculous and even laughed about it, but I still blatantly refused to listen to any of it with him.

The only other thing that annoyed me about Danny started after we had been married a couple of years. For my birthday, my brother gave me a computer that he had refurbished. Danny became increasingly obsessed with playing video games on it. Some of the games were mild like pinball, but others were rather violent. I did not really believe computer games to be harmful. What irritated me about his playing was that once he got started he couldn't seem to stop. I would have to call him to supper several times. When he finally came to the table, the food was almost cold. Eventually, I learned to begin calling for him about fifteen minutes before I actually had the meal ready so that we could eat while the food was still hot. He played computer games for hours almost every day. It annoyed me because I was busy doing household chores while he goofed off, but then again, he did mow the yard and always graciously helped me with the dishes after I cooked. Occasionally, it bothered me, but most of the time, I overlooked it with love. I am sure that there had to be things about me that aggravated him too. I just never remember him mentioning anything. The vow that we made on our wedding night was never forgotten. We always went to bed happily in each other's arms.

A New Addition

The following spring of 1999, Danny and I began to seriously consider having a baby. Since most of our debt was gone, and the house payment was decreased to normal, we felt that we were in the appropriate financial situation to expand our family. That spring, while we were remodeling our flower gardens, we planted a much more important seed. Jokingly afterwards, we often referred to the baby as a "flower child." On Monday, after Father's Day, I nervously took a home pregnancy test. With shaking hands, I picked the stick up to find two pink lines indicating positive. From the moment I discovered that I was pregnant, I developed an intense fear of the labor and delivery process. I scheduled a doctor's appointment for the following week. After the doctor confirmed my findings, I was handed an overwhelming amount of information to absorb later at home. The doctor said my due date was February 24, 2000.

I had thought that we were ready to have a baby but soon discovered that nothing was in order. Our first unexpected problem involved who would care for the baby while we worked full-time jobs. We lived over thirty miles from our immediate family. I did not want to put the baby in day care so we decided to move back closer to our parents. We quickly found a house to buy conveniently located about fifteen minutes from our parents' houses, but it took us several months to sell our other place. A young buyer put a contract on our house after it had only been advertised for a week, but the government was taking his current residence to build a road so we had to wait for months on the government to pay him for his present home before we could complete the sale.

While we waited to close on our new house, Danny and I both looked for different jobs with more conducive hours to care for the baby. Nightshift was not the best work schedule for both of us to have with an infant. I applied for a second shift opening in the Radiology Department at First Street Hospital. I wanted the position very badly because it would work out extremely well with my mother's Monday through Friday dayshift schedule. If she and I worked opposite of each other, then one of us would always be available to care for the baby. I figured my condition would exempt me from the position because of radiation exposure during the procedures. Since I did not want to chance damaging the baby in any way, I confessed that I was pregnant during my interview. The nurse manager informed me that it would not matter because my job requirements would not involve direct exposure to radiation. My duties would mainly be monitoring patients after the procedures, making daily rounds on patients in the hospital, giving instructions to patients via phone, and assisting CAT Scan and MRI in acquiring difficult intravenous sticks after hours. The only area that pregnant women were completely restricted from entering was the MRI room due to the powerful magnet, but no one could really explain why. After working intensive care for five years, I was quite ready for something new. Fortunately, a few days after my interview, they offered me the evening shift position in Radiology.

Since we were moving, Danny was also actively seeking employment at First Street Hospital. He did not really want to leave the small rural hospital, but after we moved, it would be too far for him to continue to commute there. Since Danny had already been doing some staff relief at First Street Hospital, they hired him for a full-time nightshift position in the radiology department. Incidentally, we found ourselves working together in the same area, but our hours were basically opposite of each other. Danny worked ten and twelve hour nightshifts seven out of fourteen days with every other weekend off. I worked Monday through Friday evening shift, so our shared time off was again limited to every other weekend.

While we were making all of those changes in our lives, I was dealing with the normal trials and a few added problems concerning my pregnancy. During the first trimester, I suffered from severe morning sickness. Actually, the nausea lasted all day long. On some days, all I could consume was soda and saltine crackers or bread. I tried to vomit, but I couldn't so it resulted in a constant queasy feeling. Trying to take the prenatal vitamins only made me sicker so under the doctor's advice, I took two Flintstones vitamins instead until the fourth month. At that time, she said I would have to take the prenatal vitamin every day. I prayed that the morning sickness would be gone at the end of the first trimester so I could take my vitamins correctly. Miraculously, my morning sickness disappeared as quickly as it came right after my third month of pregnancy.

The most frightening problem I experienced during the first trimester of my pregnancy was bleeding. The doctor said it was normal to spot some until the twelfth week. I did not worry about it until the spotting continued beyond twelve weeks. At my sixteen weeks appointment, I was still seeing blood almost every day so I told the doctor about it again. I was supposed to have an ultrasound at twenty weeks, but due to the bleeding, the doctor changed the date of the ultrasound to the following week. After sixteen weeks' gestation, it was possible to determine the sex of the baby so I became excited about knowing the baby's gender and health status a little sooner than we had planned.

On September 9, 1999, I had an ultrasound. Actually, the spotting completely stopped after my sixteen week appointment, but I went ahead with the early ultrasound just to be safe. I drank a liter of water as instructed making my bladder painfully full. The ultrasound technician called another non-pregnant patient that had checked in after me first. That angered me because my bladder was miserably full. I fidgeted in my seat in the waiting room for thirty more minutes because I could not be still. Finally, when she took me to the exam room, I had to empty some urine before she could do the ultrasound because my bladder was too full. That annoyed me even more because she had taken someone in front of me causing me to sit in unnecessary extreme discomfort for an additional very long thirty minutes.

I remained pretty disturbed with her until she began to show me the baby's actual body parts like a hand and a foot, then my chagrin quickly diminished and was replaced with a feeling of awe knowing that those little human parts were growing inside of me. The ultrasound revealed the reason for the spotting. I had a partial placenta previa which meant that the placenta was implanted too low in the uterus covering a portion of the opening at the end of the uterus. Since the placenta was only partially covering the opening, no treatment was indicated. However, I would be required to have another ultrasound at twenty-eight weeks gestation to see if the condition had resolved on its own. Most partial placenta previas heal without any intervention, but occasionally they do not. If it was still present on the twenty-eight week ultrasound, the treatment would be delivery by a C-section. My mother had also spotted when she carried my sister and me. When I told her the reason for it, we figured that she must have suffered from the same condition during her pregnancies, but it was undiagnosed due to the lack of availability of ultrasound during those days.

The next important question was the sex of the baby. After looking several times, the technician said that she did not see any boy parts; therefore, she guessed that the baby was girl. Her deduction was not one hundred percent accurate because boys can hide their private parts during the exam. Even though she said that the baby was most likely a girl, I still believed strongly that it was a boy. Danny also thought it was a boy. The men in Danny's family seemed to produce more sons than daughters so we figured that it would be highly improbable for us to conceive a girl on our first attempt. In fact, I was so sure that it was a boy that I decorated the nursery in a completely neutral theme—Noah's Ark.

As I progressed through the second trimester free of morning sickness, I found myself plagued by a slightly less annoying ailment, severe heartburn. I consumed countless Tums during the latter months of my pregnancy because the heartburn lasted until delivery day. Carbonated beverages irritated the indigestion so I stopped all sodas and drank only water, juice, milk, and, of course, one beloved cup of coffee each morning. An old wives tale said that severe heartburn indicated that the baby would have a lot of hair. I did not know if that saying was true or not, but if it was, I expected the baby to have a head full of hair.

At my twenty week appointment, I had experienced no further spotting. I thought that I was perfectly fine other than some sinus problems. However, when the nurse checked my blood pressure, it was high enough to seriously concern the doctor. She ordered several blood tests on me. When the blood work came back, she said that she was going to place me off work on semi-bed rest until the baby was born. I panicked because it was too early in my pregnancy to stop working. If I started my maternity leave that soon, it would be over before the baby even arrived. I would have to return to work with only a mere six weeks of bonding time. Plus, I feared that they might dismiss me from my new radiology job if I became unavailable for that many extra weeks. I pled with her to permit me to work for a few more weeks. She finally relented after much persuasion on my part with one condition. I had to promise to lie down and rest on my left side for two hours every afternoon when I got home from work. Afterwards, I struggled to comply with her instructions but found them very difficult to obey because I had so much packing to do in preparation for the move.

I think the main reason for my high blood pressure during that time was the stress of selling our home. We had to wait for months on the government to give the young man buying our house his money. Meanwhile, unbeknownst to us, other people were interested in our residence, but none of them were allowed to view it because the young buyer was a friend of the owner of the real estate company. We were left in limbo with the realtor always saying he was supposed to receive his money the next week. That went on until his contract breeched the ninety day time limit and expired. I told the realtor that since the buyers' contract had expired, I wanted the house marketed to other people. The realtor used my threats to pressure the government into giving him his money. During the week of Thanksgiving 1999, we finally completed the sale of both houses. Danny's mom and stepdad gave us fifteen thousand dollars for a down payment on our new house. They had inherited a large sum of cash when Danny's stepdad's father passed away the previous year, and they generously wished to share with us. The extra money reduced our final monthly house payment by one hundred dollars. It was truly a much appreciated gift.

We moved into our new home on Thanksgiving day. The rain poured relentlessly all day long. All of our belongings and the entire moving party were thoroughly drenched, but mercifully, no one got sick. When we arrived to our new home, the men put our bed together first. My mom placed sheets and blankets on it and told me to lie down. I know I was supposed to rest for two hours every day, but I couldn't sit still with everyone else working. I would get up and work some; then rest a little while to make everyone happy. My only regret after moving was I had to leave my flower gardens behind after tending to them affectionately for three years. Since we moved during the winter months, it was impossible to take any of the flowers that I had labored so hard on with us.

Our new home was bigger than our old one. It had light tan siding and hunter green shutters and rested in the middle of a large one acre lot. A two car drive-in garage was attached to the main level. The house had three bedrooms, three full bathrooms, and a full basement. We persuaded the builder to finish half of the basement into a huge den while we were waiting for our other house to sell. The only flaw in the house was that the three bedrooms were divided. The master bedroom was on one side of the house and the two spare bedrooms were on the other side separated by the dining room, kitchen, and living room areas. That was an inconvenience because the nursery would be on the opposite side of the house from us. Fortunately though, I received a monitor at my baby shower which would solve the problem of being able to hear the baby cry during the night.

On December 2, 1999, the following week, I had my follow-up ultrasound to see if the placenta previa had resolved. Thankfully, it was completely gone. I would be able to have a natural delivery process, no C-section. I was working feverishly at unpacking, arranging the house, and learning entirely new job duties, but somehow, my blood pressure stayed normal.

As I became visibly pregnant, my mom's dog even began to take notice of my growing abdomen. When I visited my parents, the dog would sit in my lap and smell my stomach with intense fascination. It was like she knew that something wonderful was happening inside me and she wanted to be a part of it like everyone else.

While I was pregnant, Danny had his follow-up cardiology visit related to his heart condition, Tetralogy of Fallot. He usually had to travel out of town to see a cardiologist. So that he would not have to do that, I asked one of the cardiologists that I worked with at First Street Hospital if he would see him. He graciously said that he would. I accompanied Danny to his first appointment with the new doctor. During the examination, the doctor noticed that I was pregnant. He said that we needed to be aware of the fact that Tetralogy of Fallot was a hereditary condition, and there was a chance that the baby could be born with it. With the other problems I had experienced, spotting and high blood pressure, that added yet another worry to my list. I prayed with all my heart that God would let the baby be healthy. A heart condition in an infant was very frightening. I was nervous just thinking about it; however, after I prayed, I felt at peace. I had faith that God would allow our child to be okay.

❦

Until Thanksgiving, I had been orienting on dayshift to the new radiology job. After Thanksgiving, I switched to my routine evening shift position as planned. I had hoped that the new job would be less trying than the intensive care unit, but gradually, it became much more stressful. The one and only reason for that was Dr. Peck, a radiologist that specialized in angiography procedures. He intentionally treated me disrespectfully while I worked in that department. Apparently, he enjoyed harassing and berating new employees, especially female ones. The meanest thing he did was constantly insist that I should be assisting with special procedures because my pregnancy was no valid reason to protect me from radiation exposure. It was one thing for him to be mean to employees, but an entire other matter to show no concern for the well being of my baby.

I reported his mistreatment of patients to superiors on multiple occasions, but to my knowledge, First Street Hospital never reprimanded him for his conduct. I assumed it was because he made a lot of money for them. Exasperated and not knowing what else to do, I begged Danny to corner him privately and tell him to "leave me alone or else." Danny refused to do that for me. He was so meek and mild that he lacked the gumption to confront him, even for my sanity. I tried to stand up for myself and the patients the best that I could and just tolerate the rest of his behavior. His continual harassment of me finally drove my blood pressure high enough for the doctor to place me off work about one month before my due date of February 24. I had really wanted to work until the baby was born, but the stress of being around Dr. Peck had made that impossible. In the few brief months since I had taken the much desired radiology job, I had learned to absolutely hate it. Going into work each day at three-thirty in the afternoon was a dreaded chore. I gladly took my leave of absence knowing that I would still have at least twelve weeks to bond with the baby if it arrived on time.

On February 7, 2000, I began to have some impending labor signs. As the next few days passed, my fears of delivery day intensified. I wondered how I would cope with the pain. My only consolation was in the fact that I would be able to have an epidural. Each time I felt anxious, I thought about the pain relief that an epidural would provide and I immediately calmed down. On February 10, 2000, I had a regularly scheduled prenatal checkup. When the doctor examined me, he said that I was already three centimeters dilated. He wanted to send me to the maternity ward right away, even though I wasn't experiencing any contractions. Being a nurse and therefore, very stubborn, I argued with him about going to the hospital since I was not in any pain. He relented and instead of admitting me right away, he decided to do a stress test at the office. I had to lie completely still on my left side on an uncomfortable table for over an hour with a monitor strapped to my belly and nothing to think about but my impending labor. I was in a terrible state of anxiety before the test was finally over. The machine did not detect any contractions, but did show that my uterus was very irritable meaning that I could go into labor at any time. I called my mother to tell her what was happening. She said excitedly, "We are going to have a baby soon!" I was unable to reach Danny because he was fast asleep after working nightshift. He kept the telephone ringer off during the daytime while he slept so that telemarketing solicitors would not wake him.

My biggest concern had been that the doctor would not let me return home. I did not even have my bags packed yet. However, he had finally allowed me to leave as long as I promised to go straight to the hospital when I felt the first contraction. Before

I left the office, the doctor commented, "You will be in labor before the night is over." I had an appointment for a hair cut after the doctor visit. Since my hair was a mess and I felt fine, I decided to keep the appointment at the beauty shop. After my hair cut, it was mid afternoon, and Danny was awake. I called him to tell him what was going on. As soon as I got home, I started frantically vacuuming the entire house. I had been on a cleaning frenzy all week, and suddenly it seemed a priority that I finish. Afterward, I packed my suitcase for the hospital stay.

Danny was scheduled to go to work that night at eight-thirty. He called his boss, but the supervisor was reluctant to grant him leave since I wasn't actually in labor. Being only three centimeters dilated and having my first child, as a nurse, I knew that it could be several days before the baby even arrived. I decided not to insist that he remain with me because I did not want him to get into any trouble at work. With a new baby soon to arrive, we both desperately needed our jobs.

Later that evening, we met my parents and our pastor at a hamburger specialty restaurant for dinner. I was starved so I devoured a scrumptious cheeseburger with pickles, possibly my last meal before labor, I thought. After we ate, Danny went to work. I left the restaurant with my parents. They wanted me to spend the night with them so that I would not be alone in case I went into labor.

I laid down that evening with my mom, but I was extremely hot and restless and could not sleep at all. My back was aching mildly. I waited anxiously all night to feel the first contraction, but it did not happen. At five in the morning, I had not been asleep at all so I decided to lie on the couch for a change. A few minutes later, I heard a terrible roaring sound followed by fluid running down my legs. It felt like an explosion. It took me a minute to realize that my water had broken, but when I did, I could not help but to scream out loud. My parents' dog was lying at my feet. She leaped from the couch, scared to death at my outburst. My parents rushed out of their bedroom, startled, to find me standing in the middle of the floor with my gown completely soaked. One look at me and they knew that we had to leave immediately. I quickly changed into a dry gown, robe, and house shoes and called Danny to tell him that we were on our way to the hospital. I had to brush my teeth before we left, even though my mom kept repeating, "There's no time, let's go."

On the way to the hospital, I began to experience real contractions for the first time. I finally understood the true meaning of labor and it was not pleasant. I begged my dad to go a little faster. With the hazard lights flashing, he drove as fast as he safely could. The ride seemed to take forever but was probably only about thirty minutes. As I began to feel a tremendously increasing pressure in my lower body, I decided to time the contractions. They were occurring almost exactly two minutes apart. *Surely, they can't be that close,* I thought, knowing if they were that my labor was already very advanced.

We arrived at First Street Hospital at six in the morning. Due to my insurance policy, I had to receive healthcare at the facility where I was employed. Danny was waiting for us at the emergency room entrance with a wheelchair. He quickly rolled me to the third floor maternity ward with me repeating, "Go faster!" When we reached the nurse's station, no one seemed to pay any attention to us. It was shift change (a known busy time on any hospital floor). The nurses were preoccupied with another patient (obviously not in labor) that was standing at the desk. My dad interrupted them by saying that I was in labor and needed immediate attention. A few more minutes later, one of the nurses slowly rolled me to a room at the far end of the hall. Since I was a first time mom, I am sure they just thought that I was unnecessarily panicking. The nurse handed me a lovely hospital gown that sported a couple of small holes and told me to go into the bathroom and take "everything off." I changed into the hospital gown with shaky hands in the privacy of the bathroom and then reclined back on the bed. One nurse began to ask me a series of admission questions while another one was taking my blood pressure. I could not stand their relaxed attitudes anymore. I blurted out for them to please check the progress of my labor. Several more minutes passed while they gathered some equipment. Then the lead nurse sent all of my family to the waiting room except Danny and my mom. First, she pressed on my lower abdomen several times to push some of the fluid out. Next she tested the fluid with some kind of strip to confirm that my water had indeed broken. Lastly, she reached inside me to actually check the status of my labor. Her eyes grew wide as she suddenly announced with alarm, "You are eight centimeters dilated!"

The atmosphere in the room instantly transformed into a whirlwind of activity. One nurse put an automatic blood pressure cuff on me and strapped a monitor to my belly. Another nurse grabbed my arm and started to stick and intravenous needle in it. Two other nurses began to rearrange the furniture in the room and changed the bed into a delivery table. The doctor was paged immediately. They continued to fire admission questions at me, but my pain became so intense that I could no longer concentrate on what they were saying. Danny tried to answer for me the best that he could. I begged for an epidural (the one thing that I had counted on to help me with my pain throughout the months of pregnancy), but the nurses all said it was too late for an epidural. One nurse tried to comfort me by saying that after a couple of good pushes, it would all be over anyway. When the reality hit me that I would not be getting any pain relief medication, I began to shake and cry uncontrollably.

The pressure in my abdomen became so constant that I could no longer tell when I was having a contraction and when I was between them. The nurses would not allow me to push until the doctor arrived which seemed to take hours. I asked them to please page him again. Finally, Dr. Dawdle appeared, and I began the arduous task of pushing. I mistakenly assumed that once I was able to push that it would be easier, but I could not have been more wrong. Since I was a nurse, I had skipped child birth classes, but now I would quickly learn just how little I knew about maternity and pediatric nursing. Over an hour of straining provided no results. I screamed from the pain until my voice was hoarse. My sister, only thirteen at the time, waited outside the room terrified at the sounds that I was making.

During the turmoil, I accidentally ripped my intravenous line out. Dr. Dawdle was more concerned about my hand bleeding than my labor progression which really irritated me. Danny coached me on my right side, and my mom encouraged me from the left side. I was unbearably hot and sweating profusely which was completely unusual for a cold natured person like me. I prayed out loud to God to have mercy on me and end my pain. To encourage me, the nurse said that she could see a head full of black hair, but I still cried, "I can't do this!" Everyone reassured me, "Yes, you can!" Finally, Danny said, "You have to do it because you are the only one that can." I think that helped me to realize that the only way to end the excruciating pain was to somehow muster enough strength to push my baby out into the world.

At around eight in the morning, Dr. Dawdle was relieved by another doctor, Dr. Handle. He was truly an answer to all of our prayers that morning. I begged him to help me as soon as he entered the room. Dr. Dawdle had neglected me other than a few brief visits to the labor room to announce to everyone, "It looks like we are going to have a baby here soon." We were all very aware of that fact and did not need him to remind us. He should have been helping the baby to get "here soon." Dr. Handle wasted no time. He quickly donned a pair of gloves, positioned a stool at the head of the bed, and started to work on me. Between my contractions, he gave me a pudeal block to numb the very lower part of the birth canal. I saw the four inch long needle that he intended to inject into my lower spine, but I was in so much pain that I did not even flinch.

The block alleviated my pain so much that after two more good pushes, Bryanna Faith Draper entered the world on February 11, 2000 at 8:15 in the morning. As she was born, I almost passed out from the pain and cried out, "I have torn in half!" because that was exactly how it felt. Everyone assured me that I was okay. However a few minutes later, when I tried to remove my sore legs from the stirrups, the nurse stopped me. That was when I discovered that I had suffered a third degree tear when Bryanna came out, the worst possible laceration, ripping both directions through the front and the back, completely through the rectum. Dr. Handle had tried to perform an episiotomy, but the tearing was too advanced before he arrived. She had actually tore me from the inside the whole way down the birth canal. I guess that was why I had such a hard time delivering her. With every push, I was ripping apart from the inside out. Dr. Handle asked anesthesia to come and place an epidural for pain relief while he repaired of the tremendous injury, but no one was available to insert it due to a C-section occurring in the operating room at the same time. Therefore, I was extensively sewn for well over an hour from the inside out under only a local numbing medication. They restarted my intravenous line and gave me a light dose of pain medication, but it relieved the discomfort very little. I felt almost ever stitch being placed and must have let out a hundred audible "ouches." My injury also caused something even worse than the pain. It delayed me from being able to cuddle and admire Bryanna until several hours after her arrival. I could not hold or breastfeed her while undergoing massive bedside surgery, but at least Danny was able to carry her. I can remember him proudly dancing around the room with Bryanna's tiny body resting comfortably in his arms. In my hazy, fatigued, pain infested fog it seemed like they were floating on a cloud.

Life with Baby Bryanna Faith

Bryanna arrived two weeks before her due date. She weighed six pounds and eleven ounces and was nineteen and three-fourth inches long, exactly the same height and weight that I was at birth. She was so tiny that only preemie clothes would fit her for several weeks. Her eyes were the typical dark blue, common among all newborns, and her hair was thick dark black covering her entire head. I decided that the myth about heartburn must harbor some truth. She had a tiny face with perfectly rosy rounded cheeks. I counted all of her fingers and toes to be sure they were present. She was absolutely beautiful. Dr. Handle called her "moderately gorgeous."

The origin of her name carried a unique story. While I was pregnant, I saw a thirty inch tall porcelain doll on QVC that I wanted badly, but it was very expensive. In the end, Danny ordered the doll for me as an anniversary present. She was a slender, blue-eyed, Victorian beauty with a pink and white lacy dress, parasol, and long red curls, named Bryanna spelled with a "y" instead of and "i." We had chosen both a boy and girl name just in case. Picking a boy name was easy. We quickly agreed upon Caleb from the Bible, but deciding a girl name was more difficult. At first we chose Danielle, the female form of Daniel, after her father, but after Bryanna arrived in the mail, we decided that we loved that name, especially the unique spelling. We used Faith as the middle name to signify my faith in God that everything would be okay.

I was thrilled to have her in spite of my nightmare delivery. My parents constantly commented about how she looked just like me when I was a baby. Smiling, my mom claimed that it was like holding me for a second time. Danny paraded around the room as the proud father. At lunch time, a dietary aid delivered a food tray to my room. I was starving, but unsure if I was permitted to eat yet. I decided if they were mistaken, it was their fault and quietly devoured every bite.

Due to the extensive suturing I had to undergo after delivery, my initial breastfeeding session was postponed. Danny carried Bryanna to the nursery where she remained for several hours before we were reunited. I mistakenly thought that breastfeeding would come naturally. I was mentally prepared for the pain but did not know how to perform the task correctly. She would not stay latched to the breast for any length of time, feeding only a little and then spitting it out to go fast to sleep. In a few minutes, she would wake up fussy so I would try to feed her again. Each attempt to feed her followed the same sequence of events. My mom had breastfed my sister so I thought that she could offer the best guidance, but she could not keep Bryanna latched on either. Frustrated, I feared that she was not getting enough to eat. Verbalizing my concerns to the nurse caused the appearance of a lactation specialist to instruct me in feeding techniques, but I still could not get everything coordinated. After so many incorrect attempts, my breasts were so sore that I could barely stand to do it. I spent the next day crying uncontrollably until finally, I resolved to just bottle feed. When I asked the nurse for some formula, I felt like I was letting Bryanna down, but she said that it was important for me to choose the best option for "us" because breastfeeding wasn't ideal for everyone. After talking to her, I felt some relief, overshadowed by guilt for failing Bryanna in my motherly duties.

Danny really wanted me to breastfeed. He was very disappointed when I decided to bottle feed and scolded me that I should have tried longer. In his opinion, his sister-in-law did it, and I should too. However, when I weighed the assets against the disadvantages, I concluded that formula was the best choice for us. Bryanna would eventually have to eat from the bottle when I returned to work anyway. My job, as the only evening nurse, would probably not allow time for pumping my breasts. If by some slim chance I did have an opportunity, Dr. Peck would interrupt me to be spiteful. After shedding many tears and battling feelings of guilt, I fed Bryanna her first bottle. She consumed the two ounces hungrily and slipped into a restful quiet sleep. It pleased me to finally see her full and content, but that decision would haunt me for many months.

The next day, we were discharged. During the first few days at home, I was weak and uncomfortable, but fortunately, we had a lot of help from our parents and other relatives. I experienced the normal trials and wonders of motherhood. I learned how babies wake you up at night to eat and how innocent they look resting in your arms. It was blissful just to watch her sleep. I wanted to keep her in the bed with us at night but Danny was adamant that she did not sleep in our bed at all. I suggested letting her just lie with us a few minutes on a couple of occasions, but I was met with such resistance on his part that I let it go. He said it was a bad habit to start. I decided that he was probably right. Besides, all of the literature spoke of how dangerous it was to sleep with an infant because you can roll onto them and smother them.

At age two weeks, Bryanna went to church for the first time. My mom bought her a pretty green dress and black patent shoes for the occasion. The black patent shoes were too large for her tiny feet and fell off several times. I put them back on each time just to see the smile it would bring to my mom's face. Going to church exhausted me even though I only sat in the pew. Danny sang in the choir as usual, but I was unable to participate. Our pastor introduced Bryanna to the entire congregation in a warm, welcoming gesture. I lifted my eyes to God thanking him for such a beautiful, healthy baby.

Bryanna's life fell into a predictable routine. During the day, between feedings, she laid in the living room floor listening to her Fisher Price music box. While resting there, occasionally, she would pull her own hair and then whimper about it. At night, Bryanna slept in a bassinet in our bedroom. The bassinet was on wheels and conveniently rolled to any room in the house. During those first several weeks, on his nights off, Danny would stay awake and feed Bryanna a bottle at about two o'clock in the morning so that I could rest until her usual six a.m. feeding. On those nights, we just pushed the bassinet to her room, and Danny listened for her with the baby monitor. When she woke up, he would take her to the basement and feed her at around two in the morning. Then he pushed her to the door of our room and joined me in the bed. Those arrangements allowed me time to rest and recuperate from her delivery. I went to bed early, closed the door, and switched on the humidifier for a few hours of uninterrupted sleep, fully trusting Danny to take care of Bryanna.

At Bryanna's one month well baby check-up, she was examined by her established pediatrician, Dr. Green. I chose Dr. Green because a trusted friend recommended her, and I had worked with her husband, a cardiologist, at First Street Hospital. With a weight gain of three pounds and growth of two inches, she concluded that Bryanna's developmental progress was normal. Bryanna was consuming at least four ounces of formula every four hours. My grandfather nicknamed her "little bird" because of the way her mouth constantly rooted looking for the bottle.

At six weeks of age, Bryanna began to sleep for longer periods during the night so it was only occasionally necessary for Danny to feed her in the early morning hours. She was such a good baby. I felt so lucky to have her. She fussed a little in the afternoons but generally calmed down when I put her in the swing. Since it was natural for some babies to be cranky at the same time each day, that really did not concern me.

When Bryanna was about two-months-old, I noticed a couple of small dime sized purple areas on her torso, one in the front and another on her back. I showed them to Danny and asked him if he knew what had caused them. He was as puzzled as I was at first. Then suddenly, he asked me if I remembered the previous day when she almost fell out of his lap. I did recall walking down the basement steps to the den, finding them in an awkward position, and exclaiming, "What's happening?" He replied, "I was clumsily changing positions to burp her and almost dropped her." He figured that he probably made those two marks at that time because he was really scared and accidentally grabbed her a bit too hard. His explanation made sense to me especially since his hands were so large. I did not think any more about it and the marks disappeared in a couple of days.

Around the middle of April, Danny's father and step-mom came to visit Bryanna for the first time. At the same time, Danny's brother, sister-in-law, and their three children flew in from Hawaii. Danny's brother's assignment in Hawaii was finished, and they were moving closer home for the next two years. We were once again overwhelmed with company for the weekend.

The following week, on Wednesday, April 19, Danny and I took Bryanna on a little trip to the hospital to show her off to our coworkers. It was not during the flu season, but I still avoided all infectious areas and shielded her face with a blanket. She suddenly became very fussy while we were visiting people. Even though I fed her before we left, I suspected hunger first and took her to the car to warm a bottle. She fretted and refused the milk. Since she was neither hungry nor wet, I could not figure out why she was so irritable. She had never acted that way before. We ended our trip early, and the thirty minute car ride home soothed her to sleep.

The next two days after our trip, Bryanna was okay except for she did not have a bowel movement. On Saturday, April 22, she had another disturbingly irritable episode where I was unable to console her. I suspected that she might be constipated from the iron in her formula so I called the weekend pediatric clinic for advice. The nurse told me to try half of a child's sized glycerin suppository. I sent Danny to the local pharmacy to purchase some glycerin suppositories while I stayed with Bryanna. When he returned, I promptly tried a suppository, but it did not produce a bowel movement. The only result she had was a small smear of stool in her diaper. I tried offering her extra water with Karo syrup frequently the rest of the day hoping that would relieve her constipation.

The following day was Easter. My grandmother (Bryanna's great-grandmother) had bought her a white lacy dress to wear for Easter. I was confident that she would have a bowel movement and ruin that white dress, but the day passed, and she did not. I was so consumed with worry about her stomach that regrettably, I did not take her picture in that beautiful dress.

On Monday, April 24, Bryanna's appetite decreased even further, and she still had not had a bowel movement. I decided that it was time to take her to the doctor. When I called the office, Dr. Green, her regular pediatrician, was not available. The office worker made her an appointment with Dr. Heart instead. After examining her, he decided that she was simply constipated and prescribed some lactulose, a strong liquid laxative. Bryanna was supposed to have her two month immunizations on Wednesday, but I postponed them until Friday hoping she would be better. I did not want to give her the shots while she was already feeling bad.

Later that afternoon, Bryanna developed diarrhea shortly after the first dose of lactulose. I doubted that the lactulose would cause diarrhea that soon, but I decided not to give her anymore. During the next few days, Bryanna began to vomit after eating. Her vomiting gradually worsened until it occurred with every feeding and became huge like she was throwing up the entire bottle. Concerned, I took her back to the doctor on Thursday, April 27 (my birthday). Once again, her regular pediatrician, Dr. Green, was unavailable so she was examined by another different doctor, Dr. Cloud. He seemed to think that she was suffering from lactose intolerance (an allergy to milk) and possibly a virus. I did not know where she would have caught a virus unless it happened at the hospital during our brief visit or from one of her cousins on Easter Sunday. I remembered that Danny's oldest nephew had complained of an upset stomach, but we just thought he did not want to go to church. I chastised myself for not being more cautious. Dr. Cloud switched Bryanna to a soy formula. Since she was actually even sicker than she was on Monday, I rescheduled her shots for the following week. I was far too worried about Bryanna to enjoy my birthday that year. Instead, I spent the entire day taking care of her, flushing her system out with Pedialyte and then slowly starting her on the new soy formula.

During the next few days, Bryanna drastically improved on the new soy formula, but she was not able to consume as much of it as she had been prior to the constipation problem. She was also still spitting up some significant amounts once or twice a day. I decided to take her for the immunizations on Wednesday, May 3 as scheduled. Due to no available appointments with Dr. Green, she was again seen by yet another new provider, Mr. Smith, a nurse practitioner. I had to explain to him from the beginning about her stomach problems and lactose intolerance. Her weight still remained at ten pounds, the same as the previous week. Even though she had not gained any weight, Mr. Smith administered the immunizations that day. Also, he thought that she might be experiencing some acid reflux since she continued to spit up with her feedings. He prescribed Reglan to relax her stomach.

After we got home that afternoon, Bryanna's condition gradually deteriorated. By night time, everything she ate was vomited back up directly. She was very restless during the night. The next day, I called the doctor's office and spoke with a nurse. I was quickly beginning to realize that although I was a nurse myself, I knew nothing about pediatrics. The office nurse said that it was normal for babies to suffer a decreased appetite after their immunizations for a day. If she was still not eating tomorrow, she said to call back for an appointment. Danny stayed home from work to help me care for Bryanna because I was exhausted from being up most of the previous night with her. That evening, when I was trying to feed her, she became severely choked on her bottle. Her eyes rolled back into her head, and she went unconscious for a few seconds. Frantically, I yanked her arm in the air and patted her on the back while screaming her name. Finally, she took a breath and seemed okay, but I was severely shaken. As the night progressed, she became increasingly irritable. Danny and I took turns sitting up with her so we both could get a little rest.

The following morning at around eight, I was asleep in our bedroom. Danny quietly slipped through the door trying not to wake me. I stirred anyway because I was sleeping very lightly. He looked very tired in his eyes as he told me that Bryanna was finally asleep in her bed. Since her bedroom was across the house, and the baby monitor was not on, I went to the living room and lay down on the couch so I could hear her while Danny rested for a while. Not ten minutes later, Bryanna cried out pitifully. It had been two hours since I had seen her. In that brief time period, she had drastically changed. She looked pale and lifeless and had developed a strange purple rash across her forehead. Since it was after eight, I phoned the doctor's office and took the first available appointment at 9:40 in the morning. I immediately woke Danny up telling him that Bryanna looked really sick, and we had to leave for the doctor's office in just a few minutes. I asked him if he had noticed the purple rash, but he did not recall it being present when he left her that morning.

We left the house as quickly as possible. Once again, Bryanna saw a different physician, Dr. Beverly. I had to go over the entire three week history of her illness for the third time. It was becoming increasingly complicated to explain everything. I was extremely disappointed at Dr. Green's lack of availability especially with Bryanna being that sick. I took all of Bryanna's clothes off so they could weigh her. Her weight remained at ten pounds. When Dr. Beverly pressed on Bryanna's lower stomach, she screamed in pain. Dr. Beverly said that she suspected meningitis (an inflammation in the tissue surrounding the brain that can cause strange rashes), and Bryanna would have to be admitted to the hospital. I cried uncontrollably at the thought of how sick she suddenly was. The nurses came and whisked her out of my arms, taking her to a treatment room for a spinal tap. Meanwhile, I paced the hallways wringing my hands. I found a phone at the end of the hall and used it to call my mom at work and tell her that Bryanna was being admitted to the hospital. Her voice was shaking as she promised to meet us at First Street Hospital. It seemed like they were gone with Bryanna for hours before they finally emerged and placed her in my arms. Bryanna appeared very different after the spinal tap. She was no longer fussy but actually appeared stunned and lifeless which made me even more scared.

The nurse handed me the tubes containing Bryanna's spinal fluid to take to the hospital for them. After I put Bryanna's clothes back on her, we headed for our car. I noticed that she did not wiggle like she usually does when I dress her. When we arrived at the First Street Hospital pediatric ward, the nurses again took Bryanna away from me to another treatment room. They did not allow me to go with them and told me to wait in her room. Extremely upset at them for taking her away from me again, I could not sit still in her room. Instead, I paced the hallways as I listened to her pitiful screams coming from behind that closed door. More than once, I went to the entrance with the intention of barging in, but each time I reminded myself that I needed to let them do their job. Yet, I wondered, what are they doing to my baby in there? Danny left the area to go call his mom and stepdad and let them know that Bryanna was being admitted to the hospital so I had to pace the halls and wait alone for most of the time.

It was probably the longest hour and a half of my life before they finally emerged with her. I rushed down the hall to meet them. I had to take her very carefully into my arms because she was hooked to an intravenous line. They had removed her clothes, and she was wearing a long sleeved t-shirt bearing the hospital logo. We walked slowly down the hall to her room due to the nurse pushing the IV pump. In her room, I sat down with her in the rocking chair where we remained for the next two hours while she received intravenous fluids, Tylenol for a low grade fever, and two different antibiotics to aggressively treat suspected meningitis. She appeared more alert than earlier when we left the doctor's office. As a matter of fact, she kept turning her head to the right to stare at the colored pattern on my shirt. Two hours later, the x-ray technician arrived to do her chest x-ray. As I positioned her on the bed for the exam, I instantly noticed some swelling in her right arm. The inflammation was so significant that I could see it through her long sleeved shirt. When I pushed the sleeve up, there were two puncture marks in the bend of her arm where blood had been drawn. I called the nurse immediately and questioned her about the swelling. She did not recall it being present in the treatment room and furthermore attested that Bryanna was easy to stick for the blood draw.

Four more hours passed before the pediatrician, Dr. Cloud, finally arrived to examine Bryanna's swollen arm. Danny and my parents had gone home to get some overnight items for us so Bryanna and I were alone in the room with him during the evaluation. I was upset that she was being examined by a different doctor than that morning, but at least Dr. Cloud had seen her once during her illness. He asked me if she had fallen. I firmly told him, "No." He then ordered an x-ray of her right arm. A little while after the x-ray was taken, Dr. Cloud called me on the hospital phone with the results. Danny or my parents had not returned yet when he told me the shocking news that her right arm was fractured and that the injury appeared to be at least two weeks old. How could her arm have been broken? I silently speculated. Furthermore, he said that her spinal fluid was normal and the antibiotics were being discontinued. He blamed all her fussiness on the arm fracture. However, he did mention that her blood work was suspicious for a viral infection. I asked him how the fracture could be two weeks old and not swell until today. He stated that the manipulation of her arm during the blood draw had caused the sudden inflammation. He never made any accusations toward us of harming Bryanna and even added that he "saw fractures like hers all the time." Speaking with him left me with the impression that the fracture was no big deal, but that did little to calm my nerves. I was extremely upset that her arm was broken and it was even worse to have received the news over the phone. I wished now more than ever that I would have burst into the treatment room to see what was going on. In my experience as a nurse, fractures swell within a few hours of the injury. I had never heard of it taking two weeks for a fracture to show signs of swelling. To be quite frank, the more I thought about it the more I was not buying his story at all.

Later that evening, when Danny and my parents returned, we discussed how the fracture could have happened. By that time, I was absolutely sure it had occurred in the treatment room of the hospital. After all, Bryanna was completely undressed at the doctor's office, and I noticed nothing unusual about her arm. Also, I had heard her screams while she was in that room with my own ears. Since we both worked there, Danny and I went to the radiology department to speak directly with Dr. Frank, the radiologist who had interpreted her x-ray. He gave us an entirely different story. He said that the fracture was fresh (not old) because there were no signs of new bone growth. He labeled it a "spiral fracture" which brought images of the twisting motion used when blood was drawn to my mind. Demonstrating that bending motion with my own arm, I asked him if the fracture could have been caused that way. He solemnly nodded his head. I thanked him for talking to us because under the circumstances, he really

had no obligation to tell us anything. His enlightening information along with Dr. Cloud's indifferent attitude confirmed to me
that her injury did indeed occur in the hospital treatment room,
and they were trying to cover it up.

When Danny and I returned to Bryanna's room, I told my parents and our pastor what Dr. Frank had said. Afterward, we were
all convinced that some kind of incident had occurred in the hospital treatment room. Maybe it was simply an accident, but what
made me mad was their attempt to cover it up. Danny and I did
not know how to handle the situation. We both were employed
at the hospital and feared that making a complaint would cause
us to be fired. First Street Hospital had always been very good at
keeping their workers in constant fear of losing their jobs. How
would we support Bryanna with no income? We decided to postpone filing a grievance against the hospital just yet.

Dr. Cloud said that an orthopedic doctor would come to
examine Bryanna's arm later that night. However, he never
arrived. Instead, a nurse secured Bryanna's right arm against her
chest with an ace wrap. I was furious that the injury was not
considered important enough to be treated promptly. My mother
stayed awake all night rocking Bryanna, refusing to lay her in
the crib. I was too mad at the hospital staff to sleep so we talked
almost all night long. I offered to hold Bryanna for a while but
my mom would not allow it. At four in the morning, she was
completely exhausted. I finally persuaded her to lay Bryanna in
the crib. She carefully positioned her so that her arm would in
no way be harmed, and then she collapsed on the bed beside me.
What an unsightly pair we must have been wedged uncomfort-
ably together in a bed built for one.

The next morning the orthopedic doctor came to set Bryanna's
arm properly in a splint. I interrogated him like an attorney concerning how a twist fracture could occur. He carefully dodged all
of my questions. However, he did comment about the two puncture marks in the bend of her fractured arm. His persistent eva-

sion of my questions further convinced me that they were all hiding something from me. He claimed the swelling was caused by her sleeve being pushed up creating a band of pressure (another different explanation for the delayed swelling). Correcting him, I replied that the inflammation was plainly visible before the sleeve was rolled up. I helped him make the splint for her arm because I trusted no one else to assist him.

Shortly after the orthopedic doctor left, Danny and his mom came to relieve us. After their arrival, Mom and I went home to shower and rest for a while. Later after we left, Danny called me to say that Dr. Cloud had been in to check on Bryanna. In spite of his aloof attitude, I was glad it was Dr. Cloud again so Bryanna could at least see the same doctor as yesterday. Danny said that Dr. Cloud reassured him that he treated fractures similar to hers "all the time." He made no accusations toward us for the injury. In fact he commented very little on it according to Danny. When I returned to the hospital later that afternoon, I noticed that the purple rash across Bryanna's forehead was completely gone. She was also eating the soy formula well and only spitting up very small amounts occasionally.

That evening, when we discussed arrangements for the night, it was decided that Danny and my father would stay while "the ladies" went home to rest. Bryanna had a peaceful, wonderful night in their expert care. The next day when we returned while Danny had stepped out of the room, my father commented on how impressed he was with the way Danny handled Bryanna in such a sincere gentle manner last night. He felt it truly showed Danny's deep affection for her.

Dr. Cloud discharged us home later that morning. Bryanna was significantly improved, and I was thrilled to be home at last, but my happiness was overshadowed with guilt for her stomach problems. If I had only breastfed her, maybe she would not be so sick, but it was too late to start.

In an effort to inflict as little pain as possible we decided to carry Bryanna around on a pillow to prevent any unnecessary movement of her right arm. I yearned to hold her tiny body up close to me but feared it would hurt her. We only removed her from the pillow to ride in the car seat and at bedtime because of the potential for smothering.

Bryanna improved until Tuesday evening when she threw up an entire bottle. Afterward, she cried constantly for over two hours. I gave her some Reglan with no relief. I had only been giving the Reglan intermittently because she continued to be plagued with diarrhea. I really thought she was doing better. The setback was very disappointing.

The next day, Wednesday May 10, she was scheduled for a follow-up appointment, finally, with her regular pediatrician, Dr. Green for the first time since her one month check up. At the appointment, I told Dr. Green about Bryanna vomiting and crying for two hours during the previous evening. Dr. Green told me not to worry about it as long as the vomiting did not occur with every feeding. As matter of fact, she appeared totally unconcerned with Bryanna's stomach problems. I tried to reiterate to her how bad Bryanna's digestive issues actually were, but she did not seem to listen. She was focused on Bryanna's broken arm. Since that was definitely a concern, I went along with her. She wanted us to take Bryanna to First Street Hospital for a bone survey to rule out osteogenesis (a genetic disorder where bones are brittle and break easily). I asked her if we could do it tomorrow because I had only brought one bottle of formula with me. She said that it was not urgent but should be done this week. Danny and I both told her that we suspected that Bryanna's arm had been fractured in the hospital treatment room. We assured her that we were not seeking any damages; we just wanted to know what had happened to our baby and asked her to please talk to the staff about that day for us. At the mention of that, she became very cautious, insinuating that we were irrational for even suggesting "such an absurdity." "Nothing like that has ever happened on that ward! I can promise you that," she barked at us defensively. I requested that she check out the hospital for two reasons. First, I had a small spark of hope that she would actually do it for her patient. Second, I wanted to see what her reaction would be to our petition. Her response convinced me that the hospital staff had done something to Bryanna's arm, and they feared a malpractice lawsuit.

Later that evening at home, Bryanna vomited a large amount of milk again. I was worried in spite of Dr. Green's lack of concern regarding Bryanna's stomach issues. As a matter of fact, I was very upset with Dr. Green in general. The whole time Bryanna had been sick and even in the hospital, she had been totally unavailable. Now, she completely dismissed our beliefs that the injury occurred at the hospital. I was seriously beginning to question her abilities as a pediatrician.

The next morning, Bryanna had a follow-up appointment with the orthopedic doctor. After he x-rayed her right arm, he concluded that the bone was not exactly positioned correctly, but that hopefully, as it healed, it would fall into the appropriate alignment. Since the break had occurred on the growth plate (According to him an easy place to fracture. I wondered why he felt compelled to add that information), a chance existed of experiencing complications later in life including the possibility of surgery. The new information caused me to again contemplate seeking legal counsel in regard to her injury.

After the orthopedic appointment, we went to First Street Hospital's Radiology Department for the bone survey. Bryanna was extremely wiggly and difficult to position for the x-rays. She screamed the entire time. It broke my heart to think how much we were hurting her. I put on a lead apron and remained in the room with her during the shooting of the films. At least she was so small that several bones could be taken on one slide. The two technicians performing the study were Danny's coworkers.

They discussed with Danny the difficulty of obtaining the exam. Together, they decided to take only a minimum number of shots; thus, they did a baby gram rather than a true osseous survey. The two technicians developed the films and hung the x-rays on the viewing screen so they could inspect them for quality before taking them to the radiologist to read. As we were all standing around the room examining the x-rays, Danny exclaimed, "Look, her right clavicle is fractured." Danny and the two technicians all looked closer at the film and confirmed that indeed the right clavicle was broken. In shock, I asked really no one in particular, "How could that have happened?" One of the technicians explained, "That injury is common during a traumatic child birth. You did have a traumatic birth, right?" I replied, "Yes, I did." Danny agreed that it probably occurred during delivery because he said the fracture appeared "old." I could not read x-rays at all and I certainly would not know if a fracture was old or new so I took his word for it. Knowing that it was old and probably occurred during child birth relieved some of my initial anxiety. Still, she had two fractures! Maybe she did have a bone disease. Only the radiologist could confirm that. We asked the two technicians if we could accompany them to the radiologist's office so that we could know the results promptly. They said it would probably be okay since we both worked in the department.

We waited at the door of the radiologist's office while the two technicians asked him if we could come in while he read the films. He immediately recognized us and motioned with his hand for us to enter his office. As he studied the films for a few seconds, he took a pen and traced it down her legs on the x-ray a couple of times. Then he mumbled, "No, it's nothing," and concluded that she did not have any signs of osteogenesis. However, he did note the fractured right clavicle without specifically aging it.

I left the hospital so relieved that she did not have brittle bone disease that I naively did not consider the fact that she had two completely separate fractures. I believed that the arm fracture had occurred in the hospital treatment room, and that the clavicle injury resulted from her traumatic birth. Those explanations seemed logical to me. I knew that I had not done anything to Bryanna and neither would Danny or anyone else in my family. With those thoughts in mind, I trudged blindly toward the future.

Accusations

The next morning, Friday, May 12, 2000, Dr. Green's nurse called me at home. She said that we needed to report to Dr. Green's office at 1:10 p.m. for an appointment to discuss the results of the bone survey and further diagnostic tests. I asked for more information on why we had to come so quickly, but she would say no more except that it was urgent but not life threatening. Yesterday, the radiologist said that Bryanna did not have any signs of osteogenesis, leaving me with the impression that she was medically fine. My mind raced with terrifying thoughts as to what the new undisclosed information could be.

We arrived promptly at 1:10 in the afternoon as requested. The nurse took us straight back to Dr. Green's office instead of an exam room. After the door was securely shut, Dr. Green informed us of the real reason for the specially called visit. She said that since Bryanna had two unexplained fractures, she was forced to report us to the Department of Children's Services (DCS). As we were speaking, an officer and a social worker from the DCS were waiting in another room to question us. Danny asked Dr. Green if the clavicle fracture was present on Bryanna's chest x-ray from the previous Friday, May 5, 2000. Dr. Green admitted that she had not even checked last Friday's chest x-ray for comparison. She shuffled through papers on her desk until she found the report of Bryanna's May 5 chest x-ray and read it. She said that it did not mention a clavicle fracture; thus, she told the DCS that the clavicle fracture had happened after Bryanna was discharged home the previous Sunday. When we asked Dr. Green if she had questioned the hospital staff pertaining to Bryanna's arm, once again, she simply dismissed our concerns as outrageous, saying, "There is really no reason for me to do that." Dr. Green took Danny and Bryanna to an exam room while I was escorted by her nurse down the hall to another room where a social worker, Mrs. Blakely, and a detective from the County's Sherriff's Department, Detective Gray, were waiting to question me. Dr. Green said that they wanted to talk to Danny and me separately. I nervously took a seat on the bench next to the exam table across from the two of them. They were sitting in chairs at an angle from me. It seemed strange to be questioned in one of the pediatric examination rooms.

After brief introductions, Detective Gray began, "It must be really hard taking care of a colicky baby. I had a cousin whose baby had the colic. It cried all of the time and kept them up all night long. It was very stressful for them."

I was confused because none of the doctors had ever mentioned anything about colic. I gave him a blank bewildered look as he continued, "You must be very tired. I remember my cousin talking about how exhausted they were. My wife and I watched the baby once for them so they could take a break. Their baby cried a lot while we took care of it. I felt sorry for them."

"What are you talking about?" I asked, perplexed. "I have been taking Bryanna to the doctor about two times a week for the past several weeks because she keeps vomiting up her formula. The doctors diagnosed her with lactose intolerance and a virus. None of them have ever mentioned colic. Who said that she has the colic?"

He did not really answer my question. Instead, he asked, "How long have you and your husband been married?"

"Almost five years. It will be five years this September. But we knew each other for about six years before we got married."

"Why did you wait so long to get married?"

"Well, I had to finish school and then Danny was laid off from two different jobs and decided to go back to school and change his career. We waited to marry until we had both finished our degrees."

"Do you get along well with him?" He continued.

"Yes, we get along very well. We rarely disagree about anything."

"Is Bryanna your first child?"

I nodded my head, looking him in the eye.

"Did you plan on having a baby or was it a surprise?" I subconsciously noticed that Detective Gray was asking all of the questions, while Mrs. Blakely was writing feverishly.

"She was definitely planned," I said firmly.

"Is Dan a violent person? I mean have you ever seen him act violently in any way?"

"Absolutely not," I assured both of them by making eye contact with Detective Gray first and then with Mrs. Blakely who only nodded and continued to write.

"You mean in all the... " Detective Gray paused to count, "the ... I guess eleven years that you have known him, you have never seen him act violently or get mad?"

I did not even have to think about my answer. "Danny is not a violent person. You just have to understand. He is not that way. He was laid off from the two management jobs for not being aggressive enough. He has never ever laid a hand on me inappropriately. You just have to know him. It is just not in his nature to be aggressive."

Changing the subject, Detective Gray asked, "Why did you decide not to breastfeed? We can see from her record that you tried it and then stopped."

Detective Gray spent a significant amount of time dwelling on the fact that I did not breastfeed Bryanna which caused me to have overwhelming feelings of guilt. I explained to them that we just could not seem to get the coordination of breastfeeding and that knowing I would have to go back to work, I ultimately decided to just bottle feed. I began to think about the benefits of breast milk and how much easier it is to digest. Her main problem seemed to be her stomach rejecting the formula. Maybe she would have been okay if only...

Next, Detective Gray asked me to speculate on how I thought that the two fractures had happened. I had been anxiously anticipating his question but did not really know what to say. Should I tell them about the hospital? I reflected back over the past week in my mind and remembered the evening when she became choked on her bottle, and I pulled her arm in the air. Could I have actually caused the injury at that time? Deciding to be completely honest about everything that I could think of, I told them about that evening last week, ending with, "I did pull her arm in the air pretty hard because she scared me, but I don't think that it was rough enough to have broken it." I looked at both of them, and the expressions on their faces made me immediately regret telling them about the choking incident.

"What about the clavicle fracture?"

"Well, Danny and the two technicians said that it was a common injury during a traumatic birth, and I did have a traumatic birth. That could have caused it. I have also thought about the shoulder straps on the car seat. If the straps were too tight, I don't know if they could have caused a fracture like that." I felt like I was rambling, sounding idiotic. I really did not know why she had two fractures and no bone disease, but I was sure that my flimsy speculations were making me look guilty. I hated it because I knew that I had done nothing wrong, and they were here to take my child!

They wanted a list of everyone who had taken care of Bryanna over the past few weeks. I told them that it was only Danny, her grandparents on both sides, my grandmother, and of course, me. Mrs. Blakely meticulously wrote down all of those names.

"Has Bryanna been with anyone else like a babysitter?" Mrs. Blakely asked. It was oddly the first time she had spoken during the interview.

I saw that as my opening to tell them about the hospital. I directed my eyes toward her as I began, "No, the only babysitters that we have are her grandparents, but she was out of my site on two previous occasions with strangers. The first time was at this office and the second time was at First Street Hospital on the pediatric ward. The swelling in her arm developed after she was in the pediatric ward treatment room for well over an hour out of my site. The nurses would not allow me in the room with her and made me wait in the hall, but I could hear her screaming like she was in terrible pain the whole time she was in that room. She will never be out of my site again. I promise you that! I was the one that pointed out the swelling in her arm a couple of hours later. She also had two puncture marks where blood had been drawn in the bend of that arm, right here," I said pointing to the area on my own arm for emphasis. "Danny and I went to speak with Dr. Frank after the x-ray on her right arm was taken because he had read the film. He told me that she had a spiral fracture. I asked him if it could have been done during the motion of twisting her arm for a blood draw and he said yes." I paused to demonstrate how an arm is manipulated for blood to be drawn. "All I can think about is how she screamed while she was in that treatment room. I have been just sick thinking about it," I finished, crying and rocking back and forth. While describing everything to them, I realized the force they must have been using with her to get her to cooperate, and it was unbearable to think about it. They wanted to know if I had reported my suspicions about her arm to anyone at First Street Hospital or the authorities. I told them that we had not because we both worked at the hospital and were afraid if we caused any trouble that they would fire us. The only person we had asked to check on it was Dr. Green, and she refused to do it.

"Do you think these two injuries could have happened at home?" Detective Gray asked.

"No, I don't think so. I always position her in the crib very carefully."

After that, they dismissed me. I returned to the exam room where Danny was holding Bryanna and immediately took her from him. I was so scared that they were going to take her away from me that I needed to hold her close. Only a minute or so passed and Dr. Green came to the door to take Danny to the room to be questioned. My interview had lasted about thirty minutes. I wondered how long Danny would be gone. While I waited for him to return, my head was spinning with thoughts. I paced the exam room with Bryanna clutched tight against my chest. My heart pounded with fear that they were planning to take my baby from me. I believed Bryanna sensed my apprehension because she was crying relentlessly despite my various efforts to soothe her. Dr. Green had betrayed my trust by summoning the authorities to take my sick baby away from me instead of trying to figure out what had happened at First Street Hospital. The hospital staff had made a mistake and now she was doing everything possible to place the guilt on Danny and me before we had a chance to sue them. It was appalling that she would lower herself to such means to cover the hospital's mistake. I wrapped my arms around Bryanna as tightly as I safely could. If they planned to take her, they would have to pry her from my arms. I would fight them physically if I had to.

I had worked myself into a nervous frenzy before Danny returned to the exam room, and he had only been gone for about ten minutes. His interview was much shorter than mine. I wondered why for a brief moment but did not dwell on it for long. More pressing issues were on my mind like they would be at the door any minute to take Bryanna. For a short time, the three of us (Danny, Bryanna, and I) were completely alone in the exam room. I used the opportunity to ask Danny something that was bothering me. Looking him straight in the eyes, I said, "Please tell me right now at this moment, have you done anything to Bryanna, even accidentally? Dropped her? Anything? Anything that could have caused these two fractures?"

Without flinching, he looked me back straight in the eyes and said, "No, I have never done anything. You know I love her."

"Never?" I questioned one more time for absolute assurance.

"Never, I promise." He confirmed and hugged both of us close to him.

"Well then they are definitely covering something up," I said my voice choking with tears, completely believing him.

"That is what I have been saying since all of this began last week."

I don't know what possessed me to question Danny that day. I had known him for so many years that it felt like we were part of one another. Besides, Danny was far too meek to ever harm anyone. He had lost two management jobs for not being aggressive enough. He had never physically hurt me in any way and rarely ever raised his voice to me. I knew in my heart that he was not capable of harming Bryanna, but I guess with all of those accusations flying around, I needed to hear him say it.

Right on cue at the end of our conversation as if she had been listening outside the door, Dr. Green entered the room and said, "Bryanna has to be admitted to the hospital until Monday for a series of tests to rule out shaken baby syndrome. She will have a CAT Scan of her brain to look for trauma, and an Ophthalmologist will examine her eyes for any signs of bleeding. A sitter will be present in your room at all times to supervise your interactions with Bryanna."

Interrupting her, I said," What about her vomiting?"

She replied, "I will only do an upper gastrointestinal study if these other two tests are negative."

"But I really think something is wrong with her stomach," I pleaded.

"Well, there is a rare condition in which the stomach twists and expulses the milk," she said, then added as an afterthought, "But it is very very rare."

She placed her stethoscope on Bryanna's tiny chest and listened for a few moments. Afterward, she stated, "I think I heard a slight heart murmur."

Instantly alarmed, I blurted out, "Danny had Tetralogy of Fallot as a child and the cardiologist told us just recently that there was a chance our baby could have it because it is hereditary."

She gave me a blank look. I wondered if she even knew what Tetralogy of Fallot was. "I don't think it is anything to worry about right now," she said simply dismissing her findings.

"But . . ." I said only to be interrupted by Dr. Green.

"We need to do the CAT scan and eye exam right now. They are top priority. Everything else can wait."

Can wait! I thought. Tetralogy of Fallot was a serious disease especially if left untreated. Dr. Green's expertise as a physician was completely gone as far as I was concerned. I felt like she did not know what she was doing. I had no confidence left in her. She had introduced the possibility of a rare stomach condition and a heart murmur but failed to order any further tests to investigate them. Her complete focus was child abuse.

After Dr. Green examined Bryanna, she left us alone in the room again. I placed Bryanna in Danny's arms and said, "Don't let them take her. I am going to go call Mom and Dad." I stepped cautiously into the hallway. No one was there. I slipped to the old familiar phone I had used last week and quickly called my mom to explain briefly what was happening. She replied that they were on their way.

Since it was really too late for Danny to call in sick that night and there was little that he could do anyway, we decided for him to go ahead and work. My parents could accompany Bryanna and me to the hospital. The door to the exam room creaked and I looked up to see Detective Gray and Mrs. Blakely peering in at us. My heart skipped several beats in fear. I freely told them that my parents were coming to the office if they would like to speak with them. (After all, they were active caretakers in Bryanna's life.) Detective Gray said, "We don't need to speak to them," and then they left the office. After my parents arrived, Dr. Green's demeanor completely changed. She acted like she was sorry for "having to report us" to the authorities. She told my parents, "I am doing them a big favor by admitting Bryanna to the hospital with a sitter because the DCS planned to take her away from them today." Then she contradicted herself and conceded that we might be allowed to take Bryanna home with us before Monday if the CAT Scan and eye exam were both negative. Bragging that she was "a really good stick," she asked for my permission to collect some blood work before we left for the hospital and proceeded to poke Bryanna's arm with a needle two times with no results. Next, she stuck her foot and slowly squeezed enough blood from her heel to fill a test tube while Bryanna screamed louder and louder. Tears were flowing freely from my eyes after watching Dr. Green sticking my baby not once but three times. However, I was afraid to protest to anything because she might call me uncooperative and summon the authorities back to take Bryanna away from me.

I expected an armed escort to the hospital, but instead, Dr. Green allowed my parents to drive Bryanna and me there. Upon our arrival to the pediatric ward, the nursing staff acted very defensively, appearing almost afraid of us. Repeatedly, they insisted that none of them had hurt Bryanna in the treatment room. They even added that the lab technicians were very gentle while drawing blood. We chose not to respond to their statements. To me, their behavior just confirmed that something did happen in that treatment room. The only question that I asked was, "Where is the sitter?" No one seemed to know what I was talking about, and no sitter ever arrived. It must have been another threat to scare us on Dr. Green's part. Dr. Green had instructed the staff that I was to accompany Bryanna during all procedures so that she was never out of my sight.

Shortly after we were checked into the pediatric ward, they called for Bryanna to have her CAT scan. I carried her to the Radiology Department and stayed in the room with her during the entire exam, wearing a lead apron and feeding her a bottle so she would be still during the procedure. Since Danny and I were coworkers with the CAT scan staff, it proved to be a very awkward experience. I asked the technicians afterwards if they could see any signs of bleeding or trauma in her brain. I simply could not wait for the radiologist to read it. They along with Danny looked at the slides. All three of them had the same conclusion. No bleeding or abnormalities were present, but then again none of them were trained as radiologists. However, the official report from the Radiologist came back about an hour later, unsurprisingly as completely normal.

After the CAT Scan, an Ophthalmologist came to examine Bryanna's eyes. I was not surprised when he determined that there was no evidence of retinal bleeding. The only abnormality he noted was a minor superficial cornea scratch on one of her eyes. We concluded that she most likely had scraped her own eye with one of her tiny sharp fingernails. After both tests were reported normal, as I had expected, I began to ask for an upper gastrointestinal study to be ordered. However, the night ended without Dr. Green or any other associate doctor returning to update us on any of the test results or even to check on Bryanna's status. The nurses were who told us about the CAT Scan results.

The main reason that Danny wanted to work that night was so he could check the actual film from last Friday's chest x-ray. After he looked at it, he came to tell us that the clavicle fracture was present on that film but was not mentioned in the report by the Radiologist. He had missed it, but that was not what mattered. The important fact was that the fracture did not occur after our discharge home Sunday as Dr. Green had erroneously told the DCS.

After Dr. Green reported us to the DCS, my focus concerning Bryanna completely changed. Instead of wondering why my child had two fractures, I worried that the authorities were going to take her away from me. At that time, that seemed like the worst alternative imaginable. Bryanna was extremely ill and needed her mother. How could she survive without me? Perhaps I would have been more receptive if Dr. Green had approached the problem like this: "We need to determine the cause for Bryanna's two fractures whether that road leads to a family member or a hospital employee." Instead, she tricked us into coming to her office under the pretense that something was medically wrong with Bryanna that required further testing. Upon our arrival, the DCS were waiting for us like a trap set by her. Her actions destroyed our doctor-patient relationship. Since I was a nurse with more medical knowledge than the average person, I knew that she was trying to intimidate us to prevent a lawsuit against the hospital and/ or doctors. If they had really suspected wrongdoing, why didn't Dr. Cloud report us to the DCS last weekend after her arm fracture was discovered? Instead, he acted very unconcerned about it. No accusations were made until after we asked Dr. Green to see if something happened to Bryanna in the treatment room. Then suddenly, we found ourselves under investigation for child abuse.

That Friday evening while we were sitting at the hospital with Bryanna after all the tests were completed, my father suggested that I start a diary detailing Bryanna's illness. Luckily, my sister handed me a clipboard and some loose leaf notebook paper that she was doing her homework on. Starting on April 24, I wrote about her first visit to the doctor, illustrating her symptoms and the doctor's instructions. I described the other doctor visits, hospitalization, and eventually ended with the DCS investigation. Reviewing the nightmare of the past three weeks was not enjoyable, but writing that diary was probably one of the smartest things that I have ever done. After that day as necessary, I continued to make brief entries concerning any changes in her status. I planned to use my notes to pursue a malpractice lawsuit against the hospital and pediatricians for breaking her arm and hiding their mistake by accusing us of child abuse.

Here we are again suffering through another fitful night in the hospital. We should be at home resting comfortably in our beds, I thought to myself angrily. It was all Dr. Green's fault for forcing Bryanna to be admitted for a battery of tests to rule out shaken baby syndrome and child abuse. Tests that were, of course, completely negative. All of that misery was being inflicted upon us because the hospital did not want to take responsibility for breaking Bryanna's arm. Danny's mother stayed with Bryanna and me our first night at the hospital. Everyone decided that it would be wise to not leave us alone anymore. At least, we had a bigger room, equipped with a bed, crib, and cot. Danny's mom insisted that I sleep in the bed while she used the cot. Bryanna rested in the crib surprisingly well considering her upset stomach and the two painful fractures. But I didn't shut my eyes for the entire night.

The next morning, after my parents had returned, Dr. Heart came to see Bryanna instead of Dr. Green. Dr. Green had flashed onto the scene one time during the month of Bryanna's illness and that was to report us to the DCS. Now, once again, she had disappeared, but after yesterday, to be quite honest, I was actually glad to see someone else enter the room.

We attacked Dr. Heart with questions. First, I wanted to know why the investigators had said Bryanna had the "colic." Dr. Heart denied any knowledge of Bryanna being diagnosed with colic. My parents and I had a long discussion with him regarding the allegations of child abuse. Danny was not there to join us. He had gone home to rest after working all night. Dr. Heart stated that they were simply investigating the two unexplained fractures and that we had not been accused of anything. He also added that no mishaps had ever happened in the hospital treatment room in the past.

"Since all of the tests for shaken baby syndrome are negative, can we please go home?" I asked him. He replied that Dr. Green's explicit instructions were for Bryanna to remain in the hospital until Monday. However, after we had talked with him for a while, he started to soften a little toward us, even stating that we appeared to be "a very caring, attentive family." He finally agreed to my request for an upper gastrointestinal study and said that depending on the results of the test and her milk consumption, he might let us go home later that afternoon or the next day. He also suggested that we change her formula again. I had to choose between nutramigen (a very expensive hypoallergenic formula specifically for infants that are sensitive to cow milk and soy based formulas) or going back to the regular formula with milk lactate. Dr. Heart no longer believed that she was lactose intolerant. He felt like her fussiness was due to the fractures. Since she had suffered such severe stomach upset, I did not want to chance the old formula again so I selected, without regard for the cost, the nutramigen.

During our lengthy conversation, he revealed a very shocking piece of information. He said that Bryanna would be inclined to rotate her head to the right toward the fractured clavicle. I recalled her looking at the colored pattern of my shirt when they brought her back from the treatment room last Friday. Suddenly, I realized that she was turning her head because of the clavicle fracture, not my blouse. That new information immediately convinced me with a good degree of certainty that both injuries had occurred simultaneously last Friday in the treatment room. Without thinking, I blurted out my suspicions to Dr. Heart, but he did not respond. As he exited the room, he commented, "I will order the upper gastrointestinal study, but I seriously doubt we will find anything."

After he left, when we were alone, my parents, Danny's mom, and I discussed Bryanna's condition in whispers. I was too paranoid to speak out loud for fear that the hospital staff might be spying on us through the nurse call system. Both fractures were present on last Friday's x-rays that were all taken after Bryanna had been removed from my eyesight on two separate occasions—once at the hospital and the other time at the doctor's office. We were all positive that they had hurt her, but the mystery remained as to what exactly had happened. I began to envision in my mind from a nurse's standpoint the positioning required for a spinal tap. I described to my parents and Danny's mom how she would have been immobilized sort of into a ball (bending the head and feet forward) to push the spine outward for easy access. It suddenly occurred to me and made perfect sense that was how the fractures had occurred. If the injuries had happened simultaneously at the doctor's office during the spinal tap, it would explain why Dr. Green was so determined to accuse us of child abuse. She must have known about an incident at the pediatrician's office and was covering not for the hospital staff but for the very practice where she worked! She did not want us to bring legal action against the doctor's office so she was trying to intimidate us by calling the DCS. I decided not to file a complaint against the hospital because I was not absolutely certain that they were the ones guilty of breaking Bryanna's clavicle and arm.

My father called a trusted attorney friend of his to see who he would suggest for the best malpractice lawyer in the area. He gave him a name, and my father called the attorney's office. Luckily, he was working half a day on Saturday. My father explained our situation to him, and the attorney recommended for us to cooperate with the doctors and hospital staff during the admission and call him back on Monday for an appointment to discuss everything in more detail at his office the following week. He further advised that it appeared like we had a strong malpractice suit.

Bryanna's upper gastrointestinal study was performed around noon by Dr. Story, the chief radiologist. I accompanied her to the Radiology Department, donned a lead apron, and remained with her during the entire procedure feeding her a bottle filled with gastrographin (a liquid substance used to highlight the path of the fluid on the x-ray films). After the exam was completed, Dr. Story said that she did not have any blockages or reflux, but he did note some gastroenteritis (an irritated stomach lining). He asked if she had recently had a stomach virus. I told him that she was diagnosed with one last week. He said that the gastroenteritis was probably causing the formula to curdle in her stomach and then come back up. Dr. Heart did not return to see Bryanna that evening, but he did order Tagamet, a medication to decrease the irritation in her stomach.

The next day was Mother's Day. When Dr. Heart made rounds, he released us as promised. Bryanna was tolerating the new formula very well. She had not vomited since being admitted to the hospital. At least we were able to enjoy Mother's Day, peacefully at home. My grandmother stayed all night with us while Danny worked his last nightshift for the weekend.

The next morning, right after my grandmother left, the doorbell rang. Sure that she had forgotten something, I opened the door expecting her but instead found the DCS social worker, Mrs. Blakely, and the police officer, Detective Gray glaring at me. Since I was still wearing my night clothes, I politely asked them if they minded to wait on my porch while I dressed. Being dressed was not the real concern. It was merely a tactic to buy time and figure out what to do. I closed the door, wrung my hands, and paced the living room floor nervously.

Danny was asleep downstairs. Should I wake him? If they were here to take Bryanna, would meek, non-aggressive Danny even try to stop them? "No!" my mind screamed. Grabbing the phone, I called the one strong person in my life, Daddy. I quickly told him that the DCS was outside waiting on my doorstep. He told me to let them in; he was on his way. Knowing it would take him at least fifteen minutes to get there, I dressed very slowly.

I reluctantly opened the door and permitted the DCS into my home. They sat, side by side, on my loveseat. I sat on the couch across from them with Bryanna clutched tightly in my arms. They asked questions about how she had been since her discharge from the hospital yesterday, and then they wanted to see her room. I left Mrs. Blakely alone in Bryanna's room to look at everything at her convenience. She asked if Bryanna had ever fallen out of the bed. I told her that Bryanna rarely slept in her bed because we used the bassinet all the time. She then wanted to see the bassinet. I showed them that as well and confirmed she had not fallen from either one of them.

They were walking toward the door to leave when my father arrived. He greeted Detective Gray with a firm handshake and asked them to please continue their investigation into what had happened to his granddaughter. Detective Gray acknowledged my father's request with a silent nod, and then both he and Mrs. Blakely exited out the front door. I finally breathed a sigh of relief to see them disappear without my baby.

As the week passed, Bryanna began to eat increased amounts of formula without vomiting. Her appetite improved until she was back to consuming four and one half ounces at a time. Any significant vomiting usually occurred with her first morning feeding so I gave her the Tagamet about fifteen minutes prior to the initial morning bottle and then made her eat it slowly. I fed her every three hours during the day to prevent her stomach from becoming completely empty. An empty stomach could cause acid accumulation which would make gastroenteritis and reflux worse. All of the strategies really seemed to work until later that week when she developed another problem—diarrhea. I was unsure if the new formula, Nutramegin, or the Tagamet was causing the diarrhea. I tried decreasing the Tagamet to three doses per day instead of four, but her regurgitation worsened so I went back to four doses each day.

During that week, I decided to change doctors because I was so dissatisfied with the treatment and actions of Dr. Green's office. I scheduled Bryanna's four month well baby visit on July 6 with an entirely different practice closer to our home. The new pediatrician only practiced with one other physician. That was important to me because it meant that Bryanna could be followed more consistently by fewer doctors. Besides, since her grandparents would be taking care of her while we both worked, we really needed a doctor closer to home.

Even though I planned to change doctors, I kept Bryanna's hospital follow-up visit with Mr. Smith, the nurse practitioner, on May 19, 2000. I did not want to give any impressions that I was not cooperating. Again Dr. Green did not have an open slot for Bryanna, her patient, and she was left to be seen by someone else. At the visit, Bryanna had gained eight ounces. I told him about the diarrhea, but he dismissed it, stating that it did not matter because she was gaining weight. He further said that frequent loose stools were common in infants on Nutramegin. He felt that Tagamet was probably not causing the diarrhea, but he said that I could use my own judgment regarding the frequency of the doses. However, his advice did not ease my anxiety about the diarrhea because I had lost all confidence in the whole practice. He ended the appointment by instructing me to continue Tagamet and Nutramegin until her four month check-up to provide adequate time for the gastroenteritis to resolve.

The next week, on Friday May 26, 2000, Danny and I scheduled an appointment with the malpractice attorney. We discussed in detail all of the events leading to the accusations of child abuse toward us. The attorney felt like the doctor's office or hospital had broken both of Bryanna's bones and then blamed it on us. He was sure that if the authorities truly believed we were guilty of child abuse that they would have taken Bryanna away from us by now. I signed a form to obtain a copy of her hospital and pediatric records, and he promised to take it from there. As a matter of fact, he concluded, "If you were guilty of anything, you would not have been allowed to leave the hospital with her on Mother's Day."

The next week on Memorial Day, May 29, 2000, I was off because it was a holiday. Luckily, Danny managed to get the day off as well. We spent a lovely evening dining with our family. I dressed Bryanna in a darling little dress with ladybugs on it. The red colors made a beautiful contrast with her thick dark hair. It seemed like her hair was getting much longer. She was my little lady bug. I remember my grandmother rocking her after we had supper. Bryanna seemed so alert as she looked around at each of her family members especially focusing on her daddy. That night, after we got home, it suddenly occurred to me that I had not taken Bryanna's picture for several weeks because I had been so consumed with caring for her. I grabbed the camera and snapped several pictures of her with the splint on her arm, anticipating the need for them in my malpractice suit.

The next day, I had to return to work at three-thirty in the afternoon. I really wanted to stay with Bryanna, but I had already missed so much. I laid her on our bed that morning while I took a shower. When I finished my shower, she was still fast asleep. Her little angelic face looked so peaceful. I was absolutely exhausted from the past several weeks of stress. I suddenly wanted to rest a while too. I started to move Bryanna to her bassinet, but I was overcome with the urge to cuddle up next to her. Danny was always explicit that we were not supposed to sleep with Bryanna, but he was downstairs still resting. He would never know the difference. I snuggled her against me on our bed and fell asleep. We took a nice little nap together that day and shared a special secret stolen moment that I will never forget.

The following day, Wednesday, May 31, 2000, shortly after I reported to work, I called Danny to check on Bryanna. He said that she had vomited a large amount of formula back up with her last feeding. That night, after my mother picked her up, I called her to check on Bryanna. My mom said that Bryanna was unusually drowsy and had developed a strange red speckled rash on her forehead and cheeks. Extremely upset about her condition, I left work early. After I arrived at my parent's house, I immediately examined at the rash. It had spread from her cheeks to her shoulders and upper arms. She was restless throughout the night. At six in the morning, she drank some formula only to throw it back up. I checked her temperature, and it was 101 degrees.

At eight in the morning, I attempted to call for an appointment with the new pediatrician, but his office was closed. I knew she needed medical treatment so as much as I hated to, I called Dr. Green's office. Fortunately, I was able to get an appointment with Dr. Heart at 10:40 in the morning. I was actually glad that Dr. Green was not available because Dr. Heart was familiar with her, and I trusted him much more than any of the other doctors in that office.

Since I was afraid to take Bryanna to see Dr. Heart alone, my grandmother went with us. Before the appointment with Dr. Heart, Bryanna had a previously scheduled check up with the orthopedic doctor. After repeat x-rays on her right arm, the orthopedic doctor removed the tiny splint and said that her arm had healed "perfectly." We left the orthopedic doctor's office and headed to see Dr. Heart. When the nurse checked Bryanna's temperature upon our arrival, her fever was completely gone. Her weight remained right at ten pounds. As Dr. Heart examined her, he expressed complete bafflement by the strange rash. He called it petechiae (or bleeding under the skin) and wanted to admit her to the hospital because she appeared seriously ill. Without thinking, I blurted out, "I hope you don't think that we have hurt this baby again." He responded with compassion. "There is no way that anything physically could be done to cause a rash of this nature," and further explained that more than likely it was related to a disease process such as leukemia, meningitis, an immunity disorder, or a blood infection. He recommended a spinal tap to check for meningitis. My grandmother interrupted him by saying, "Only as a last resort because I think that is where our problems began the last time." I agreed with her completely by nodding my head. No way did I want to repeat that episode. Since we were so resistant to a spinal tap, he decided to just do some lab work to look for an infection in her blood stream. We waited in the exam room for the results. He returned a short time later to say that it only showed anemia which was pretty normal at her stage of development. The blood test to look for infection in her blood stream would not be back for twenty-four hours.

Since her lab tests were essentially normal, Dr. Heart decided to let us take Bryanna home and return to the office in the morning for a re-check. If she were to worsen during the night, then we were to report immediately to the pediatric ward at First Street Hospital for admission. While we were there, I told him about Bryanna's persistent diarrhea and subsequent diaper rash. He stated that the diaper rash looked like a yeast infection, and he prescribed some cream. Since Dr. Heart was off the next day, he asked Dr. Cloud to come and look at the rash before we left so he would be able to evaluate it for any changes tomorrow. We made a follow-up appointment with Dr. Cloud for Friday morning. I could not believe that we would have to see a different doctor yet again! Their office certainly had no continuity of care. I would be glad when we were finally switched to the new pediatrician.

That evening, I stayed home from work to take care of Bryanna even though I had already missed a lot of days during my maternity leave. Dr. Heart had suggested alternating formula with Pedialyte for the rest of the day which worked very well because Bryanna retained most of the fluids. Danny reported to work that night for his final shift that week, and I stayed with my parents. I did not want to be alone in case Bryanna worsened during the night.

The Worst Day
of My Life

Bryanna improved during the night and was more alert the following morning. Because I was so reluctant to return to Dr. Green's office after everything they had put me through, I called them to ask if it was truly necessary for her to be re-checked. The office insisted that we keep the appointment with Dr. Cloud. I complied because I did not want to be labeled as uncooperative. Again, so that I would not be at Dr. Green's office alone, Danny's mom accompanied us there. Danny had worked the previous night and was resting so he could take care of Bryanna that evening while I worked, and he could not go with me.

At the office, Dr. Cloud concluded that since the rash was improving, it may have been related to a viral illness. He said that unusual rashes were fairly common with viral illnesses. He felt like she was doing much better, and no longer needed a spinal tap or hospitalization. I decided to go ahead and try to work that afternoon since Bryanna appeared to be doing okay. Danny and his mom both planned to take care of her. Danny's mom was feeding her when I left. I called to check on her after I got to work. Danny said that she had eaten well, kept the formula down, and was sleeping.

I tried to stay busy at work to pass the time until I could return home and be with Bryanna for the weekend. My mom promised that she and my dad would stop by my house to check on Bryanna later that evening. Knowing that eased my mind. My mom was very good with babies, and I trusted that she would truly be able to make a good assessment of how Bryanna was doing.

At around five in the evening, as I was preparing a patient for discharge, my pager beeped displaying my home phone number. Since Bryanna had been so sick, I stopped what I was doing to call home immediately. Danny answered breathless on the first ring, shouting that Bryanna had choked on her bottle. Afterwards, she had become unconscious and stopped breathing. Danny said he had performed CPR until emergency personal arrived and took over. At that very moment, they were loading her into the ambulance to take her to our local hospital, which was not First Street Hospital where I was working. I screamed and dropped the phone. When I realized what I had done, I grabbed the dangling phone and told him that I was on my way to the local hospital. He said if he wanted to ride with her in the ambulance that he had to leave now and hung up. My coworkers mistakenly thought I had screamed because something had happened to my patient, and they all ran into the room. I told them that I had to leave immediately because my baby was unconscious, not breathing, and being rushed to the emergency room. I fumbled with my key ring trying to unlock the cabinet that contained my purse. As I desperately tried to force a key to fit, a coworker placed her hand gently on my shoulder and informed me that I was using the wrong key. I moved aside, and she opened the cabinet for me in an instant with the correct key and handed me my purse. She looked at everyone else and said, "She is way too upset to drive. I will take her to the hospital." I objected that both of us really should not leave, but the charge nurse had the final word and told her to take me.

My coworker turned on her flashing hazard lights and sped us to the hospital as fast as she safely could. I looked at her on the way there and said several times, "I think my baby is dead."

She tried to reassure me, "Don't think that way. You don't know yet."

I listened to her words, but somehow, I already knew in my heart that Bryanna was gone. Maybe it was a mother's instinct or perhaps, I was just mentally preparing myself for the very worst.

My coworker used to work in the emergency room at the hospital so she took me in through the back door. She approached the nurse's station and asked where Bryanna Draper's room was. The nurses pointed to a door carefully guarded by two security personnel. No one was permitted inside her room at that time. Instead, they took us to a private waiting area where we found only Danny, hysterical, trembling and crying. No one else from our family had arrived yet. I had never seen him that upset in my entire life. I knew immediately that Bryanna was in very bad shape. His appearance frightened me both for Bryanna and him. I wanted to calm him, but instead, I felt myself falling to the floor. My coworker grabbed me by the shoulders and lowered me gently to the ground. For a few seconds everything was black. I weakly opened my eyes and began to shiver all over, feeling freezing cold. My coworker shouted "she is going into shock!" I faintly remember her propping my feet into the air on a stool and covering me with warm blankets.

My parents, my sister, Danny's mom, Danny's stepdad, and our pastor and his wife gradually arrived sometime while I was collapsed in the floor. My mind was in a fog, and I saw everyone in the room in a haze. Danny's mom was wringing her hands and repeatedly saying, "I had been gone for no more than an hour when he called me and said she had choked. How can this be happening? She was fine when I left. The doctor said she was much better this morning. I hope they don't try to pin something on Danny. What if they claim he did something to her?" She sat next to Danny with her arm around him worried that he was so upset that he might have a heart attack. Even though I was in a very weak state of mind, her words stirred a new fear inside me that they would blame something on Danny since he was the last person to be with Bryanna while she was alive. Part of the reason that I worried about that was because of the earlier child abuse allegations.

We waited for what seemed like hours with no update on Bryanna's status. Since my coworker had previously worked in that emergency room, she left to see if she could convince the doctor to speak with all of us. She returned to the private waiting room a few minutes later with a tall very young looking doctor. He explained that so far all of their attempts to revive Bryanna were unsuccessful. She had demonstrated no heart beat since she had arrived to the emergency room. He promised that they would continue their resuscitation efforts for a little longer but gave us no real hope. Before leaving, he asked for the name of her pediatrician.

I knew from my years of nursing experience exactly what they were doing to Bryanna in that room. Vivid pictures raced through my mind of them sticking needles in her, pumping on her chest performing CPR, and placing a breathing tube down her tiny throat. I was torn between wanting them to revive her and wanting them to stop torturing her. When the doctor said that she had no heart beat since arriving to the emergency room, it meant she had been without signs of life for at least an hour. I knew in my heart that she was already lost. He was simply preparing us a step at a time for the inevitable. I myself had done the same thing during the years that I had worked intensive care.

About thirty minutes later, the doctor returned to tell us that she was gone. The physician on call for Dr. Green's office accompanied him to the waiting room. I looked at her and realized that she was yet another different doctor that Bryanna had never seen. She never spoke a word to us, not even "I'm sorry for your loss." In an attempt to avoid the reality that Bryanna was truly dead, I fainted. My coworker snapped an ammonia inhalant under my nose. The noxious, repulsive odor immediately revived me. I pushed it away, almost fighting. I wanted them to leave me alone and let me die with her. How was I supposed to go home without her? How could I make it through tomorrow without her? I learned the meaning of surviving one minute at a time.

While we waited for the nursing staff to prepare Bryanna's body for viewing, my dad took Danny to the bathroom. When they returned, Danny was quietly composed, no longer crying or hysterical; then, he saw his mother. As she approached him sobbing uncontrollably, he instantly became distraught again.

A few minutes later, the staff took us to view her body. In spite of my protests, my dad rolled me in a wheelchair because everyone was afraid that I would faint again. I was the first to enter the room. As he pushed me through the door, I could see her tiny lifeless body on the table. I grabbed the sides of the doorway to stop the wheelchair and screamed, "I can't stand it! I can't look at her. Take me out!" He started to back me out of the room when I suddenly realized that I did need to tell her goodbye. "No, wait, I'll go," I barely whispered. My dad pushed me to the huge exam table where her tiny body rested without movement. I brushed my fingers against her cheek and looked at everyone else as they gathered in the room in a circle around the exam table. "My baby is so cold!" I told them. She had always felt so warm making the coldness seem very unnatural. It consumed my thoughts until I noticed a portion of her hair had been shaved away and an intravenous line was planted in the top of her pretty little round head. A breathing tube was protruding from the corner of her mouth. Because I was a nurse, I knew that all of the foreign tubes would remain in place until they asked us if we wanted an autopsy.

My coworker told the emergency room staff that I was a nurse and would understand medical language so they could speak plainly to me. I asked them what was done and what she had been given during the resuscitation process. The staff named the medications that had been used. The intravenous line had to be placed in her scalp because they could not get one anywhere else. I felt like I was watching someone else's life, not really taking part in the events. The nurse said, "Go ahead and pick her up. It is okay to hold her." I gently lifted her limp lifeless body from the table properly protecting her head and neck as if she were still alive and breathing thinking, *my life will never be the same again.*

My boss in the Radiology Department at work entered the room while I was holding Bryanna. She kindly said to me, "You take as much time off as you need, and I mean that. Don't worry about your job. It will be waiting for you when you are able to return." All of Bryanna's family members and friends that were present held her for a few brief moments. She was passed from one person's arms to the next all in the same gentle fashion that we had held her in life. It was extremely solemn with each person speaking a few words about how pretty she was, how sick she had been, or just saying goodbye.

When they were all finished, she was returned to me so that I could hold her one last time. The room was filled with audible sounds of sobbing from everyone. After I placed her gently back on the exam table, one of the nurses clipped a curly lock of her beautiful dark hair and preserved it in an empty specimen tube for me. The emergency room doctor gave me a few valiums to help me sleep that night. I thanked all of the staff for their efforts to revive her and their kindness for allowing us adequate peaceful time to spend with her.

As we left the exam room, we were approached by a police officer, Detective Sharp, and a department of children services worker, Mrs. Campbell. After they introduced themselves, Detective Sharp apologized for bothering us at such a difficult time and explained that it was a necessary requirement to speak with the family when a minor died at home. Once again, we were escorted to a private room to talk with them. Only Danny, my father, and I were allowed in the room. The door was closed behind us. Detective Sharp did not really question us about anything. He just said that she would have an autopsy because it was required by state law. I told him that was good because I wanted an autopsy to be performed whether it was mandatory or not. I needed to know what had happened to my baby. Since she died at home, they had to inspect our house and take some photographs that very night because nothing could be moved or changed before their assessment. I felt like a criminal. My dad volunteered to go with them to our home so Danny and I would not have to face it that soon after her death. I asked my dad to gather all of her stuff scattered throughout the house, put it in her room, and close the door. After talking to them, we left the emergency room. Danny and I rode to my parent's house with our pastor and his wife.

When we arrived at my parents' house, I became bombarded with suicidal thoughts. I wanted to die so that I could be with her but lacked the strength or the means to perform the act. More relatives and friends arrived to speak their condolences. My mother said that I collapsed to the floor and prayed for God to take me. However, I don't remember doing that. All I can recall is being consumed with the desire to join her. Every aching minute seemed like an hour of agony without her. I would have gladly given my life in exchange for hers, but unfortunately, God made that decision for me. During her entire illness, I prayed with faith for God to heal her. Now she was dead. No number of prayers could bring her back. God had betrayed me and I was angry. I felt guilty for being mad at God, but I could not control it. Yet, without him, how would I survive the next few days? A turmoil of emotions flooded my mind as I studied various ways that I could end my misery. I counted the valium that the emergency room doctor had given me—only four pills, far from enough for an overdose. I thought about sitting in the garage with the car running. I slipped quietly to Danny and whispered that plan to him, inviting him to join me. He told me that death was not the answer. Since he did not want to go with me, I would just find a way to do it alone.

The valium proved useless because I did not sleep at all that night. I could not eat anything either. It required too much effort to swallow solid food over the lump constricting my throat. Then I decided, subconsciously, that if I did not eat, I would eventually starve and die.

Many people offered sympathetic words, but few understood my feelings. A lady that worked with my mom visited us the next morning. She shared her story of giving birth to a stillborn infant with me. She knew how it felt to lose a child. I also had an aunt that had lost two pregnancies. Of all the people who offered condolences, only those two people truly understood my grief enough to comfort me.

The lady that worked with my mom told me it might help if I held a baby doll. My sister went through her closet until she found one of her plastic dolls and brought it to me. I wrapped it in a blanket and sat in my mom's rocking chair cuddling the plastic doll. It did seem to provide some relief for my empty arms, although it was cold and lifeless. My days had been consumed with caring for Bryanna. Now suddenly, I had literally nothing to do.

Danny and I decided to go home around lunch time that day. The house was strangely dark, desolate, and quiet. My dad had done a decent job hiding most of Bryanna's things but a few stray undetected articles remained visible. I opened the refrigerator absentmindedly for a drink and found several bottles filled with unused formula. No longer thirsty, I snuck away from Danny and my family so that I could go to the basement den where she had actually died. I needed to know exactly where it had happened. On my hands and knees, I crawled around the room in front of the couch rubbing the carpet until I found a large stiff patch where the regurgitated formula had dried. Daddy had attempted to clean it, but it had evidently been there long enough to leave a stain. I felt something touch my shoulder and turned to see Danny kneeling beside me. "Is this where she died?" I asked, my voice cracking. Tears streaming down his cheeks, he could only nod his head as he embraced me. He pulled me to my feet and almost had to carry me back upstairs away from that dreadful place.

Afterward, I sat in the living room very still for long periods of time holding the cold plastic doll in a trance like state until someone would arouse me by yelling my name. Whoever it was said, "We've been saying your name several times. What's wrong?" I just stared at them. I did not know what was wrong. I was weak from not eating but could not have swallowed a bite if my life depended on it. Sitting extremely motionless helped me to empty my mind and relieve some of the pain. Slowly, I was becoming what psychiatrists call "catatonic"—a state in which one stops moving or talking, usually instigated by some type of severely stressful event. The stillness was pleasant and I wanted to stay there but my family kept calling me out of it. Then suddenly, my parents loaded me into their van. "I don't want to go anywhere," I protested, but they took me to an afterhours clinic anyway because my behavior and suicidal thoughts were really scaring everyone.

We checked into the clinic and were quickly taken to an exam room. When the doctor entered, Danny and my parents told her about Bryanna's death and that they were afraid that I might harm myself. They wanted her to put me on an anti-depressant. I listened to them quietly. The doctor asked me if I planned to harm myself. I told her I just missed my baby and wanted to be with her. She said that was understandable and wanted to know if I would like to try some medication to help me. I answered with only a nod. I would have taken anything to ease some of my pain. Danny and my parents promised her that they would see that I took whatever she recommended. She prescribed Paxil (an anti-depressant) and Xanax (an anti-anxiety medication), advising that the Paxil would take about two to three weeks to be effective and the Xanax would compensate until then. Due to the serious nature of my threats, she said that I would have to be evaluated by a mental health therapist before I could leave. That woke me out of my trance like state. They were going to try to lock me up!

We had to wait an hour for the therapist to arrive, but hey, what else did we have to do anyway? There was no way I was going to let them lock me up because if they did, then I could not kill myself. I gave all the right answers to her questions to prevent them from confining me in a psychiatric hospital. I told her I simply wanted to be with my baby and that death was the only route. I denied having a plan to kill myself (That, of course, was a lie. I had at least four or five ideas, but if they detained me on a psychiatric ward, then I could not do them.) After my family promised to keep me safe, and I answered all the questions to her satisfaction, we were finally allowed to leave.

During the rest of the weekend, every minute seemed like an eternity while we waited for her autopsy to be done on Monday. Many visitors offered sympathy and brought enormous amounts of food. Even my close friend from King College, who was living in Colorado at that time, flew in for the funeral. I truly appreciated everyone's kind gestures, but sometimes, I could not face anyone and had to hide in my bedroom. The one thing I wanted was my baby back, and no one could do that for me. No real comfort existed for my empty arms. Danny's father and step-mom arrived from out of town on Sunday to stay with so we were not left alone at night.

Sunday night, I woke up in the middle of the night and could not go back to sleep. For a change of scenery and not to disturb Danny, I decided to go lie on the couch in the downstairs den. Still, I could not sleep. Suddenly, thoughts and phrases entered my mind from some unknown place. The words came together to form a beautiful poem to dedicate to Bryanna. I hand wrote a special copy and signed it "love, mommy" to be placed in the coffin and buried with her.

Monday finally arrived. Her autopsy was scheduled to be performed in the afternoon. If the funeral home did not receive her body by seven in the evening, they would not have enough time to prepare her for the services on Tuesday, and it would be postponed by another day. Danny's dad made several phone calls throughout the day to check on the progress of the autopsy, but he could never get through to anyone at the medical school. Finally, at seven that evening, he spoke with someone from security that said the autopsy was finished, and the funeral home was on the way to get the body. We would be able to have the wake on Tuesday after all.

As soon as we knew that she was going to the funeral home, my father rushed over there to ensure that she did indeed arrive. I was a zombie and could not concentrate on anything long enough to make a decision about the details of her funeral. Danny was busy caring for me and consumed in his own grief. The duty of arranging the services was designated once again to the strongest person in my life, my dad.

My dad returned with instructions for me to choose a dress for her to wear. "I can't do it," I sobbed. "I can't go in her room."

"Yes, you can," my pastor's wife said. "Come on. I'll go with you and help you."

She wrapped her left arm around me and my mom grabbed my right arm. The three of us, arm in arm, took slow, steady steps across the house to Bryanna's closed bedroom door. The door had remained shut since Friday night. I had to do the task myself. No one could do it for me.

The room was in disarray. Evidently, my dad had just thrown everything inside the door and pulled it shut. We had to step over a variety of toys to reach the closet. I looked at several different dresses before I decided on her white Easter dress that I was positive she would soil on Easter Sunday. I debated on burying her in the beloved black patents that my mom had bought her, but I just could not give them up. I choose white cloth shoes and white hose instead. We were about to leave the room when Daddy said that she would need a sweater and bonnet also. "Why does she need a bonnet and a sweater?" I asked, distressed. My mind raced with terrible thoughts. My dad tried to calm me by explaining that her arms and head could not be exposed due to the autopsy. That did little to relieve me. I found a tiny white lacy bonnet, but she did not have a sweater (other than one that someone had made for her, and I did not want to give it up). We decided to just buy one, but later, my mother found a really small sweater that had belonged to my sister as a baby. My dad took all of the clothes to the funeral home that evening. I sent the handwritten copy of her poem with him to be sealed in her coffin.

Early the next morning, my father went to the funeral home to see if Bryanna was ready for me to view. He returned to my house to take us to the funeral home to finalize all the arrangements. On the way there, we stopped at Kmart to pick up a roll of film that contained the pictures I had taken on Memorial Day. I decided to wait to open them until we arrived at the funeral parlor. I had also brought a stack of pictures of the first two months of her life. After I viewed the body that morning, I would have to decide whether I wanted an open or closed casket. If I chose a closed casket, I planned to display several of my favorite pictures of her on a bulletin board.

⟨⟨⟨

We entered the large viewing room. On the opposite side rested a tiny white coffin engulfed by beautiful flower arrangements, most of them powder light pink, the color used at a baby shower. Someone had even purchased a white teddy bear with a pink bow. Surrounded by several close family members, I walked across the long room to her awaiting casket. She seemed so still and peaceful, adorned in the white Easter dress, sweater, and bonnet. I noticed immediately that something was horribly wrong with her eyes. The outside corners were unnaturally pinched or pointed. It almost looked like a stitch was holding them shut. She did not remotely look like my Bryanna.

Turning to the other family members in the room, I exclaimed, "This is not Bryanna." My dad assured me that it was definitely her. I asked him several times, "Are you sure they haven't confused her with another baby?"

"No honey, it is her," he answered consistently every time.

My dad finally just took me by the arm and moved me away from the coffin to a nearby couch. As I sat down, I said, "I want a closed casket funeral." With trembling fingers, I slowly opened the new package of pictures and looked through them. The recent pictures compared to the older pictures revealed a major change in her appearance. The pictures from the first two months of her life showed a round, pink, healthy infant face. Two months had passed before another picture was taken of her on Memorial Day. In those most recent pictures, she looked pale, waxen, and gaunt. Being with her every day, I had not noticed the gradual decline in the way she looked, but it was quite obvious when I compared the two sets of pictures. I announced loudly to everyone, "Oh my gosh, she really was sick!" The room was so quiet that my words seemed to echo off the walls. No one said anything in response. It was like I was talking to myself. I carefully chose a dozen pictures to display on the board. Then I returned to her casket and kissed her forehead one last time. It was so cold that it chilled me to the bone. I looked at the funeral director and said, "Please close it now."

On the way home, I realized that I did not have a black dress for the funeral. My mom drove me to Sears where I found a black dress with small white roses embroidered onto the collar. Afterward, we rested until time for the evening services. Danny hovered over me intently all afternoon. Many people commented on his devotion to me and how brave he was to put his grief aside and attend to me.

The services started at six-thirty in the evening on Tuesday, June 6, 2000, with the funeral scheduled to be first and visitation to follow. I swallowed a Xanax on the way to the funeral home.

I didn't have any water so I almost choked on it. Wringing my hands, I prayed for the strength to survive the next few hours.

My family had to almost carry me into the funeral home. I felt so weak that I could barely walk. I had to stop at the bathroom on the way to the chapel because I felt sick to my stomach. I almost passed out in the bathroom. My mom had to yell outside for Dad. She thought he was going to have to come in the ladies room and help her pick me up from the floor, but she quickly put a cold wet paper towel on my forehead, and it revived me enough to get me safely to the chapel. My family was probably glad to secure me in a pew where hopefully I wouldn't faint again.

Pain was evident on my pastor's face as he preached a wonderful message for her funeral. She had only briefly touched our lives, but her loss was so great. He concluded the ceremony by reading the poem that I wrote for her as follows:

My Little Piece of Sunshine

June 5, 2000
I had a little piece of sunshine
Within the depths of my womb it grew,
Then one day through agony and pain
My little sunshine came through.

※

This little ray of sunshine
Was really a gift from heaven above;
I thanked God every day
That he gave me her to love.

※

Then one day I had her
And the next day she was gone;
I screamed to God Why! Why me!

His reply, she was simply on loan.

⁂

I had a little piece of sunshine,
But God took her away;
I guess that heaven wasn't bright enough
Without her extra ray.

I was very upset when he first started to speak because I had not intended for it to be read aloud in her service, but afterward, I realized that it created the perfect final touch, making a way for me to contribute my thoughts to her eulogy. As my pastor read the words to the poem, audible sobbing could be heard throughout the chapel.

At the conclusion of the poem, my pastor asked everyone to bow their heads for prayer, and then we moved to the visitation room to greet people. The line of family and friends lasted for two solid hours. I was greeted with hugs, kisses, and tears as each person came to pay their respects. The funeral home director commented that he had never seen such a large number of visitors for a baby. Usually, baby funerals were very small. Even though a few people were still streaming through the door, I asked my dad to take me home. I was so exhausted that I just could not talk to anyone else.

The next morning, we concluded her memorial with a graveside service at ten in the morning. I wore the same black dress as the night before, and I didn't care. My pastor spoke a few brief but poignant words; I realized that my only hope to ever see her again was in the afterlife. We, the immediate family, were supposed to exit first. As I stood up to leave, I had an overwhelming desire to touch her coffin one last time before it was buried in the ground forever. I reached my hand toward her casket, but my family tried to pull me back. I guess they feared that I was either about to fall down again or go completely nuts. All I really wanted to do was bid her little tiny body farewell. Somehow, I found the strength to pull away from their grasps. Grabbing the casket with outstretched hands, I barely whimpered, "Goodbye, my love." My chest was physically aching from the mental pain of her loss. The memorial services were now concluded. I had to learn to live without her and somehow deal with my sorrow.

Adjusting

Danny and I took two weeks off work after Bryanna's death. During that time, I felt lifeless and mostly slept. I did not know if the fatigue was related to the antidepressant medication or the intense stress that I had endured. Danny's dad and step-mom returned home on Wednesday morning after the graveside services, and we found ourselves all alone and lonely after the rest of the visitors had left.

We had so much food and no appetites. I knew that we would never be able to eat all of it so we decided to donate the food to the Haven of Rest. I wanted to do a good deed in her honor by feeding hungry people.

The next day, I began to clean my house to occupy my mind. It was rather messy from so many visitors coming and going over the previous several days. My mom and Danny's mom were supposed to be arriving at any moment to help me. When the doorbell rang, I figured that it was one of them and absentmindedly opened the door. To my astonishment, it was Detective Sharp and Mrs. Campbell from the emergency room the previous Friday night. Seeing them on my doorstep left me speechless and faint. Detective Sharp said, "We want to discuss Bryanna's illness with you." I did not know what to say so I yelled for Danny. He immediately came to my side. Detective Sharp repeated his request. Danny said, "We just buried our daughter yesterday and do not feel like talking to anyone right now." He gave them our lawyer's name and told them to contact him with any questions. Thankfully, they just nodded and left after that. How inconsiderate of them to want to question us the day after we buried our daughter! I was appalled!

That morning marked the second time I had opened the door with unwelcome guests waiting on the other side. After my mom and Danny's mom arrived, I sent Danny to Lowe's to buy a peephole for the front door so I could see who was there before I opened it the next time. Meanwhile, I called my father and told him about our morning visitors. He contacted our lawyer who advised that we cooperate with the authorities if they only wanted to ask about Bryanna's medical history. My father then called Detective Sharp and set up a time to speak with him the next day. While on the phone, my dad asked him if he had attempted to obtain her medical information from the pediatrician's office. Detective Sharp replied that they had been to the office once, but everyone was too busy to talk to them. That made perfect sense considering that they were guilty of doing something to Bryanna's arm and then accusing us of child abuse to hide it. Of course, they would avoid the authorities.

My mom, Danny's mom, and I cleaned the house for the rest of the afternoon so that it would be presentable for the meeting with Detective Sharp the next day. As we worked, our paranoia gradually increased until our voices lowered into barely audible whispers. We conjured the idea that Detective Sharp had bugged the house Friday night when Daddy brought him to take pictures and completely stopped speaking out loud about anything concerning Bryanna's death, sure that they were somewhere secretly listening to our every word. That day marked the beginning of a paranoid state of mind for me that would only worsen as time passed. Looking out the window for anything odd or unusual, I noticed a strange dilapidated Winnebago parked on a vacant lot in the distance. Afterwards, we all took turns peering between the slants in the blinds at the unidentified vehicle that had suddenly appeared from nowhere. We imagined Detective Sharp and Mrs. Campbell sitting inside that Winnebago listening to our conversation, waiting to hear one of us confess to harming Bryanna. The Winnebago would have been a perfect place to spy on us because it looked very roomy for their equipment and the windows were darkened. Plus, they would be near us to make an immediate arrest if anyone confessed to anything. The more we thought about it, the more our imaginations surged.

❧

Friday afternoon Detective Sharp and Mrs. Campbell arrived to our house promptly at one in the afternoon. For emotional support, my parents, Danny's mom, and Danny's stepdad were also present for the meeting. Detective Sharp began by stating it was unusual for them to speak to all of the family members at the same time like that, but he was willing to do it. He then told us that only he and Mrs. Campbell would be working on the task from now on. Detective Gray and Ms. Blakeley had been mistakenly assigned to our case earlier because Dr. Green thought we lived in the county. Instead, we actually resided within the city limits which fell under Detective Sharp and Mrs. Campbell's jurisdiction.

After we were comfortably seated in my living room, my father stood up in the center of the room and faced everyone. He said sternly, "Before we get started, I want to say something. All throughout Bryanna's illness, the doctors have tried to intimidate us and threaten us, and they have used your department to help them."

Detective Sharp responded by saying, "Well my job is to find the truth, wherever that road my lead."

After they finished, I recited my handwritten diary notes from the beginning to the end. As I read, other family members added extra details to my story. I recorded their remarks in the margins of the notebook paper. Detective Sharp asked occasional questions for clarification. He and Mrs. Campbell were both writing in their own tablets as I talked. When I reached the last doctor's visit, Friday June 2, I stopped. I asked Danny to finish the story after that point. I felt he could describe it better than me because I was not actually present. While he recounted her death, I left the room for a mental break. I could not bear to listen to the details of that horrible afternoon again.

When I returned to the living room, Detective Sharp asked us a few vague questions, one of which struck me as rather odd because I did not see how it related to Bryanna's death at all. The question was directed specifically to me. Detective Sharp wanted to know what I thought of Dr. Story, the chief radiologist at First Street Hospital who had performed Bryanna's gastrointestinal study. I replied with my true feelings at that time, "I think he is a very good, thorough doctor from what I have seen."

We asked him when we might know the autopsy results. He said, "You are not going to like hearing this. There will be a preliminary report in about two to three weeks, but it will probably take at least five months to obtain the final results." I quickly calculated the time in my mind and realized that would be about November. Five months seemed like an unreasonably long waiting period for an answer as to why she died. Yet, we should still have the report in adequate time to meet the one year time limit from the date of the incident to file a malpractice lawsuit. Before they left, my father said a prayer asking God to guide Detective Sharp during his investigation to find the truth. As he spoke, I nodded my head, convinced that the truth involved a massive cover-up by the pediatricians and hospital. I prayed silently and perhaps a little vindictively that they would be exposed for exactly what they were.

After Detective Sharp and Mrs. Campbell left, my mom took me to the cemetery for our first visit since Bryanna was buried. I gathered some beautiful wild flowers from my backyard to put on her grave. My grandmother had seen a baby bunny sitting on Bryanna's grave the day before so I also took some lettuce for the rabbit hoping that it might stay near her resting place.

Bryanna's plot was next to my great-grandmother's grave. I had several different choices for her final resting place, but quickly decided upon the plot next to my great-grandmother for three important reasons: her death was the first great loss I can remember, she had also experienced the loss of a child, and the two other plots beside it were vacant. My grandmother gave ownership of those two additional plots to my father so that one day, Danny and I could be buried close to Bryanna. Her grave was marked only by a huge mound of freshly shoveled earth. With no monument placed yet, her resting place appeared desolate and meaningless. I decided to place a headstone as soon as possible. I arranged the wildflowers and lettuce on top of the roughened dirt, thinking sadly that I should be holding her instead of visiting her grave. It was all so wrong.

⁂

During those first two weeks after Bryanna died, my dangerous suicidal feelings slowly decreased until they almost disappeared. I guess it was partially due to the antidepressant medication, Paxil, but mostly due to prayer. I realized that I had to be strong for Danny and my mom. I could not leave either one of them alone. My mom suffered horribly over the loss of Bryanna. If I killed myself, it might ease my pain, but it would compound her sorrow terribly. That thought helped me recognize that I needed to live in order to take care of those around me. The therapist at the weekend clinic had recommended further counseling, but I chose not to follow up with it because I had good emotional support from my family, church, and Danny who were constantly available to console me.

Another great source of comfort during that time was our dog, Annie. I found that I could sit in the backyard, stroke Annie, and block out my shattered life for a short while. She eased my sorrow so much that I decided to get another dog. The week after Bryanna died, Danny and I went to the kennel and adopted a black lab named, Baxter. He was young, energetic, and affectionate. Now I had something to take care of again. It certainly did not replace Bryanna, but it was helpful in my healing process.

Another task that we needed to accomplish before returning to work was to choose a grave marker. Unfortunately, we did not have any life insurance on Bryanna when she died. I had planned to purchase it but became so preoccupied with caring for her that I forgot to do it; therefore, we had no extra money to pay for the funeral or burial. My parents took care of the funeral home expenses. My grandmother gave us the grave plot, and Danny's mom and stepdad volunteered to purchase the monument. Thankfully, those three things combined covered all of the expenses of her death. Danny and I did not have enough in savings to begin to cover the costs.

The day after we adopted Baxter, Danny's mom and stepdad took us to the cemetery office to purchase the marker for Bryanna's grave. There were basically two kinds to choose from: simple concrete stones with just a name and date or fancier bronze markers with a vase. The price difference between the two kinds was phenomenal. I really wanted the one with a vase so that we could keep flowers on her grave all year. During the summer without a vase, the flowers would be thrown away or destroyed during mowing season. Danny's mom and stepdad bought the expensive bronze marker without regard to the cost with the money that they had inherited from Danny's stepdad's father (They still had a large portion of those finances left). We discussed at length what to engrave on the monument. Selfishly, I suggested "Mommy's little angel." Everyone else said why not "Mommy and Daddy's little angel." Realizing that I was being inconsiderate, I agreed wholeheartedly to that inscription. Since her life had been so short, I also wanted her exact birth and death date engraved onto it. It would be two weeks before it arrived. When it did finally come and was placed in the ground, this is how it looked:

Bryanna Faith Draper
Feb. 11, 2000 – June 2, 2000
Mommy and Daddy's Little Angel

I cannot begin to describe the generosity that everyone extended to us during our time of grief. I spent a lot of time the two weeks that we were off work writing thank-you cards. We had flower arrangements scattered all over the house; my mom took most of them home with her because she has a true "green thumb", and I did not want them to die. I planted a couple of them outside our house so that I could watch them come back year after year. A lot of family and friends gave us money. I offered the money to my dad and Danny's parents to offset their contributions to the funeral expenses and marker, but they all refused it. They said that paying for that stuff was the last thing that they would ever be able to do for their granddaughter and advised us to use the money to catch up on bills. Danny began to talk about what we could buy with the money. That struck me as odd because I felt like the money we were given was "blood money" and should be used only for a good purpose. Since I took care of the bills, I told him that we needed the money for her hospital expenses and that was exactly how I used it. I did not feel right spending that money on anything frivolous.

Two weeks after Bryanna's autopsy, my father contacted Detective Sharp to inquire about the preliminary results. Detective Sharp stated that they were "inconclusive." We would have to wait until the final report was back, probably in November, to know what had happened to her. My mind was filled with huge question marks. It must be something very bad or very rare for the report to be "inconclusive." Confused and frustrated, I wanted a copy of the report, but Detective Sharp said it would not be helpful because it did not say anything. I had hoped for some answers in two weeks, but we were left to wait for five more months.

Knowing that child abuse charges were in place before her death, I felt my anxiety level slowly start to rise. However, there was nothing I could do but pray. I did notice one thing that kind of relieved my mind. The strange Winnebago that had appeared across the street around the time of Bryanna's funeral had mysteriously vanished. If the detective had been using the vehicle to spy on us like we imagined, maybe the preliminary results did not indicate any wrong doing on our part, and they had left.

In order to stay busy, on June 19, 2000, Danny and I returned to work. During our two weeks off, I had only moped and slept most of the time. If I did not do something soon, I risked falling into a deep depression. I thought that the best therapy that we could give ourselves was to reach out and help others through our jobs. When we returned to work, Danny started a new job with the hours of twelve in the afternoon to eight-thirty at night. I was still working two-thirty in the afternoon to eleven at night. His new schedule made our hours almost the same again. That was great because neither one of us would be at home alone for a long period of time. We would also be together at work to help each other make it through the day. I was truly trying to take just one day at a time, and staying busy proved to be beneficial in passing the time and easing the pain.

The first several weeks back at work were very difficult because of initial confrontations with my coworkers since Bryanna's death. Most people offered sympathy, but really were at a loss for words. Just letting us know they loved us and were praying for us was always enough. Words cannot alleviate the pain anyway.

The worst moments were when people were not aware that she had died, and they asked, "How's that baby doing?" It was not their fault because, by all means, she should have been doing wonderful, but in reality, she was not. I usually responded by turning pale and not saying anything. They generally guessed what had happened and apologized. It created an extremely uncomfortable situation, but I couldn't help it. However, it did expose one dreadful fact. Her death was unnatural for everyone.

The Waiting

When I returned to work, I quickly discovered that a lot of people were gossiping about what had happened to Bryanna. Worst of all, none of the individuals that were talking should have even legally known about Bryanna's medical history. For example, a previous coworker from my old cardiac unit at First Street Hospital was discussing Bryanna's condition and illness with Dr. Green's husband, a cardiologist, and the wife of Mr. Smith (the nurse practitioner that saw Bryanna twice at Dr. Green's office). The three of them worked together in the cardiac catheterization lab. They were spreading rumors about intimate details of Bryanna's case that Dr. Green's husband and Mr. Smith's wife should not have even known about unless Dr. Green and Mr. Smith had told them those things. As a nurse, I knew the seriousness of maintaining privacy of medical records, and the correct term for their behavior was breeching confidentiality. All through nursing school, we were taught that you do not discuss a patient's records with anyone not involved in their care, not even your spouse. Dr. Green and Mr. Smith's behavior was unprofessional and unethical and punishable by the medical boards.

Through the grapevine, I found out that the same previous coworker was interrogating some of my closest friends in the cardiac unit for more details about Bryanna's death such as autopsy results and lab values. When my friends warned her to stop meddling, she told them that Dr. Green's husband had said on several occasions, "it doesn't look good for the parents" and "it is going to be long and drawn out and possibly go public." Mr. Smith's wife was bragging to everyone that she knew something really important about it, but she could not tell what it was. Regardless of exactly what Dr. Green's husband and Mr. Smith's wife were saying, they discussed information that could have only been obtained through their spouses breeching patient confidentiality. I had not spoken to my ex-coworker in over six months so any propaganda that she was spreading was not from me. She even attempted to call me at home to get more details, but I ignored her messages. Plus, I had not shared the child abuse accusations with anyone apart from close family members so no one at First Street Hospital should have known about that.

All of the rumors that I was hearing pointed toward some type of charges being filed against Danny and me. My anxiety level increased another notch. I had no idea what Dr. Green's office was plotting behind our backs especially now that Bryanna had died. Bryanna had obviously had some type of disease process that Dr. Green had ignored and instead accused us of child abuse. Now Bryanna was gone, and I was sure that Dr. Green would not want to accept the blame for her death. Maybe she had even put her husband up to making comments like "it does not look good for the parents" to further scare us from filing a lawsuit against her.

I also heard a completely contradictory rumor that involved Dr. Cloud saying that a vital lab result on Bryanna was overlooked, and she had a rare bone disorder that was deadly if not detected early in life. All of the chatter was very disturbing so I did the only thing that I knew to do. I called my lawyer and reported their unethical behavior to him so that he could document it. When I sued Dr. Green's office for malpractice, I planned to include breeching confidentiality as well.

Since all of those unnecessary individuals were prowling through Bryanna's records, I decided to do a little research of my own. I began by going to the medical records department and asking to read her chart. To my surprise, it was locked away in legal files, and I had to schedule an appointment to look at it. Legal files could only be accessed on specific days at certain times so I had to wait two days to see it. Meanwhile, I obtained lab and x-ray results on my own via the hospital computer.

Around ten o'clock one night, I was reviewing the x-ray reports and encountered a very puzzling piece of information. On the day of Bryanna's autopsy, June 5, 2000, at about five-thirty in the afternoon (which was during her autopsy), an addendum was written to her CAT scan report by Dr. Story, the chief radiologist. The addendum stated that Bryanna had "a fluid collection" or "hygroma" in the front of her brain and "minimally widened sutures" (sutures—the long immovable joints connecting the bones in the skull). I had no idea what a "hygroma" was, but I did know that a "fluid collection" and "widened sutures" meant increased pressure in her brain and possibly swelling or bleeding. Extra fluid in her brain would push the sutures away from each other, thus, causing them to widen.

I immediately called Danny at home to ask him if he knew what a "hygroma" was. He had no idea either. Next, I phoned my parents to tell them about what I had accidentally found. The radiologist that originally read it had either missed an abnormality, or Dr. Story was falsifying Bryanna's chart to make us look guilty of child abuse. Either way, I was furious. As soon as I arrived home, I searched the internet and all my medical text books for a definition of "hygroma," but could find very little information about it. In the neck area in small children, a "hygroma" could be a cancerous tumor, but her "hygroma" was in the head so that did not fit the profile. It could also result from trauma. That was about all that I could find, and none of it really made any sense. Dr. Story was on vacation that week so I planned to talk directly with him about it one evening as soon as he returned.

On June 23, 2000, I was finally able to review her entire hospital chart. I had to sit in an office and read it and was forbidden to have a copy. Her spinal tap at the doctor's office was described as being "traumatic," confirming my suspicion that both fractures had occurred there. Her spinal fluid was not normal as I had been told, and she had multiple abnormal lab results including E.

Coli (infectious bacteria) present in her urine. The progress note written by Dr. Green for Bryanna's second hospital admission portrayed Danny and me as foolish, like we had asked silly, uneducated questions. It did not reflect at all what had really happened. She even wrote that I had handled Bryanna too roughly when I pulled her arm up to unblock her airway and insinuated that had caused the arm fracture. Dr. Green's notes really tried to implicate us with child abuse, but the other doctor's notes failed to support her allegations. I loved my baby, and her accusations were unjustified and infuriating. In my heart, I knew that I did not break Bryanna's arm that night. I now regretted even telling them about that incident. I was just trying to be honest, and Dr. Green had used it against me.

None of the abnormal lab results were ever treated or followed up on, and her antibiotics were discontinued during the first day of her admission. Her fussiness and stomach problems were all blamed on an arm fracture that occurred either at the doctor's office or hospital. The only treatment ever administered by Dr. Green was a child abuse investigation. The chart was stamped on June 5, 2000 as "under investigation for child abuse," with a photocopied picture of Mrs. Blakely's identification card attached to it. Only Detective Sharp and Mrs. Campbell knew about Bryanna's death on June 2. On June 9, Detective Sharp stated that he had assumed the entire case. How did Mrs. Blakely even know about Bryanna's death? The only way I could think of was if Dr. Green had specifically sent her to the hospital to mark the chart as "under investigation for child abuse" to implicate Danny and me with the crime. I had to say one thing for Dr. Green. She was good!

Dr. Story returned to work the next week. On June 28, 2000, Danny and I were both working, and Dr. Story was pulling the on call/evening shift. I knew it was our best opportunity to speak with him privately about the CAT scan. I was ready to go, but Danny hesitated. I thought I was going to have to physically drag him to Dr. Story's office. Danny was so meek that he lacked the courage to confront Dr. Story. On the way to the office, I reassured Danny, "We have nothing to hide. He is in his office alone right now. It is our best chance to talk to him. Let's go." The shy little girl that I used to be would never have had the confidence to go to a doctor and ask questions like that, but in my quest for answers to what had happened to Bryanna, I was driven by forces that gave me a new boldness. I knocked gently on Dr. Story's door, and he said "come in." He seemed very surprised to see us, almost as if he had been caught off guard. We slipped quietly inside the door, and I closed it softly behind us.

"I want to ask you about the addendum that you wrote to our daughter's CAT scan," I began. "Dr. Bass said that it was normal, but on June 5, you added that she had a hygroma and a fluid collection."

"How do you know about that?" he barked at us defensively.

I firmly replied, "I have read her chart. Why did you write that addendum?"

He stuttered, "Someone from the College of Medicine called me that day and asked me to take a second look at the CAT scan, but I can't remember their name. It was a long title and sounded important."

"Why did Dr. Bass say it was normal?"

"He simply missed it."

"What could cause a hygroma?" I asked

"Why trauma, of course!" he snapped. "It's no big secret that you both are under investigation for child abuse."

My mind exploded with rage, but my voice remained calm. "Could an infection cause a hygroma or fluid collection?"

"Yes, but she would have had a very high fever and been very sick."

She was very ill and had a fever the day before she died, I thought, but I did not say it out loud. I gave him a final silent hateful glare and left his office with Danny trailing behind me.

I completely changed my former opinion of him (that he was a good, competent doctor) that day.

After leaving Dr. Story's office, Danny and I had a quick discussion about what he had said. We were both really angry that he had basically called us child abusers. I asked Danny if he remembered seeing any of those things on her CAT scan the night it was done. He said he could not recall anything abnormal about it at all. We decided that we should look at the CAT scan again and see if Danny could detect any type of fluid collection or tumor. Even though he was not a radiologist, I figured that those two things should be fairly obvious to a trained eye.

Danny left me to continue with my duties while he went downstairs to the big file room to pull her entire jacket of films. He returned to where I was working a good bit later and said that he was unable to locate any of Bryanna's x-rays. Evidently, her jacket of films had been checked out on June 5 (the day that Dr. Story made the addendum) and never returned. For all we knew he still had her x-rays in his office. Well, we certainly could not go and ask him for them. Now we could add to the mystery of her chart being locked away in legal files that all of her x-rays were missing. My anxiety level climbed another notch.

Danny said that there was one other way that we might be able to look at the CAT scan film. He explained that the slides are kept on tapes for about ninety days after they are done. The original CAT scan films might still be viewable on the old tapes, but one of the CAT scan technicians would have to pull it up for us.

Danny and I went to the CAT scan room and asked one of the technicians that we knew fairly well if he could pull her CAT scan up for us to look at on the big screen. It took him a little while, but he was finally able to locate the exam. He and Danny scrolled through each of the films very slowly at least two times. I stood behind them anxiously awaiting their verdict. I could not read x-rays at all and would not have been able to spot any abnormalities. I knew that they were not doctors, but they looked at films all the time and would surely recognize something as obvious as a collection of fluid. Besides, I trusted their opinion more than any of the radiologists in that department.

After several minutes of intense scrutiny, both Danny and the other CAT scan technician concluded that there was nothing abnormal about Bryanna's study. The other CAT scan technician did point to a place at the back of Bryanna's head and said that might be something, but then, they both decided that it was just artifact or movement because it was only present on one slide. The questionable abnormalities in Dr. Story's addendum were in the front of her head not the back anyway.

The CAT scan technician then looked at both of us and asked, "Are they trying to accuse you guys of something?"

We nodded yes simultaneously.

"I am not one bit surprised that they would try to do something like that," he said, shaking his head with disgust at the doctors and radiologists. We decided not to say anything more to him about what they were doing to us because he had already went out of his way by showing us the films, and I did not want to get him into any trouble.

Was her CAT scan normal or had something been missed? It was all very confusing. I went home that night and took what I learned from studying her chart, lab work, and x-ray results and began an extensive search on the internet and through medical textbooks to try to figure out what had happened to Bryanna. I spent hours every night after I got home from work searching on the internet, looking for an answer until I was completely exhausted. There were several diseases that she had symptoms of, including meningitis (characterized by low grade fever, vomiting, diarrhea, irritability, and strange rashes such as petechia), uremic syndrome (a disease associated with vomiting, diarrhea, paleness and E. Coli like she had in her urine), osteogenesis (brittle bones), osteopetrosis (a condition where the bones have increased density and fracture easily. The infant will also be anemic.), immunity disorders, SIDS (sudden infant death syndrome), leukemia (defined by frequent infections, fever, stomach pain, and petechia), and liver problems.

During my multiple searches, I came across a most strange and intriguing article. It dealt with infants and small children receiving routine immunizations and then showing signs of shaken baby syndrome within a few days. Shaken Baby Syndrome is a form of child abuse where the caregiver picks the infant up and shakes it violently in an attempt to make it stop crying. The lack of well developed muscles in an infant's neck causes it to tear away from the brain during the acceleration/deceleration motion created by swinging the baby back and forth; thus causing bleeding in the brain and eyes. The arms and legs are left dangling and often fracture as a result of the vigorous jerking motion. Considering the possible bleed in her head (if it really was there) and the broken bones, that explanation fit her symptoms so well that it was eerie. I read the article several times and showed it to Danny, my parents, and my lawyer. Out of everything that I had discovered so far, that one document was the closest explanation to what may have actually happened to her since she became ill after receiving her immunizations. I believed that the doctors were guilty of malpractice, but the extent of their negligence could not be determined until the final autopsy results came back. In the end, my hours and hours of research provided no definite conclusions.

In early August 2000, I was finally able to review Bryanna's records from Dr. Green's office. Her office had refused to turn them over to my lawyer for two months. He had to call us several times because the staff demanded more information about her before they would release them. I went to the lawyer's office to read them one day before work. The notes contained a lot of the same material as the hospital records, but they also included some different information. Dr. Green had further twisted what we said to her to imply child abuse. After reading the file, I was sure that Dr. Green had held the records back on purpose to change the chart and frame us with child abuse.

The more I thought about the notes written by Dr. Green, the more convinced I became that the injuries had all occurred simultaneously at her office during the spinal tap. If Bryanna really did have bleeding in her brain, it was highly possible that someone had dropped her in the treatment room. Whatever had happened, I was sure that Dr. Green knew exactly what it was. All of the child abuse allegations were a massive cover-up to scare us from filing a lawsuit. I was positive that I had not harmed Bryanna, and neither would Danny or anyone else in my family. To accuse us of anything was absurd. I wished that Dr. Green's office would have been honest about their mistakes instead of creating all that deception. Now it was too late for them to rectify their error because she was dead. Dr. Green accused us of child abuse instead of looking for what was really wrong with Bryanna. Her actions were beyond reproachable. I planned to sue them for all that they were worth just as soon as I had the final autopsy results.

While I was reviewing her medical records and establishing my own conclusions, Detective Sharp was conducting his investigation as promised. He made several visits to the Radiology Department to interview the various radiologists that had read Bryanna's x-rays. Danny was stationed near the front of the department and knew each time that Detective Sharp was there. Later, Danny confessed to me that he did not always tell me every time he saw the detective because it upset me so much. I also found out from the other x-ray technicians that Detective Sharp had taken a copy of all of Bryanna's x-rays. Why did he keep returning to the department? This question would haunt me for the next several months.

I called my attorney several times to report to him that Detective Sharp was again at the Radiology Department. His reply was always the same, "Relax. He is just investigating her death. Let him do his job. If anyone was going to arrest you, they already would have." He still felt like we had an excellent malpractice suit. We just had to wait for the final autopsy results to know how good it would be.

One day, Danny accidentally overheard that Detective Sharp was returning to interview one of the radiologists at two in the afternoon. I was getting tired of Detective Sharp coming to the department, asking questions, and basically making me a nervous wreck. Danny guessed that Detective Sharp might be coming to talk with Dr. Frank who did not arrive until two. I called my dad to see what he thought I should do. My dad suggested that I simply confront Detective Sharp and ask him why he kept returning to the department. I knew that I had nothing to hide so his idea seemed perfectly reasonable. In the past, I would never have dreamed of confronting Detective Sharp, but in my quest for answers about what had happened to Bryanna, I was definitely emerging from my shy shell. At about two in the afternoon, the clerk overhead paged Dr. Frank to the front office. I knew that meant that Detective Sharp was there. In order to catch him before their meeting, I rushed to the front of the department and found him standing in the hallway.

"May I speak with you privately a moment?" I asked, approaching him with a boldness that I certainly did not feel.

He seemed surprised to see me. We moved to an empty side hallway to speak more discreetly. "Have you found out anything during your investigation?"

"I have not made any final conclusions yet," he replied.

"I have noticed that you have been here several times, and I was just wondering why or what you may have found out."

"I have to talk with everyone who had any contact with the baby at all. I don't want this investigation to end with unanswered questions. I really want to find out what happened to Bryanna." With that response, he walked away from me and entered the front office.

Our conversation provided no relief to my growing anxiety; in fact, it confused me even more. Was he investigating the doctors or us?

⟨⟨⟨

After exhausting every available angle, I began the long and arduous task of waiting for an answer. In order to maintain an ongoing accurate record, I documented in my diary each time that I was aware of Detective Sharp visiting the Radiology Department at First Street Hospital and the conversation with Dr. Story. Since my handwriting was so difficult to read, I decided to type my diary into the computer. Using the extra notes that I scribbled during the June 9 meeting with Detective Sharp, I formulated the text into complete sentences and a more detailed account of her entire illness and the ongoing investigation.

Without answers, closure, or resolution, I coped with my grief the best way I knew how—by staying busy. I started an exercise program of walking and lifting weights. I even bought a punching bag to release some of my frustration. My long daily walks gave me time to talk to God and pray that he would reveal the truth about what had happened to Bryanna.

I could not concentrate on my previously enjoyed hobbies of sewing and reading any more. Working meaningless word puzzles passed the time for me. I bought several new dolls, expanding my already large collection in a feeble attempt to somehow replace Bryanna with porcelain dolls, but it did not work.

I continued to attend church regularly where I frequently volunteered in the nursery. Rocking and cuddling the babies and toddlers seemed to provide me some brief pleasure. Most people would have probably avoided being around children in my position, but their company was a comfort to me.

I passed the long days with one single hope—we would have some answers in November. As soon as we found out what happened to Bryanna, I wanted to try for another baby. With that expectation in mind, I slowly began to wean myself off Paxil around the first of October 2000.

Without the Paxil to keep me calm, it seemed like my anxiety and paranoia surged out of control. After our conversation with Dr. Story in June and Detective Sharp's multiple visits to the radiology department, I began to imagine our coworkers and the radiologists all talking about Danny and I being guilty of child abuse behind our backs. Danny told me that some of the technicians had disclosed to him that some people were indeed gossiping. They shared that information with him because they were angry at those particular people for what they were saying. For the most part, the people that Danny and I worked with were very defensive of us, especially Danny. They had known him longer than me. They were very angry at the doctors and hospital because they felt like we had been accused of child abuse to cover the mistakes made by the medical staff. It was very reassuring to know that other people could see what was really going on too.

Due to all the stress, I desperately wanted to leave the First Street Radiology Department and find a new job. Through the grapevine, I heard that the local government hospital was hiring nurses. I had always wanted to work at the government hospital so in October 2000, I submitted an application for employment there. After completing a list of prerequisites including reference letters and a comprehensive medication test, I interviewed for both the intensive care unit and the emergency room. Afterwards, I did not feel confident about either interview but prayed that God would make a way for me to get out of the radiology department at First Street Hospital. Walking those halls, weighed down by those whispers was slowly driving me crazy. Dr. Peck was harassing me more than ever as the days passed. I thought he must be a wretched person for treating someone who had just lost a child so dreadfully. However, Dr. Story had openly called us "child abusers" and said "it was no big secret."

Maybe Dr. Peck justified his despicable behavior by assuming that I deserved it.

After patiently waiting for a month to hear a response from the government hospital regarding employment, I decided to contact them. To my pleasant surprise, they planned to hire me as soon as they completed a "boarding process." The "boarding process" consisted of an examination of my credentials by a panel of professionals who would either approve or reject my employment. I also had to satisfactorily complete a physical examination, so for the time being I remained trapped in those wretched radiology halls in the grips of worsening paranoia, hoping there was light at the end of my tunnel.

Thanksgiving came and went, and we heard nothing from Detective Sharp about Bryanna's final autopsy results. At my insistence, my father contacted him only to be informed that no autopsy results were available yet. Detective Sharp asked us to patiently wait a few more weeks for the final report. Another month passed, and still, no report. The waiting was becoming unbearable.

Around the middle of December, I had almost given up all hope of being hired at the government hospital. Finally, one afternoon while at work, I received a phone call from their human resources department offering me a position in the emergency room. I had no emergency room experience, but I did not care. I was so happy that I started jumping up and down for joy. My coworkers demanded to know why I was so excited. I told them that I had been hired by the government hospital and would be turning in my two week notice that very afternoon. As a bonus, I received a two dollar an hour pay increase. Luckily, what the government hospital did not know was that I would have gladly taken a two dollar per hour pay cut to have gotten out of that dreadful radiology department.

The year 2000 passed into the year 2001. I managed to survive the holidays without Bryanna, but her birthday loomed in the near future. The final autopsy results were still not back. The funeral home director that my dad knew said that they were running about five months behind schedule on releasing autopsy reports. The state had reprimanded them for it but that had done little to change the situation. My dad made multiple phone calls to Detective Sharp, but his answer was always the same—no final report yet. My anxiety level increased to the point of being intolerable. I phoned my attorney to ask if anything could be done to expedite the process. I was concerned about the June 2 deadline for filing a malpractice lawsuit. However, he assured me not to worry, that we still had plenty of time.

At least I was making a fresh start at the government hospital where no one knew about my past. I described to Danny how pleasant it was to be away from that radiology department and all of the gossip. I asked him if he wanted me to check into radiology technologist positions at the government hospital, but he was very content at First Street Hospital. After the first of the year, he was promoted to the evening shift radiology supervisor. His hours changed to two-thirty in the afternoon to eleven at night, Monday through Friday. My new work hours at the government hospital were a mixture of day shifts and evening shifts including most weekends so once again we did not get to spend a lot of time together. That was the only bad thing about my new job. I really encouraged Danny to consider joining me at the government hospital, but he always refused to leave the First Street Radiology Department. He said that since none of the gossip was true, it did not bother him at all. His confidence in our innocence must have helped him to hold his head high among those nasty rumors. I wish I could have ignored them the way that he did.

One of the bonuses with my new job at the government hospital was better health insurance. Their network provided more choices for doctors and hospitals than First Street's medical plan. Since Danny had a heart condition that could become serious at any time, I decided to add him to my health insurance at the government hospital. It doubled the premium costs, but If anything significant were to happen to his heart, it would be a valuable resource.

❦

Sunday, February 11, 2001 should have been Bryanna's first birthday. It was impossible for me to imagine that one year ago she entered the world, and now had been gone for so long. Danny and I stayed home all day unable to face anyone. We did not even go to church. We took both of the dogs for a long walk in the brisk cold air to clear our minds. Later in the day, we visited the cemetery placing a single red rose on her grave.

A few weeks after Bryanna's birthday, I wandered into her room for the first time alone. Danny was downstairs in the basement den playing computer games (something that he was doing more and more of those days). I had kept one of her undershirts preserved in a zip lock bag after she died. Taking it out of the sealed container, I deeply inhaled her still lingering scent. It smelled strongly pleasant of baby powder and soured milk. The power of scent can be a keen reminder of someone. I started to cry uncontrollably, thinking about how much I missed her. For a long time, I was stuck in her room overwhelmed with grief and memories. I hoped that Danny would miss me and come to see where I was at, but he never did. He was too consumed in his computer game. Finally, I crawled out of her room on my hands and knees a few inches at a time and went downstairs to seek out Danny for comfort. I slowly approached him weeping and shaking, interrupting his computer game. Instead of consoling me, he scolded me for going into her room alone and made me promise not to do it again; then continued to play his game, appearing annoyed that he had been interrupted. I had expected comforting arms and received only harsh words. His strange behavior confused me, but I decided that maybe he was having a difficult time as well.

When I filed the federal income taxes for that year, we received an unexpected large refund due to being able to count Bryanna as a deduction for the year 2000. Danny was very excited, anticipating the arrival of the refund check. While we waited for it, almost every day, he approached me with lists of things we could buy with the refund money, wanting me to choose an item from the list. I just told him, "Whatever you want is fine with me." To me, they were just material things. He replied, "I want to get something we can both enjoy." I could not force myself to be excited about the refund. As a matter of fact, it hurt me to write her name on the form. It seemed unfair that we could count her for tax purposes, but not have her physically with us.

Finally, I chose a new computer from Danny's list to make him stop bothering me. The computer we had was fine with me, but Danny wanted one that would play more advanced video games faster. He was becoming obsessed with video games and bought a new one about every other week. He stopped mowing the yard, working on his ship models, and reading books to spend hours in front of the computer. I assumed that it was his way of coping with the loss of his child, but I still could not understand why he was so excited about spending the tax refund money.

March 2001 arrived with no autopsy results. One Sunday, I asked Danny to take me to the cemetery because we had not been in about two weeks. He responded by saying, "Don't ask me to go to the cemetery anymore. If you want to go from now on, you will have to go by yourself." I was shocked by his answer. He had been catering to me for months; now, suddenly since her birthday, I sensed a change in him. It seemed that he no longer wanted to indulge me. In fact he acted like he expected me to get over her loss and go on with my life. The problem was I could not move on without some answers. Danny no longer appeared as disturbed as I was over the lack of resolution concerning her death. I wanted to have another baby, but we could not until we knew the cause of Bryanna's death.

Another strange occurrence happened on a Sunday afternoon. Danny and I went to the mall. While looking at Sears, I wandered to the children's cloths and found a display of little girl's fancy Easter dresses. Danny found me looking at them crying. He grabbed me by the arm and took me to the car. I was still sobbing when he started the engine. Instead of being sympathetic, he scolded me for looking at the dresses. I said, "I did not mean to look at them. It just sort of happened." He replied, "You should know that something like that is going to upset you. You should never have gone over there. From now on, don't look at things like that." I was surprised by his harshness. He had always tried to comfort me about Bryanna, but over the past few weeks, it seemed that his attitude was gradually changing. I figured that he must have progressed further in the grieving process than I had. Maybe it was harder for the mother?

Due to Danny's unusual behavior and the stress of waiting for the autopsy results, in March 2001, I belatedly decided to seek counseling regarding Bryanna's death. Several months had passed and Danny seemed to be doing better than me. I felt like I was dragging behind him and needed some professional help. I saw a therapist twice in March and once in April. When I told her about the details of Bryanna's illness, especially the addendum to the CAT scan report, she agreed with me that the hospital and radiologists were hiding a huge mistake that they had made. Again, it gave me a good feeling to know that other people outside of our family could see through the doctor's scheme.

⟫⟫

After numerous phone calls, around the first of April, Detective Sharp informed my father that the completed autopsy results had finally arrived, but he could not disclose the report yet. Evidently, "a big question" remained on the autopsy that required the expertise of a pediatric neurologist to resolve. Detective Sharp said, "If we have a question, then you will have a question." What could the "big question" be? I wondered. She must have had something extremely rare and very serious. Detective Sharp also said that when they were ready to discuss the findings with us that they wanted to speak with only my father and me. Danny was the last person to see Bryanna alive. What his mom said in the emergency room that night thundered in my mind, "I hope they don't try to pin something on Danny." Were they going to attempt to falsely accuse him of something? The question loomed over me like a black cloud. I did not even speak it aloud to Danny for fear it would upset him. After giving it more thought, I felt sure my father had misunderstood Detective Sharp and that he meant he would talk only to Danny and me (the parents) about the results.

A few days later, I went to visit my parents in the evening. Danny was working second shift and therefore, did not go with me. While I was there, my father took me to their sunroom for a long serious talk. He said that we needed to be prepared for the possibility that Danny and/or I could be falsely accused of child abuse. I was terrified at the very thought of them incriminating one or both of us and shook uncontrollably the whole time we talked. My dad said if that happened we would have "to get from point A to point B" meaning first, we would have to prove our innocence and then second, sue them for the unjust charges. He told me not to worry about the expense of it because he and my mother were prepared to mortgage their home and cash in their assets to defend us if necessary. I tossed and turned in bed that night fearing that the doctors were plotting one final explosive conspiracy. My father advised me not to upset Danny with the details of our conversation just yet. I wanted to discuss it with him terribly, but instead I struggled to remain silent.

A few days after that conversation, for some reason, I felt compelled to ask Danny about Bryanna one more time. While he was getting ready for work I cautiously approached him, "Did you ever do anything to Bryanna, even accidentally?" That topic had remained closed since May 12, 2000 in the Pediatric office when he assured me that he would never do anything like that. The uneasiness I felt in my soul after the conversation with my dad prompted me to want to hear him say it again. Almost too quickly, he replied, "No." I noticed that he averted his eyes to the floor as he said it. I tried to make eye contact with him, but he avoided me by hastily leaving for work. I chased after him, tripping over myself with apologies, even adding that I was unsure of why I had asked him that question. He still acted angry toward me. I assumed he was mad at me for doubting him, but the incident left me feeling troubled and uncertain.

Another two weeks passed with no word from Detective Sharp about the autopsy results. On Friday April 21, 2001, my father contacted a state representative that he knew personally and asked him to have the State Bureau of Investigation initiate an investigation into the police department, hospital, and doctors concerning Bryanna. About two hours later, Detective Sharp called my father and arranged to meet with him alone, on Monday, April 24, at ten in the morning at the county courthouse to discuss the results of the autopsy. I was puzzled as to why Danny and I (her actual parents) were not allowed to participate in the meeting. However, we decided to cooperate with them and only my dad would go; otherwise, they might not tell us anything. By that time, almost ten months had passed since her death, and we were almost insane from waiting for an answer. Plus only two months remained before the time limit for filing a lawsuit would be up. I was willing to do anything for some answers. Three more days and hopefully some of this anxiety would end. What I did not know was that it was only the beginning of something far worse.

Confrontation

Monday morning, my mother and I planned to wait on my father in the parking lot of the courthouse while he met with Detective Sharp so that we could know something just as soon as they finished. Danny did not want to go and complained that it would be pointless for us to sit in the parking lot waiting. After he drove me to the courthouse, Danny stayed with us for about an hour and then he went home to get ready for work because he had to go in early that day for a mandatory supervisor meeting.

At noon, my dad had been in the courthouse for two hours. Anxiously, I thought surely they would break for lunch soon. I did not know how much longer I could stand to wait, not knowing. I wanted to go inside and look for him, but that was crazy because I had no idea where to find him. My mom and I watched the front door intensely because that was all we could do. At 12:15, my dad finally emerged from the courthouse with a frown on his face that was so deep it caused his eyebrows to crease. We questioned him as soon as he climbed into the truck. All he did was shake his head and say, "It is not good," refusing to explain anything right away. He drove away from the courthouse to an empty parking lot. Then he shut the motor off and shared the details of the meeting with us.

He began by saying that at death, Bryanna had multiple injuries—more than the clavicle and arm that we knew about including seven fractured ribs in various stages of healing, two broken legs, and a fractured scapula (shoulder blade). She also had two separate bleeds in her brain. The "big question" on the autopsy that required the expertise of a pediatric neurologist was to determine which one of the two bleeds in her brain had actually caused her death to pinpoint exactly who was with her when she died. The pediatric neurologist's answer was unexpected—-neither bleed resulted in her death; instead, she was smothered to death. That critical piece of evidence placed Danny, and Danny alone, as the perpetrator. The district attorney allowed my father to listen to the actual 911 call that Danny made on June 2, 2000. He said that Danny's voice showed no emotion, and he repeated calmly at least three times, "I think she has choked. Yes, that's it, she choked." The pathologist speculated that Bryanna may have been dead for a period of time before Danny even called 911. Her death certificate stated that the cause of death was multiple trauma due to battered child syndrome and was stamped "homicide."

Based on all the evidence, the district attorney and Detective Sharp were sure that Danny had murdered her. They did not think that I knew about it because each time she was sick, I was the one who always took her to the doctor. The physical evidence that my dad presented to us that afternoon in the truck was beyond what my mind could comprehend. To me, it was unbelievable to think of Danny as a murderer, but the district attorney and Detective Sharp had convinced my dad, and I knew that had been no easy task. Two weeks ago, my dad was prepared to mortgage his house to defend us. The evidence must have been very persuasive to have changed his mind. I wanted to know if any of the doctors or radiologists from First Street Hospital had participated in any way on her autopsy. My father had already posed that question. None of the doctors involved in Bryanna's autopsy had any connection to physicians associated with First Street Hospital. There was absolutely no reason for any of the results to have been falsified to cover mistakes made by the pediatricians. Still, I asked my dad, "Do you believe them? Do you really think that Danny did it?"

"Yes, I do," he responded sincerely. If my dad believed them, then I had to too because I trusted my dad with all my heart.

One other puzzling question lingered in my mind, "Why haven't they arrested him yet?"

My dad said it was because the district attorney was waiting to present the evidence to the grand jury when they convened in two weeks. The grand jury would then issue a warrant for Danny's arrest. Before my dad left the meeting that morning, he had asked them, "What if I do nothing with this information that you have just given me?"

Detective Sharp replied, "You don't have to do anything with it. We are giving you the autopsy results that you have been requesting for months. In two weeks, we will have an arrest warrant, and we will come for him." No matter what happened Danny was going to jail soon.

While we were talking, Danny called my mom's cell phone to see if we had heard any news. Daddy advised her not to say anything to him just yet so mom told him that we were still waiting. Daddy said that we needed some more time to figure out what we were going to do. Thus, we began a series of events at that moment that I can only explain as God's divine intervention.

"I have to talk to him," I said. "He has to tell me the truth. How owes me that."

We began to make a plan. First of all, my dad did not feel that it would be safe for Danny and me to talk alone. We decided that Danny and I should talk at their house. My dad wanted to lock our shotgun and pistol in his safe because as he put it so well, "We have had enough tragedies in this family, and I want to prevent any more." We went to my house first to get the guns. While there, I called Danny and asked him to leave work immediately and meet me at my parent's house. He wanted to know why. I replied honestly, "It is not good, but I prefer to discuss it in person." After I hung up the phone, we went to my parent's house to wait on Danny.

About thirty minutes later, Danny pulled up in his little maroon truck. He joined me in the sunroom where we could talk privately and safely while my mom worked outside in her flowers and kept an eye on us through the large glass windows.

I wasted no time in getting straight to the point and confronted Danny with the autopsy results. I told him that her death certificate stated homicide caused by multiple trauma and battered child syndrome. He listened to me quietly without saying a word. I asked him several times, "Did you ever hurt Bryanna?" He consistently denied ever harming her. I then asked him why his voice was so emotionless during the 911 call. He replied, "I was trying to remain calm to deal with the situation." I told him that the police thought he did it and that they were planning to arrest him. He did not respond. As I persisted in questioning him and presenting him with all of the evidence that the district attorney had against him, he continued to deny harming Bryanna in any way.

"Why don't you just leave me alone," he said, his voice filled with frustration.

After an hour of questioning him with no results, I was exhausted and ready to do just that—give up. Looking him dead in the eye, I said, "She was my baby and I deserve to know the truth."

"Why?" he responded, turning away from me, but I grabbed his face in both my hands and made him look me directly in the eyes.

"This has nothing to do with the investigation or being charged. I deserve to know the truth about what happened to her because she was my baby and I loved her."

Silence followed for what seemed like a long time. He appeared to be thinking very intently about what I had just said. Finally, he relented. "Okay. Okay. I hit her in the head."

I was speechless. All of the evidence said that he had hurt her, but to hear him admit it was another matter entirely. I don't think that I really believed he did it until that moment when he actually confessed it to me, and maybe not then. "Once or more than once?" I asked, my voice trembling.

"More than once."

"How hard did you hit her?" I demanded.

"Like this," he said and took the palm of his hand and slapped the side of my head. The blow was slightly painful and exerted enough force to knock my head some distance to the side. The Danny I had known for over twelve years had never laid a cruel hand on me. Now suddenly, he had smacked my head. That was a side of Danny that I never knew existed. To think that he had done that to Bryanna was more than my mind could comprehend. *He must be insane*, I thought.

The belated admission of guilt finally opened a bolted door to his mind. Shaking uncontrollably and wringing his hands, he went on, "It was like I was watching myself do it. I lost control. I prayed that God would stop me, but he didn't answer my prayer. I guess he didn't hear me. Sometimes when this came over me I would leave the room so I wouldn't hurt her. Other times, I couldn't control myself."

"Why didn't you tell me about it? I could have helped you and her."

Tearfully, he replied, "I was afraid that you would leave me."

I sat quietly listening to him thinking that he must be mentally ill. What he had done to her was buried so deep within him that it was almost impossible to wrestle the truth out. He continued to explain defensively, "I never hit her with my fist, only with the palm of my hand, and I never did anything to her that would break her bones." Who was the man sitting across from me? I wondered.

"Now what do we do? Do you want to go to tell your mother?" I suggested out loud.

"No, I can't face her. My life is over. I want to drive off in my truck, take one of our guns, and kill myself. We would all be better off."

I snatched his keys from the couch where they rested between us and crammed them in my pocket revealing firmly, "Daddy has locked all of the guns up. They are no longer at our house. You have nothing to harm yourself with."

At that point, I was torn between protecting him or letting him drive off and do what he felt like he needed to do. So fearful of false accusations, it had never occurred to me that he had really done something to Bryanna. I decided to discuss it with my dad and see what he thought about the situation. I went out the door of the sunroom and told my mom to keep an eye on Danny because he was threatening to harm himself. She wanted to know more, but I told her that I did not have time to explain it right then because I needed to talk to Daddy.

I went to the body shop where Daddy was working and took him by the hand. Not telling him anything at first, we walked far away behind the body shop to the end of the property line. I was worried that Daddy might snap and do something horrible to Danny when I told him that Danny had hurt Bryanna. At a safe distance away, I told him that Danny had confessed to hitting Bryanna in the head and was saying that he wanted to kill himself.

"I brought you all the way out here to tell you because I was afraid that you would kill him," I admitted.

My dad answered very calmly, "I am not going to do anything like that." His composure surprised me, but upon reflecting back to that day, I think that we were all really numb. "Well, you certainly can't go back home with him." I had not really thought that far into the situation yet. "Let's go back and see if he wants to go tell his mother what he has done."

When we returned to the house, Daddy asked Danny, "Do you want to go tell your mother what you've done?"

"No, I can't face her. I just want to die. I need help," he replied still wringing his hands and shaking all over.

"Do you want to go see your lawyer?" Daddy asked him two or three times. Danny always replied, "No, I just need help. I need help." At that point, we were all convinced that Danny was insane and did need some professional help. He was still part of the family, and we loved him, but we really did not know what to do.

"Well I don't know what to do. Do you want to talk with Detective Sharp? Maybe he could help. He gave me his pager number in case we needed him for anything," Daddy said wearily.

"Yes, I will go talk to him."

Daddy then paged Detective Sharp who promptly returned his call. Detective Sharp said that he would meet us at the police station downtown. The three of us climbed into my dad's truck and drove there. Before we left, my dad offered one more time to call our lawyer, but Danny said, "No, don't call him."

It was a very quiet ride to the police station that day. The only thing I remember Danny saying was, "I did hit her in the head, but I swear to God I didn't touch her on the day that she died." I sat in the back seat and patted Danny on the shoulder the whole way. Before we got out of the truck, Daddy warned Danny sternly, "Be careful of what you say."

Upon our arrival, Detective Sharp and Detective Light were waiting for us at the entrance. Detective Light had been assisting Detective Sharp with Bryanna's case. It was strange because actually all three of us knew Detective Light from different ways. Danny and his family used to go to church with him, my dad had fixed his car, and I knew him from working at the fast food restaurant years ago because he came by daily for complimentary ice tea given to police officers.

The two detectives took the three of us to a private room and shut the door. Detective Sharp handed Danny and I each a piece of paper with the Miranda Rights written on it. He proceeded to read it verbatim to us. Upon finishing, he asked us to sign it, indicating that we understood. Detective Sharp said that we had a right to an attorney at any time.

My father asked referring to me, "Why does she have to sign the Miranda Rights?"

Detective Sharp explained, "Because she is Danny's wife."

I reassured Daddy that I was okay with signing it. I knew in my heart that I had done nothing wrong. The only thing that I could confess was what Danny had told me that afternoon.

After Danny and I signed the Miranda warning, Detective Sharp looked at my father and me and said, "You two can leave now."

"You don't want to talk to me?" I asked, puzzled.

"No, we would rather speak with Danny alone," he replied. Danny asked if he could be excused to go to the restroom. When he left the room, my father and I were alone with Detective Sharp.

"I know that you said you don't want to question me, but I have something that I want to say. Danny confessed to me that he did not tell me he was hurting Bryanna because he was afraid that I would leave him, and I would have," I said, my voice cracking as I started to cry.

Detective Sharp then responded gently, "Yes, we know that you would have."

As I broke into a flood of tears, my dad and Detective Light led me out of the room. Detective Light took us to the main area of the police station to wait. He pulled some chairs around his desk and told us we were welcome to sit there. He stayed with us for a little while. We showed him Bryanna's one month old picture so he could see how beautiful she was and place a face with the case that he had been working on for so long. Detective Light offered me a piece of cake because I was feeling faint from not eating all day, but I could only eat two or three bites. The food seemed to stick in my throat again like it had right after Bryanna died. Shortly afterward, he left us alone (other than an unfriendly secretary that was working in the office) to join Detective Sharp and Danny in the interrogation room. The hands of the clock seemed to inch forward at a snail's pace. My dad and I waited at the desk feeling helpless until about five in the evening. At that time, we decided to go home and check on Mom because she had no idea what was happening. We had left her hastily without telling her what Danny had confessed to me in the sunroom.

We returned home to find Mom a nervous wreck. She said that Danny's mother had called her several times and asked her what was going on. My mom had truthfully told her that we were at the police station, but she didn't know why. Danny's mother did not believe her. She told my mom, "You are keeping me in the dark." What she did not realize was that Danny was the one guilty of keeping everyone "in the dark" for almost a year now.

After telling my mom what was going on, we returned to the police station around six-thirty. Our pastor met us there a few minutes later. The police station door was locked and when we knocked, no one would let us in. We had to stand outside in the parking lot near a creek that ran by the road. While we waited, we took the opportunity to fill our pastor in on the afternoon's events.

His immediate response was, "Danny shouldn't be in there talking to them without an attorney."

His words caused me to panic inside thinking that Danny really needed an attorney with him. I rushed back to the door and knocked again. Detective Light heard me and let us back into the police station. We again sat down in the chairs around his desk. Detective Light returned to the interrogation room with Danny and Detective Sharp. The door to that room remained shut so we had no idea what was going on in there. Again, we were left alone to wait.

Sometime after eight, the chief district attorney, General Steele, arrived. He took my dad aside to a back hallway to speak privately. I waited for them to return until I could stand it no longer. I searched around the corner and found them speaking to one another in very low voices. Approaching them boldly, I said, "I have the right to know what is going on. He is my husband after all."

General Steele gently began to explain to me, "Daniel will be arrested tonight and charged with first degree murder."

I couldn't believe my ears. I turned ghostly pale and felt faint. That reality was worse than anything I had ever imagined over the past ten months. General Steele looked at my dad and said, "She is probably more of the victim in all of this than even Bryanna was."

Detective Sharp and Detective Light came around the corner to get us. They were taking a brief break from the interrogation to speak with General Steele. I looked to Detective Light for some answers because Danny and I faintly knew him.

"Did Danny say he hurt Bryanna?" I asked him.

"Yes, he did," Detective Light replied, nodding his head with a sad distant look in his eyes.

I looked at both of them and asked, "Why is Danny being charged with first degree murder? Is it because he is cold and calculating?"

"No, it is due to aggravating factors," Detective Sharp said.

What are aggravating factors? I thought. I didn't understand any of it. The legal language was very confusing.

"Can I request for him to have an attorney present with him?" I asked.

"It does not make any difference now if he has an attorney present or not," Detective Sharp replied firmly.

"Is he mentally insane?" I wanted to know.

"No, he is not." His answer surprised me. I was sure that Danny was insane when we brought him to the police station that afternoon. The detectives had to be wrong. Everything that was happening was out of my control. I felt powerless to help him or myself. Detective Sharp said, "There is nothing you can do here. Why don't you go home and rest for a while. We still have to write the confession. Then he will have to read it and make any changes that he wants to before signing it. We can't allow you to speak with him right now, but we will call you when we are finished. Then you can see him for a few minutes."

Taking his advice, we went home sometime after nine at night. My brother was waiting for us with my mom. He took me to my house to get a few of my necessary belongings so that I could spend the night with my parents. While we were gone, my dad and my pastor visited my grandparents to update them what was going on. Afterward, my grandparents (since my grandmother and Danny's mom were old friends) volunteered to go to Danny's mom and stepdad's house and fill them in on what was happening with Danny.

Sometime after ten that night, Danny's dad called and wanted to know what was happening. He knew that my dad had a meeting with Detective Sharp that morning and no one had thought to call and update him. My father informed him of Bryanna's multiple injuries, her death certificate stating multiple trauma/ battered child syndrome, and Danny's confession that he had done it. Danny's dad wanted to know how we could be sure that Danny had indeed harmed Bryanna. My dad then shared the most convincing piece of evidence that he had personally witnessed at that time concerning Danny's guilt—Danny's emotionless voice on the 911 tape the night Bryanna died. Danny's dad declared, "Well, if he did it, then he needs to pay for it. If you need me, call me."

We waited at my parent's house until after midnight with no update from the detectives. My dad paged Detective Sharp several times, but he did not answer. My parents, brother, sister, pastor and his wife decided to return to the police station and try to find out what was happening. Upon our arrival, we found Danny's mom, stepdad, and aunt all waiting outside the police station. Danny's mom was crying, shaking, and repeating over and over, "How could he hurt that little baby? He didn't hurt that baby. He must be insane." I was in shock and disbelief and did not know how to respond to her other than a hug.

At around one in the morning, Detective Light came to the police station door, looked directly at me, and said, "Danny would like to talk to you first. Is his pastor here? He has requested to see him." My pastor confirmed that he was present.

Detective Light took me back to the interrogation room where we had signed the Miranda Rights what seemed like years ago. On the way, he advised me that I should take any valuables that Danny had on his person with me. Danny was sitting quietly in a chair at the table gazing down at his lap. He looked up at me as I entered the room with sad, strange eyes. His face was red from crying but did seem to brighten a bit when he saw me. Detective Light closed the door to provide us with some privacy.

"Angie, my life is over," he said, taking both my hands into his hands. "Detective Light promised if we make it brief, you can come back one more time after I see everyone else."

I asked the main question that was bothering me. "Did you twist her arms?"

He nodded yes. "I was awfully mean to that baby." Feeling light-headed and weak, I screamed loudly and clutched my heart in pain for what he had done to her. I will never forget what he said as long as I live.

"Take everything that I have and sell it," he pleaded sincerely. "I want you to go on with your life. My life is over."

"My life is over too," I said as I sobbed. "Detective Light said I should probably take your wallet and any valuables you have with me."

Danny placed his billfold in my hand and removed his watch. Lastly, he deposited his gold wedding band into my palm and closed my fingers around it.

"Were the officers good to you?" I asked.

"Oh, yes. They treated me very well," he said with the closest thing to a lopsided smile I would see on his face that night.

Taking his few possessions with me, I left the room so other family members could visit him. The detectives only allowed two people in the room at a time. Danny's mom and stepdad went next, followed by our pastor, and finally, my parents. After my parents were finished, I was allowed to go back and see him one last time. Very few words were spoken. I grabbed him, and we held each other tight for a few minutes. I planted a light kiss on his lips, but it felt strangely cold like kissing a corpse. I did not realize at that time that I was telling him, our marriage, and life as I knew it, goodbye forever. All of the long months of waiting for an answer had turned into a nightmare. I was in too much shock to comprehend the actual weight of what he had done. We all were.

I left the room glancing back one last time at Danny's tear-streaked face. He looked like an empty shell sitting at that table staring down at the floor. I felt like the man that had just told me he was "awfully mean" to our baby was a stranger. Was he insane or not? I did not know the answer, but I prayed for the sake of his soul that he was.

I joined the others back outside while Detective Light was explaining to everyone that Danny would be arraigned in the morning when court convened. An arraignment was when he would appear before the judge to have his charges reviewed and set bond. The detectives planned to take Danny to the county jail where he would remain for the rest of the night.

Danny's mom asked, "What do you think the judge will set bond at?"

Detective Light replied, "That is very hard to predict. It could be only five thousand dollars or it could be five hundred thousand dollars. I have seen it vary significantly in murder cases."

My dad said, "Danny expressed some thoughts of harming himself. You all will keep an eye on him in that respect, won't you?" Detective Light promised, "He will be placed on a suicide watch so that he cannot harm himself in any way."

I then asked him, "When will his arrest be made public?" I dreaded the publicity that would surround all of us when the

news media found out about his crime. The rumor that I remembered hearing Dr. Green's husband say echoed in my mind. "It is
going to be long and drawn out and possibly go public."

"It becomes public knowledge after he's arrested."

Since he was being incarcerated that night, it would be all
over the news the next day. We arrived back at my parent's house
around two in the morning. In spite of being exhausted, I could
not sleep at all. My mind was consumed with the pain that
Bryanna had endured during her short life and how deceived I
was by Danny. I had been so positive that the two injuries had
happened at the doctor's office. Danny had played along with the
story and used it to cover up what he was doing. Then to find out
that she had many more injuries besides the two known fractures
and even worse, they were all done by hands that should have
loved. It was more than my mind could comprehend. Why had
God let that happen to her, to me? I could not understand any of
it, but I could see that God had not forsaken me. I had prayed for
the truth, and God had delivered it. My prayers were answered,
but not at all as I imagined they would be. I had been expecting a
major conspiracy on behalf of the doctors. Instead the culprit was
sharing my bed and my life. The truth was a nightmare I wanted
to forget, but could not. It would define the rest of my life.

> If we confess our sins, he is faithful and just to forgive us
> our sins and to cleanse us from all unrighteousness.
>
> 1 John 1:9

Loss

The next day, I began to cope with the second greatest loss of my life in less than a year. That morning just as I had dreaded, Danny's arrest was broadcasted as the top news story. It was replayed every hour all morning long displaying his mug shot across the television screen. He was crying in the picture and had a pained look on his face with his mouth half open. The press had somehow gotten our home address and went there and made a picture of our house. Later that day, as I watched the news, they showed our house and announced our address as the place where he had murdered her. I had made a large wreath and decorated it with green magnolias for the front door. On the television, that wreath stuck out like a sore thumb. I was very upset that they had the right to display our house on television like that. It seemed like a terrible invasion of my privacy.

Later that morning, my brother accompanied me to my house to help me move some of my most important personal possessions temporarily to my parent's house. I planned to stay with them for a while. There was no way that I could live at my house knowing what Danny had done to Bryanna there. The first thing that I did was jerk that conspicuous wreath off the front door and throw it in the trashcan. Then I gathered all of Bryanna's pictures into a box to take with me. I could finally look at her picture and start to mourn her loss, but oh what that grief would entail. While we were at my house, I called Danny's mom to ask about his arraignment that morning. At some point last night, while we were out of her earshot, Detective Light had advised me to not go to court because the media would harass me for an interview. Danny's stepdad answered the phone.

"The bond was set very high at two hundred and fifty thousand dollars," he said.

I could faintly hear Danny's mom in the background saying something.

"What did she just say?" I asked him.

I heard her say it again, much louder. "Tell her that I expect her to stand behind Danny through this." Danny's stepdad repeated what she said but he did not have to. I had heard her loud and clear. How could she expect me to "stand behind him" after he admitted to stealing the most precious gift I had ever had, not to mention destroying our marriage and wonderful life together? But at that time, I was still too numb to have thought that far ahead into what I planned to do.

While we were packing my belongings, I decided that I should return the computer that Danny had purchased for us with the tax refund money. My old computer was fine, and I really did not need it. Forethought helped me realize that I was going to need the tax refund money just for mere survival. It was three days passed the time limit to return the computer. My brother called Gateway and explained my precarious circumstances. Thankfully, they agreed to accept the return so we carefully packaged the computer for shipment.

When we were finished at my house, my brother took me to the doctor's office to obtain another prescription for Paxil. The counselor that I had seen a few times advised me to use Paxil "like a life raft if I was drowning." Since it had helped me once, I shouldn't hesitate to "grab onto the life raft" if necessary. The doctor prescribed some Paxil and wrote me an excuse to be off work for two weeks which I hoped would be adequate time to pull myself together.

When we returned to my parent's house, my dad was wondering if he had done the right thing by taking Danny to the police station, even though Danny had went of his own free will. My dad called General Steele and told him that he was having second thoughts about taking Danny to the police station yesterday. General Steele replied, "Let me read some parts of his confession to you" and proceeded to read select excerpts of the confession to my dad over the phone. As he read, my dad could hear pages flipping and realized that the confession must be several pages in length. Some of the things General Steele read to him were: Danny had twisted her arms and legs while dressing her, folded her body in half making her chin touch to her stomach when changing her diaper, squeezed her forcefully around the chest, and threw her several times. The abuse began when she was only one month old.

On the way to the police station, Danny swore to us that he did not touch Bryanna on the day she died. General Steele said that Danny admitted to picking her up by the head, smothering her with his hand over her face, and throwing her onto the floor before she died on June 2, 2000. Danny described how her arms and legs would flail back and forth as he smothered her. His confession confirmed the neurologist's determination that she actually died from suffocation, not the bleeds in her brain. The mysterious petechiae rash that developed two days before her death was a result of the lack of oxygen in her system. The neurologist had suspected that Danny suffocated her with a pillow; in reality, his confession revealed that he had smothered her with his own two big hands.

Daddy hung up the phone with General Steele and said to me harshly, "Don't you ever feel sorry for Danny again." He then began to tell me the details of Danny's confession that General Steele had read to him. "Stop!" I screamed before he could finish, "I can't bear to hear anymore." The part where Danny described her arms and legs flailing as he held her out in the air smothering her made me gag.

General Steele asked if I had filed for a legal separation. The thought of divorcing Danny had not yet crossed my mind, but after hearing the details of how he tortured her for the majority of her short life and lied about it, I realized that our life together was truly over. He had committed unspeakable acts on a helpless infant and refused to admit them for eleven months. Only when he was completely cornered with no escape did he confess. Somewhere deep inside he had to have known that he was guilty; yet, he allowed me to torment myself and analyze everything that I had done. There was no way to describe that kind of betrayal.

The next day Wednesday April 25, 2001, Danny's arrest was publicized on the front page of every newspaper in the area. The articles described some of the abuse he perpetrated but not in great detail. Detective Sharp made a statement to the press: "The father was alone at the time of the abuse. The mother did live there, but it was found the mother did not have knowledge of the abuse." I was thankful to him for saying that but was sure that readers would have a difficult time understanding how I could not have known. I wish with all of my heart that I could have known, but I did not. Being the prudent person that I am, I can guarantee that if I had any suspicion that Danny was hurting her, I would never have left her alone in his care again.

I was able to obtain an emergency appointment with my therapist that afternoon. During our session, she arranged for me to see a psychiatrist to manage my antidepressant medication, Paxil, and recommended long term counseling with someone very experienced in grief and divorce. She gave me the name and number of a therapist that she highly recommended. I called that person afterward to schedule an appointment. Unfortunately, she did not accept my insurance, meaning I would have to pay an upfront two hundred and fifty dollar deductible, but after talking with her for only few minutes on the phone, I was so impressed with her demeanor and qualifications that I decided she would be worth the extra expense.

The next morning, Thursday April 26, 2001, Danny's aunt called my parents' house. We recognized the number through caller identification and did not answer the phone. She left a message on the answering machine, crying and begging, "The next time the phone rings, please let Angie answer it because it will be Danny calling from the jail. He wants to talk to her very badly."

She then called my father at his shop, and he told her, "Right now, she is not able to talk to Danny. What does he want with her?"

She replied, "He wants to wish her happy birthday and tell her that he loves her."

Mom took the phone off the hook for the next thirty minutes so that he could not call their house. After hearing only pieces of his confession, I had no desire to talk to him. As a matter of fact, I was beginning to feel very angry toward him. If he truly loved me he would not have killed our baby and ruined my birthday for the past two years in a row. Last year, she was sick on my birthday because of the abuse, and I had to take her to the doctor. The next year, he was arrested for her murder right before my birthday. Thus, I entered the second stage of grief-anger—and there I would remain for a long time.

Later that day, I went to my house and discovered that Danny had tried to call there two times that morning. The caller ID box read "County Jail" and the answering machine had captured two separate messages saying "to accept a collect call from the County Jail please press one; to decline this call, please press two." The final message on the machine was Danny's mom crying and pleading for me to answer the phone because Danny needed to talk to me "so badly."

⟨⟨⟨

The next day, April 27, 2001, my birthday, I had an appointment with a divorce attorney. I liked him from the first time that we met. He had a way of making me feel at ease. He filed for my divorce on the grounds of inappropriate marital conduct with cruelty. The divorce papers asked for me to receive all of the marital property as alimony considering Danny would never be able to pay me anything in prison. The bailiff would deliver the documents to Danny in jail on the following Monday.

My new divorce lawyer further advised me to cancel all joint credit cards and open new checking and savings accounts in my name only. If Danny were to post bond, he would be jobless and in desperate need of some money. He could quickly accrue a lot of credit card debt in our name and drain our savings account. Then, I would be responsible for paying any joint debt. I left his office happy with the impression that I would have a divorce in about thirty to sixty days. I thought it might take longer than that so I was very pleased with the short time frame. I went straight to the bank to open new accounts. Afterward, I started making multiple phone calls and writing letters to close all joint credit card accounts as soon as possible.

In spite of my festering anger toward Danny, a big part of me still cared about him. I was mainly concerned for the spiritual condition of his soul. He had always professed to be a Christian, but his actions toward Bryanna were evil and ungodly. When I shared those thoughts with my family and my pastor, I discovered that they were experiencing the same mixture of emotions. My Dad and my pastor decided to check on Danny at the jail. My pastor had visited a couple of other people there and knew the routine. They planned to go Sunday evening at eight after church. I debated about joining them but ultimately decided that I was not ready to face him. At least if they went to see him, I would know if he was okay.

Sunday night, April 29, 2001, when my dad and my pastor returned from seeing Danny, they shared the details of the visit with us. First, they described how they had to empty their pockets and be searched before entering the visitation room. A huge glass partition separated them from Danny. They had to yell through the glass to communicate because other inmates had vandalized the phones until they did not work anymore. Danny had been assaulted shortly after his arrival to jail by someone who had seen on the news what he had done to Bryanna. The beating had left him with a black eye and some bruised ribs. After the attack, the guards moved him to protective custody where he was confined with inmates bearing similar charges. I had mixed feelings about Danny's injuries. Part of me ached for him because he was meek and mild and had never really been in a fight. Then Bryanna came along, and suddenly, a demon erupted from him and he was unforgivably mean to her. That part of me felt like he deserved a black eye—maybe even a little worse. Daddy and our pastor warned Danny that he would have to be tough and watch his back in jail. They described him as "strange" and "different," not at all like the Danny that we had known for years.

When Danny first saw them, he said, "I am surprised but pleased to see you two."

Daddy replied, "Well, I don't hate you, but I hate what you've done."

"Tell Angie that I love her with all my heart, and I always will. I want her to take everything I have, sell it, and go on with her life," Danny instructed them tearfully.

In an attempt to prepare Danny for the divorce papers without actually telling him about them, Daddy said, "There may be some hard things for you to face in the upcoming weeks. I want you to remember that they are not being done out of malice."

"I shouldn't have talked to the police without an attorney present." Danny's remorse was already diminishing because that statement revealed regret for his confession.

Our pastor volunteered to be the contact person if Danny needed to talk to us, but Danny would never take advantage of his offer. Danny asked if I was living with my parents, but Daddy skillfully evaded answering his question. Before they left, Daddy did ask Danny why he had done it, but he gave no response.

On Monday morning, April 30, 2001, my divorce lawyer contacted me to say that he had reviewed Bryanna's medical records and the police investigation reports. With my permission, he wanted to pursue a wrongful death suit on her behalf against the radiologists, First Street Hospital, and Daniel Draper. According to him, the medical reports plainly showed that she had multiple fractures present on the x-rays taken at First Street Hospital on May 5, 2000 and May 11, 2000 prior to her death. Also, the CAT scan on May 12, 2000 had shown a bleed in her head! The radiologists had misread all of those films. Obviously, I had a strong malpractice case after all. Danny could never pay me money in jail, but my divorce lawyer included him so that he would never be able to profit from his crime by selling his story. An associate lawyer would be assisting him with the suit because it involved more work than one single attorney could do.

The suit cited negligence against the radiologists interpreting Bryanna's films. My lawyer used evidence from the autopsy, police investigation, and a special x-ray report. The report was written by a pediatric radiologist expert, located in a different city than the other First Street Hospital radiologists. She reviewed all of Bryanna's x-rays made prior to her death and wrote an extensive letter to the district attorneys on July 17, 2000, detailing all of the fractures visible on the films. On the May 5, 2000 chest x-ray, the radiologist overlooked the left clavicle fracture, a left upper leg (femur) fracture, and an area suspicious for a fracture on the left sixth rib. On the May 11, 2000 bone survey films, fractures were missed in both upper legs and the right lower leg as well. All of these undiagnosed injuries were indicative of "non-accidental trauma."

The CAT scan on May 12, 2000 that was described as "normal" in reality, showed an "acute subdural hematoma" (bleeding) located in the "left occiput" (the back of the head). The late addendum written by Dr. Story on the day of Bryanna's autopsy was not even correct. He completely missed the true injury in the back of her brain and commented instead on fluid collections and widening sutures in the front of the brain that according to the pediatric radiologist specialist may not have even been abnormal. The suit stated:

> "That on or about May 16, 2000, Defendant Story represented to law enforcement authorities that the May 12, 2000 x-ray should have been read as abnormal, but that the abnormality was not of great concern, and inferred that it did not indicate abuse by a third party. The Defendant Story did not file an addendum to the report noting an abnormal reading until June 5, 2000, three days after the death of the Child."

The bottom line to the entire lawsuit was if her x-rays would have been read properly, her death would have been prevented because "she would have been in the care, custody, and control of the State Department of Children Services." The suit included First Street Hospital on the basis that they allowed Danny to be an active participate in the "x-ray process," "reading of the films," and "transportation of such films" to the radiologists. Postmortem x-rays done during the autopsy revealed that Bryanna had five old rib fractures and one fresh rib fracture when she died. The five old rib fractures were not visualized on the original bone survey because the pictures were taken using improper techniques. There should have been side views of the ribs. The side views were never completed because Bryanna was so fussy, and Danny knew the technicians and talked them into stopping the exam after acquiring only a minimal number of films. The reading radiologist also knew Danny and did not question the lack of an adequate quantity or variety of films. It was scary to think that perhaps Danny suspected she might have rib fractures and stopped the exam early on purpose to hide them.

My lawyers requested ten million dollars in compensatory damages and ten million dollars in punitive damages. Compensatory damages involve "compensation" for financial loss, mental anguish, pain, and suffering. Punitive damages are intended as a "punishment" to hopefully discourage other potential wrongdoers from committing the same acts.

My lawyer volunteered to proceed with the case without any upfront charges to me. If we won, the earnings would be split on a 2/3 basis to me (minus any expenses incurred) and 1/3 basis to my lawyers. I told him to go ahead and file the suit since we were rapidly approaching a June 2, 2001 deadline. Twenty million dollars does not seem like much money in exchange for a life. How do you put a price on a human being? Can you put a monetary value to pain and suffering? There was absolutely no way that you could. I guess I finally had a malpractice suit, but it was not at all how I had imagined it would be.

On Monday afternoon, April 30, 2001, my parents and I met with General Steele and an assistant district attorney, Mrs. Good, who had been helping him during the past year on Bryanna's case. During the meeting, General Steele explained more about Danny's charges and his possible intent to seek the death penalty. He wanted to know if we opposed Danny facing the death penalty as punishment for his actions. General Steele was stern and very matter of fact as he spoke. I would not want him to be prosecuting me.

Danny was charged with first degree felony murder. Felony murder meant that he was committing a crime (child abuse) when he performed the crime (murder). General Steele presented three aggravating factors that he had compiled against Danny: "the killing was committed against a person under age twelve and the defendant is over the age of eighteen," "the murder was especially heinous, atrocious, or cruel in that it involved torture or serious physical abuse beyond that necessary to produce death," and "the defendant knowingly committed the offense." In the state where we resided, only two aggravating factors were required for the prosecution to seek the death penalty, and Danny had three—giving them adequate reason to pursue the maximum punishment allowed by law.

My heart ached at the thought of Danny facing the electric chair; yet, I was angry at him for hurting Bryanna for no reason, deceiving me, and destroying our life together. The district attorneys expressed their immense concern for justice for Bryanna. She was only an infant. In today's society with rampant abortions, infants many times were not treated as important, but those individuals—perfect strangers—never ceased to show just how valuable her little life actually was. Even though their interest for her occurred after her death, it impressed me because it was more regard than any of her doctors had demonstrated for her while she was alive. That day, my family and I developed a deep confidence in General Steele and Mrs. Good. We told them since they had done an exceptional job so far in handling our tragic situation; we trusted their judgment on the matter whatever that was.

General Steele explained to us that his final decision regarding the death penalty depended on the ruling in a somewhat similar case, the Godsey case. Bobby Godsey was sentenced to death for killing his girlfriend's son by throwing him against a wall. The murder involved one single incidence of abuse rather than the continuous abuse that Danny had committed. Godsey's death sentence was currently being appealed in the State Supreme Court. The Supreme Court's ruling in the Godsey case would influence the district attorney's determination on whether or not to seek the death penalty against Danny.

General Steele informed us that Mr. Hood would be representing Danny. Mr. Hood was an expensive criminal lawyer with a reputation notorious for being ruthless. He was sure to plan a flawless defense and pursue any possibility of reducing Danny's charges or sentence. Instead of just letting Danny be represented by a court appointed attorney, his family had spent thousands of dollars in an attempt to get him off lightly.

"Do you think he will try a mental insanity plea?" I asked

General Steele replied, "They might, but I doubt it will work. The signed confession seals the case for the prosecution. I do anticipate that he will try to get the confession statement suppressed, meaning that the jury would not be able to hear it. If they attempt that, we will have to deal with it when the time comes."

"What if he posts bail?" I wanted to know.

"We do not feel that to be a threat because the judge set bond very high."

"But his family has enough money to pay his bond. His mother and stepdad received a large inheritance, well over one hundred thousand dollars, when Danny's step-grandfather passed away a few years ago."

The district attorneys had erroneously assumed that after paying an upfront fee of fifty thousand dollars to retain Mr. Hood that Danny's family would not have enough money left to post bond. After telling them that they would indeed have plenty of money, General Steele promised, "If his family tries to post bail for him, we will do everything possible to stop it, and we will make a condition of his bond that he is not to have any contact with you." His words reassured me a little, but I still felt uneasy. I knew his mom would not like him in jail especially after he was assaulted, but Danny did not deserve to be free after all he did to Bryanna.

The following day, May 1, 2001, Danny appeared in general session's court and waved a preliminary hearing. The preliminary hearing was a proceeding where the judge must determine if a crime was indeed committed in the court's jurisdiction and if there was adequate reason to believe that the defendant committed the crime. The signed confession provided that unquestionable evidence so there was really no reason for him to protest.

Danny entered the courtroom for the hearing wearing the black and white striped jail uniform bound in handcuffs and leg irons. Once again, his face was plastered across the television stations and newspapers—now sporting a black eye. The newspapers officially announced that Danny had been fired from First Street Hospital after his arrest, and General Steele confirmed publicly that the prosecution was considering the death penalty. Danny's lawyer, Mr. Hood, did not make a motion during the court appearance as expected to reduce Danny's bond, but the district attorneys requested that if Danny did post bond that a condition be made for the record that he was not to contact his wife. The general session's court hearing marked the beginning of the long legal process.

Later that week, Detective Sharp asked me to come to the police station and prepare a written statement about the events on the evening of Danny's arrest. He said that we would need it in case Danny's lawyer attempted to suppress his confession statement at a later date. It would be very important for the prosecution to show that Danny presented to the police department of his own free will. Cooperating with the authorities in all matters, I went to the police station and wrote a two page summary to the best of my memory detailing the exact sequence of events as they transpired from the moment my dad exited the court house until the time we took Danny to the police station.

Autopsy Results and Confession

The week after Danny's arrest, Detective Sharp delivered to us a copy of Bryanna's autopsy and Danny's confession. I took a few hours alone to study the two documents. The details contained in them were mind boggling and sickening.

The preliminary report of the autopsy released on June 19, 2000, that Detective Sharp told us was inconclusive, actually stated something else. The pathologist cited that Bryanna possibly suffered from Shaken Baby Syndrome and Munchausen Syndrome by Proxy. Munchausen Syndrome by Proxy is defined as a form of child abuse in which a caregiver, usually the mother, produces real or fabricated symptoms of a disease in a child. The caregiver is often a health care professional, such as a nurse, and very helpful to the medical staff tending to the child. The motivation for the behavior in the caregiver is to obtain a form of gratification from the attention that is gained when people care for the sick child. That presumption contained in the preliminary autopsy report identified me as the main suspect in her murder, not Danny. The very thought of it caused chills to go up my spine!

Her autopsy report was very complicated and lengthy. At death, Bryanna had three separate bleeds in her brain (one was old and two were new). The old bleed in the back of her head was present and missed by the radiologist on the CAT scan dated May 12, 2000. The pathologist estimated that injury to be about three to six weeks old. Fresh bleeding was present in both of her eyes. Seven injured ribs were noted on the report, in addition to the broken left clavicle and right arm. The accumulation of those injuries, some being old and others being new, resulted in the diagnosis of Battered Child Syndrome. According to the pathologist in the autopsy report, Battered Child Syndrome was defined as "several injuries involving different areas of the body that occurred at more than one point in time." Including the autopsy and the x-ray report generated by the pediatric radiologist specialist, Bryanna had a total of fourteen fractures during her short life——seven ribs, a left clavicle, right humerus (elbow), right wrist, both femors (upper legs), one tibia (lower leg), and the left scapula (shoulder blade).

Bryanna also suffered from Shaken Baby/Shaking-Impact Syndrome, a type of child abuse where the perpetrator squeezes the infant around the chest area and violently shakes the baby back and forth. This vibrating motion causes an acceleration/ deceleration injury similar to whiplash in car accidents but worse. Since a baby's neck muscles are not well developed, the gyration causes tearing of the blood vessels in the head and subsequent bleeding in the brain. This hemorrhage can be worsened in Shaking-Impact Syndrome where the perpetrator shakes the infant and then throws them onto a surface. Even if the surface is soft such as a pillow it can still cause brain damage. The other fatal injury most frequently elicited by the jerking motion is bleeding into the eyes due to the tearing of the blood vessels. The fractures commonly associated with Shaken Baby Syndrome are ribs (from the squeezing) and long bone (arms and legs) fractures because the arms and legs are riveted back and forth without support increasing susceptibility to injury. From her autopsy results, obviously, Bryanna had the three main elements essential to the diagnosis of Shaken Baby Syndrome. Although she endured an immense amount of physical pain, thankfully, there was no evidence of sexual trauma on the autopsy.

Danny's confession to all of that was truly the most horrible statement that I have ever read. He began with "his problems" starting when Bryanna was about one month old. Those nights that he stayed awake to feed her during early morning hours for me so that I could sleep was when the abuse began. Many of the incidents occurred in our spare bedroom at the far end of the house and in the downstairs den, which explained why I never heard anything. He purposefully performed the deeds at the most distant points in the house from our bedroom, not to mention that he also benefited from the white noise of the humidifier that I ran while I slept.

Danny claimed that her crying caused him to "go into a rage." To make her "stop the crying," at first, he struck her with his fingers and later with the palms of his hands. Eventually, he tossed her "no more than three feet" into the air onto the bed. Another thing he confessed to doing about five times was, "I would place my hand on her upper back while her body was across my lap and fold her up. Better described as causing her chin to go into her chest and also bend some at the waist." His behavior contradicted natural human response and good common sense. By hurting her, he was causing her to cry even more, not stop. She was a good baby and probably would have fussed very little if she had not been in such excruciating pain. Actually, I don't remember her being very fretful at all before the age of one month. Also, if he could not console her, all he had to do was walk a few feet across the house to the bedroom and wake me. I would have gladly gotten up and taken care of her. If he was alone with her and did not know what to do, he could have picked up the phone and called my mom. He was always only a hand reach away from help.

He also admitted to twisting her arms and legs on several occasions "to get her to comply with changing her or get her to stop crying." He even "twisted" both of her arms behind her back "once or twice while in a rage." Around the age of two months after she was given her shots, he said that Bryanna vomited on him in the spare bedroom, and "I again got into a rage and I struck her pretty hard in the back. That may explain the broken scapula." His explanation for the broken ribs was that "I squeezed her really hard around the ribs when I was in a rage...I really did not feel like or realize that I used that kind of pressure but, I was in that rage that came over me. It was like I was watching this happen. I just can't explain this."

Evidently, the abuse worsened significantly after I returned to work when his time alone with her also considerably increased. I believe that was when he began to smother her. He admitted to three separate occasions of smothering her until she lost consciousness by placing his hand over her face. After he suffocated her on those three occasions, he threw her onto the couch or floor where she stiffened and jerked in a way he described as similar to seizure activity. Afterward, her breathing became very slow. Twice, he revived her from that condition by patting her face with a cold wash cloth and calling her name. On the third and final time, he was unable to arouse her with the cold cloth. That was the day she died.

"Mom left about four p.m. I know I did nothing to her between four and five p.m. At five p.m., I went to the den to watch the news. Just after the newscast came on, I heard Bryanna cry and went to check. She had thrown up and I cleaned her up and gave her some water and then took her downstairs. She was still irritable as she was before I brought her downstairs. I laid her on the floor and she was crying. I picked her up as she was still crying. I picked her up by her head. I placed one hand behind her head and one hand over her mouth and nose. I held her there for maybe ten seconds as her arms flailed back and forth. I then put her back on the floor on her pillow and went upstairs to warm her formula. I was gone for six or seven minutes before returning to her in the den. She was alive at that time. I picked her up and sat with her on the couch and attempted to feed her. She was very irritable but she took some formula and I burped her on my shoulder. I then tried to give her more formula and she was still very fussy and I just lost it. I threw her and her pillow to the floor where the other pillows were located. She and the pillow struck one of the pillows and she bounced over onto her left side and then rolled back on her back. Bryanna again stiffened as though she was having a seizure. I tried to revive her but she had really slow breathing. Every ten seconds she exhibited a moaning type breath. She did that and I went to get a wash cloth and returned to find her not breathing at all. I washed her face with the wet cloth, called her name, but she did not respond. I got the cordless phone and called 911 and started CPR. I breathed into her and her chest would rise and fluid came from her nose and mouth which appeared to be formula."

Although Bryanna exhibited all the major signs and symptoms of Shaken Baby Syndrome, his confession, in my opinion, did not really confirm that diagnosis. The abuse he inflicted was much more severe than just shaking and throwing her. Generally, a perpetrator of Shaken Baby Syndrome suddenly looses their temper, picks the infant up, and shakes them violently during a single isolated event. Danny on the other hand behaved more like a person who was actually very much in control of their actions; so restrained, in fact, that he never slipped and did it in front of anyone, and he denied it completely when questioned by various people. His lies even convinced personnel trained in detecting deceptions such as the Department of Children's Service and detectives. Worst of all, he had no valid reason to ever hurt her. Even worse than that—she was his flesh and blood. He tortured and killed a part of himself. How does someone do that?

Was he sorry for what he did? I don't know the true answer to that question. I can only quote what he said at the end of his confession: "We did have some good times also. Not every time that I had her did these bad things happen. She had the prettiest smile. She was absolutely beautiful. It's unthinkable what I did to her...I was stupid enough to believe that the things I had done to her had not killed her. I actually denied what I had done until today when I realized the evidence you had. I guess I was just in denial of the whole thing. Also, it was a factor that Detective

Sharp had not come back to talk to us. I guess I really didn't realize I had killed her until today. You know I'm sorry for what I have done. I wish I had this to do over. As an educated person that I am and have a loving wife that I have and the support our families have given us over the years, I would give my life to have hers back. I would like to re-live last year. I'm very, very sorry for what I have done. The real Danny Draper would not have done anything like that, ask anybody. I feel like I have been treated courteously and fairly and I appreciate it very much. Today, I came into the detective office of my own free will. I have not been pressured or coerced to talk, to give this statement."

For days after reading his confession, I was consumed with thoughts of her pain and suffering when I tried to rest at night. I cried into my pillow until sleep finally rescued me from the horror of her death. I wished over and over again that he would have hurt me instead of her. She was so fragile and could only tolerate so much of his abuse. I am stronger and could have withstood it better and maybe even been able to fight back. She was helpless at his mercy. She could not even tell anyone what was really happening. Perhaps on judgment day, she will have a voice and proclaim to all. I think it would have been easier for me to have cut off one of my arms or legs than to have lost her.

During the eleven months that we were waiting for the autopsy results, my father knew a very disturbing piece of information, but he did not share it with my mom, Danny, or I. My dad was good friends with the funeral home director where Bryanna's services were held. The director told my dad that Monday night when they received Bryanna's body that it might not be presentable for any type of viewing at all because the pathologist had kept the bones inside her right arm and her eyes. My dad did not tell me about that for eleven months fearing that it would upset me too much. After Danny's arrest, when he revealed that information, it caused several things to finally make sense.

The fact that the pathologist had kept her eyes was probably the reason that they appeared strange and pinched to me at the funeral home that morning when we first viewed her body. It also explained why my dad returned to our house the evening before the funeral and said that she needed a sweater. The sweater was used to hide the missing bones in her right arm.

Bryanna being returned to us without her eyes and right arm was very distressing for my dad because he felt like "we were only being given back a partial baby to bury." If he had shared that information with me, I would have known something very bad was wrong. From a nursing standpoint, the keeping of her eyes would have caused me to suspect bleeding in the brain and Shaken Baby Syndrome. Keeping her arm might have alerted me to consider that they were gathering evidence against us, but then again, I may have only thought that she had a rare bone disorder causing them to retain it for further study. The pathologist and detectives evidently did not realize that my dad knew the funeral home director and probably never imagined that the family would know anything about the missing right arm and eyes.

After Bryanna's services, my dad asked the funeral home director to fax him a copy of Bryanna's death certificate as soon as it arrived. Many months passed after their conversation, but her death certificate did, in fact, reach the funeral home about three weeks before Danny's arrest. As promised, the funeral home director faxed a copy to my dad. Three weeks before my dad spoke to the district attorney's office, he knew that Bryanna's death certificate stated the cause of death was Battered Child Syndrome/Multiple Trauma/Homicide. Shortly after he received the death certificate was when he talked to me in the sunroom about what we would have to do if Danny and I were falsely accused of harming Bryanna. After he told me that he knew about the death certificate three weeks before Danny's arrest, the conversation we had that afternoon in the sunroom finally made sense. My dad was trying to prepare me for the worst outcome that he could imagine at that time. He agonized for three long weeks that his daughter and son-in-law were probably going to be falsely accused of murdering Bryanna.

The death certificate was signed by a physician at First Street Hospital causing my dad to suspect that the doctors were staging a mass cover up to wrongfully blame us with her death. Even after seeing a copy of her death certificate, my dad still did not fathom that Danny had ever purposefully harmed Bryanna. At the most, he thought Danny may have accidentally or unknowingly hurt her. None of us ever suspected that Danny did something to Bryanna intentionally until he confessed. That was how well he fooled everyone including those closest to him.

When Detective Sharp brought us a copy of the autopsy and confession, he also shared some frightening revelations about his eleven month investigation into Bryanna's death. Detective Sharp was present in the room when Bryanna's autopsy was performed. The pathologist noted nothing unusual about the outside of Bryanna's body. She did not realize that Bryanna had been murdered until she began the internal investigation where she found the rib fractures by feeling them. When she shared her autopsy findings with others present in the room, Detective Sharp phoned Dr. Story at First Street Hospital and asked him to take another look at Bryanna's CAT scan and write an addendum concerning his findings which explained why Dr. Story made the incorrect addendum to the CAT scan. He had lied to us the day we questioned him about it. He said that someone from the College of Medicine with a long important sounding title had called him and asked him to do it. It was, in fact, Detective Sharp that had requested the addendum.

Up until the day Danny confessed, I remained a prime suspect along with him. Detective Sharp and Detective Light did not completely exclude me as a suspect until they witnessed my reaction first hand after Danny signed the confession. When Danny and I were alone in the interrogation room, and he admitted to me that he had twisted Bryanna's arms and legs, I cried out in pain and almost fainted. Neither of us were aware that we were being watched, but Detective Sharp and Detective Light were monitoring us in a separate room via a camera. It was not recorded; but being thorough investigators, they simply wanted to observe my reaction when we spoke for the first time after the confession. When they saw my genuine anguish, they realized that I was innocent and did not have any idea that Danny was hurting Bryanna. I cannot adequately describe my reaction that night, but to onlookers it must have been something that could not have been faked.

That was the most frightening part of the entire story for me—to realize how close I was to being implicated with Danny if he had not confessed. I am glad that we took him to the police station that Monday afternoon. Confessing was the only decent thing he did for a whole year, and unfortunately, he quickly regretted doing that.

Detective Sharp also told us that my diary was an important piece of information to the investigation. The Friday afternoon that he interviewed the entire family, and I read it to him, he thought it was irrelevant to the case. As the investigation progressed, my diary began to reveal a pattern to him that Bryanna was alone with Danny, and then became sick, and then I (the mother) took her to the doctor. That pattern exposed Danny as the abuser instead of me, especially since I was the one who always took her to the doctor. What Detective Sharp, at first, thought were the insignificant ramblings of a potential murder suspect developed into the missing pieces of the puzzle. Thus, writing that diary was probably one of the smartest things I have ever done in my life.

The fact that Bryanna died when she was in Danny's care also helped to implicate him as the main suspect. Wednesday night,

May 31, 2000, when my mom picked Bryanna up after Danny had been taking care of her, Bryanna was very sleepy and developed the petechia rash. Most likely, Danny had been smothering her before my mom arrived that evening. She could have potentially died with my mom that night instead of two days later when she was with Danny. How different events could have developed by changing that one simple fact.

Another relevant factor that played into Bryanna's ultimate demise was the dynamics of today's health care environment. Each time she went to the pediatrician's office, she was examined by a different provider. If the same doctor had seen her at each visit, maybe, that consistent physician would have been better able to determine what was going on and develop a trusting relationship with the parents. However, she had no continuity of care, meaning she was followed by so many different practitioners that she was "lost in the system." I think that anyone familiar with today's health care environment can relate to exactly how that break down in the system happened.

I could continue to study the facts of Bryanna's case indefinitely, but the truth remained that there really was no valid reason or excuse for what Danny did to her. That was the hardest part for me to accept. I found it very difficult to envision the Danny that I knew and loved inflicting such pain upon a helpless infant. As I speculated on why and how he could do such a thing, one possibility occurred to me. What if evil had entered his mind through heavy metal music and violent computer games? I had never really believed that wickedness could invade someone by those means, but Danny's actions left me to wonder. On the remote possibility that those items were indeed harmful, I gathered all of the hard rock CDs and violent computer games and burned them. It was actually a very healing experience for me to watch those things blaze. I could have sold them for money to pay bills, but if they did contain something evil, I wanted it to end with Danny.

Danny's unnecessary actions had crumbled my life into pieces. My child was dead. My marriage was over, and Danny was locked away probably forever. It would have been easier if they both had died in an unfortunate accident than to have to face the reality of the crime he committed. I was experiencing the worst tragedy of my life left to choose between two roads. I could surrender to self pity and ask why me; or I could embrace the pain, learn from it, and chose to go on with my life. Where there is life, there is hope and I hoped to find happiness and joy again.

Photos

Prom Picture

Graduation

Wedding day

Spike

Annie

Hawaii

Expecting Bryanna

Bryanna Doll

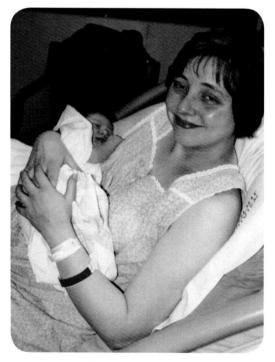

Bryanna at birth

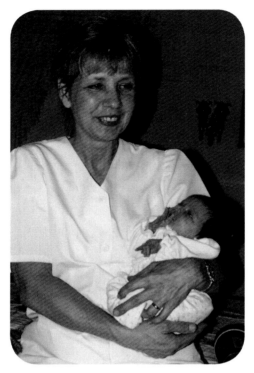

Bryanna with her grandmother

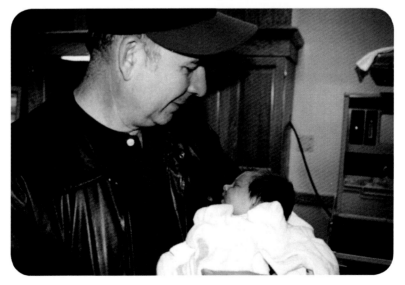

Bryanna with her grandfather

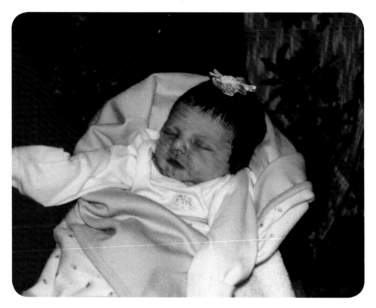

Bryanna Age 3 days

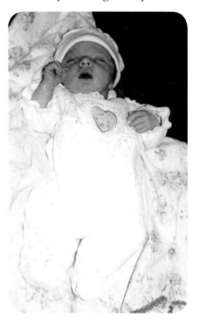

Bryanna Sleeping, Age 1 week

First Time to Church

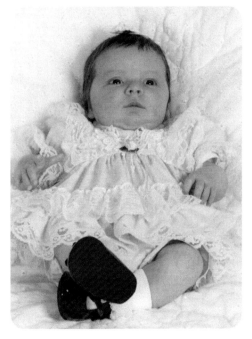

Bryanna's One Month Picture

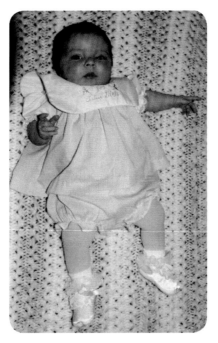

Bryanna at 6 weeks

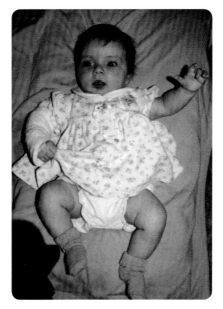

Bryanna with her cast

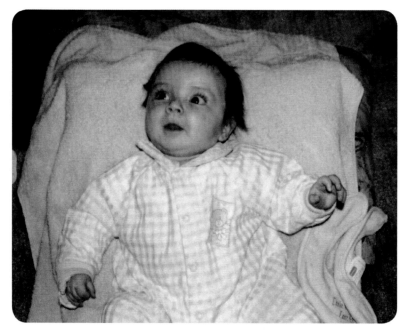

Bryanna looking up at her dad

Life Goes On

Once again, I discovered that the world continued around me in spite of my personal tragedies. At first, people offered sympathy and assistance, but eventually everyone forgot my pain. It would be nice if the world would stop for a while to give one time to grieve, but unfortunately, it does not. Suddenly, I found myself surrounded by people getting married and having babies. I probably really was not; but in my emptiness, it seemed worse than it actually was. I did not want to see their wedding and baby pictures, but in their excitement, they showed them to me anyway. What I really wanted to do was crawl into a hole and die. What I actually had to do was let life go on.

When Bryanna died, going back to work had helped me; so about two weeks after Danny's confession, I again returned to work to help keep my mind occupied. Returning to work after his arrest was even more awkward than after Bryanna's death due to the nature of his crime and the publicity. I worried that the media would find me at the government hospital and harass me for an interview. I also wondered how people would react to me since I had known my coworkers for only a few months. Surprisingly though, my colleges were very supportive and understanding. In reality, Danny had left me to pay all the bills alone so I really had no choice but to work, especially if I did not want to foreclose the house, declare bankruptcy, and destroy my own credit.

My shattered life quickly fell into a new routine. I continued to walk about four times a week; I worked evening shift five days per week. In my free time, I packed my belongings at our house, anticipating putting it on the market. The house would have to be sold, mainly because it held too many bad memories for me to enjoy living there. Also, I really could not afford the payments on one income. Sorting between what I intended to sell and what

I wanted to keep, I planned to store most of the items in my grandfather's garage, but the amount of available space would be limited. As I packed, I quickly realized that I would have to get rid of a lot of stuff.

I resolved to have a huge yard sale in the near future, but from my experience, some items do not move well at yard sales so I placed those things on Ebay or advertised them in the classifieds ads. A lot of CDs, computer games, and unopened ship models left my possession via the World Wide Web. Eventually, I also auctioned our wedding bands and my engagement ring on Ebay, receiving only a minute return in comparison to what Danny had paid for them.

One of my classified advertisements was answered by a man who offered to purchase all three of Danny's telescopes for five hundred and fifty dollars, which was only fraction of what Danny had paid for them. I hated to trade them so cheaply, but I doubted that I would find the opportunity to sell all three at once like that again. Not to mention, the money was desperately needed for accumulating bills.

All of the proceeds from my sales were used to pay for the house and Danny's truck. Each day, I feared filing bankruptcy. I may have sold a lot of Danny's stuff, but I sold much of mine as well. Several of my porcelain dolls were placed in the yard sale, in addition to my dishes, collectibles, clothes, and shoes.

A few years prior, Danny's dad gave us a bed and dresser for our spare bedroom that had belonged to Danny's grandmother. Thinking that Danny's dad would probably want to have the furniture back for sentimental reasons, I sent him an e-mail asking if he would like to have them returned. He answered yes that he would, and we planned a time via e-mail for him to pick them up. My dad and I met Danny's dad and stepdad at my house at the prearranged date and time. The two pieces of furniture had already been moved to the basement for easy loading onto Danny's dad's truck quickly.

I cannot begin to describe how cold and indifferent they treated us that day. They acted like we had committed the crime, and they were the victims instead of the way it really was. Danny's dad did not speak a word to me. As a matter of fact, he did not even look at me. He treated me like I did not exist. Even though Danny's dad and I had seen each other infrequently while Danny and I were married, we had always talked and enjoyed a good relationship; therefore, I was rather surprised that he would show me such disdain. He only spoke a few words to my father all related to loading the furniture onto the truck. While they were there, I asked Danny's stepdad if he wanted a chest of drawers that he had given Danny and me to use for storage in our basement. Danny's stepdad replied yes that he did want it back.

While they finished loading the bed and dresser, I emptied the contents of the chest onto the floor in a huge heap. Lastly, they carried the chest out of the basement den and placed it on the bed of the pickup truck and were gone. Neither one of them said "thank you." They acted like we owed them that furniture and a whole lot more. However, I was glad to see them leave and take the chilled, icy atmosphere with them, but when I looked at the pile of misplaced belongings from the dresser on the floor; it sadly reminded me of my life.

That incident was only the beginning of a huge rift that would develop between our two families. Danny's family was angry at us for taking him to the police station that night. They blamed us completely for his arrest without ever stopping to realize that no one in my family put Danny in jail. His own actions put him there. Evidently, they could not accept that fact and instead searched desperately for someone else to blame with Danny's sin. We just happened to be the best available candidates.

Danny was fired from his job so he had no income, but his family could have offered to help with the house payment with some of their inheritance money; however, they never once did. They also never helped with any of the packing, moving, or mowing. My paternal grandfather maintained our yard that summer. Danny's stepdad had given us his old riding lawn mower just weeks before Danny's arrest. Danny's stepdad never volunteered to mow the yard, but he did ask for his lawn mower to be returned on several occasions. My dad tried to explain to him that we really needed it for a short time period to keep the yard looking presentable so that the house would sell. Danny's stepdad still insisted that we return it immediately. My dad finally told him that he would gladly give it back to him, but not until after the house was sold.

❧

During the first two months after Danny's arrest, I met with my counselor on an almost weekly basis. Her office became a safe place for me to vent and discuss my grief. She suggested that I write a letter to Bryanna and also to Danny expressing all of my feelings to them. Those letters, of course, were never sent but did create a therapeutic outlet for my despair. She further recommended that I start journaling my thoughts and emotions every day. I had always loved to write and thought perhaps a record of what had happened to me might help someone else one day.

I had not written anything except the poem for Bryanna in several years. After Danny and I were married, I really did not have time to write. Working full-time and keeping house consumed most of my free time. Now suddenly, my muse had returned. My writer's block was gone. Not only did I keep a journal; I also felt inspired to compose poetry again.

Upon my counselor's advice, I began to read a lot of self help literature about death, grief, losing a child, and divorce. I read one book right after another. I even found a book about people who had a lost a loved one to murder. As relevant as that book would seem, none of them really fit exactly what had happened to me which reinforced the importance of recording my story.

Early in therapy, my counselor discussed with me that I faced a very rough task in the near future—sorting through Bryanna's belongings. I had not really thought about that. Her room had remained shut for months in hopes of another baby occupying it. Now that would never happen. After considerable thought, I decided to keep only her belongings that held sweet, special memories and to donate the rest of the items that were new or barely used to the Children's Advocacy Center (CAC). It created a way to honor her life for her belongings to be used by another child that might have been abused. I never wanted her to be forgotten. I chose the CAC because Detective Sharp said the employees there had truly grieved for Bryanna after her death. To them, she represented the worst consequence of child abuse—an untimely death.

I could only tolerate sorting through her possessions a little at a time. Some days, the very thought of it caused me to completely break down before I even started, and I could not do it all. There were special items that I really wanted to save, but keeping everything would be selfish with other needy children in the world. If I were ever fortunate enough to have another child, I would probably want to start fresh anyway, but honestly, having a family again felt like a precious dream that would never come true. Even thinking about it caused me to have such feelings of hopelessness that I really just tried not to.

As I looked through Bryanna's belongings, I found her baby book. I had faithfully recorded in it before her birth and during the first month of her life, but after that, sadly, all of the pages were blank. Obviously, I was so busy caring for her that I did not have time to write in a baby book. I wondered sometimes why we could not see that Danny was hurting her. One reason was we were all so exhausted from caring for a sick child. Another important factor was how fast everything happened. Bryanna was dead less than one month after the first fracture was discovered. We did not have enough time to see the sequence of her being with Danny and then becoming really sick. It had actually taken Detective Sharp weeks to discern that pattern in retrospect. The empty pages of the baby book clarified those two facts. My mom had even planned to keep Bryanna at her house during the summer while she was off work. If God had granted us just a little more time, maybe we could have seen the evidence more clearly as she passed from one house to the other, but it was not meant to be.

After I packed all of Bryanna's belongings that I wanted to keep, her life was reduced to the contents of four boxes and five large items that had been significant in her short life: her baby bed, Noah's Ark bassinet, swing, car seat, and favorite Fisher Price music box. I sent everything else to the CAC, and it was given to a young mother trying to raise her daughter away from an abusive relationship.

※

Each time I visited Bryanna's grave, I was reminded about the horrible mistake I had made by engraving "mommy and daddy's little angel" on it. She was definitely mommy's little angel, but she was, by no means, daddy's little angel. I hated the fact that I had allowed Danny and his family to talk me into including him on her permanent marker. That became an incredibly sore spot for my family and me.

※

My dogs had been such a comforting presence that I took them to live with me at my parent's house. I also had to decide what to do with our pet cockatiel, Spike. Spike had always really been Danny's bird. When we moved, we put his cage in our den downstairs. The thought of him being in the downstairs den watching Danny abuse Bryanna was very disturbing for me. After Bryanna died, Spike had several episodes of squawking and flapping all over his cage. Birds are fairly intelligent creatures and I thought back then that maybe he realized that Bryanna was gone and was asking, in his way, what had happened to her. Now, I wondered if he was trying to tell me what Danny had done to her in the only way he knew how. Since a lot of the abuse and her actual murder had occurred in the downstairs den, Spike was the only living eyewitness to what had happened. Knowing that, I could not endure looking at him every day and thinking about what he had seen. A young guy that worked with my dad in the body shop said he would be happy to take Spike home with him. I packed Spike's belongings and sent him on his way, far from me. Sometimes, I wonder if Spike will have a human voice on Judgment Day and testify before the Great White Throne of God as to what Danny did—his most lethal condemner, next to God and Bryanna.

❧

On June 29, 2001, Danny was indicted by the Grand Jury on three charges: premeditated murder, felony murder, and aggravated child abuse. His lawyer, Mr. Hood, entered a plea of not guilty on his behalf. It seemed strange that after confessing, Danny would be allowed to enter a plea of not guilty. However, General Steele explained that was to be expected. A plea of not guilty was what permitted Danny to have a jury trial. Judge Strong set the trial to begin on January 22, 2002 and estimated that it would take about two weeks to complete. "I'll expect it to be tried and not be reset," Judge Strong concluded. January 2002 seemed like a long time to wait for the matter to be resolved.

During Danny's June 29, 2001 court appearance, Mr. Hood also requested a hearing to discuss another mental evaluation for Danny. The prosecution had already completed a "screening process" that concluded Danny was competent to stand trial. Mr. Hood was seeking a more "in-depth examination" to determine his mental condition at the time the crime was committed. I still had hopes that Danny might be insane, but General Steele reassured me that he was not mentally ill at all. It was very hard for me to accept Danny as a cold-blooded murderer after the love we shared, but that was how he was viewed by the prosecution. My emotions changed so much throughout the day that I felt like I was riding a psychological roller coaster. At times, I was angry and bitter. Then I would become extremely down and depressed. However, overall, anger at Danny and his family began to dominate my life.

I was constantly agitated and worrying about something. Most of the time, it was how I was going to pay the bills. Danny had left me in a financial disaster paying for a two income family on one paycheck. When I created the new bank accounts, I left our joint checking account open for a few weeks to manage any pending transactions. In that joint account, I received Danny's final paycheck from First Street Hospital and his payout for vacation time via electronic deposits. Those two checks were the last of Danny's assistance with our monthly bills. Then, I was left on my own. George Bush issued a six hundred dollar tax refund that summer. I anxiously awaited the arrival of that much needed money.

I was trapped with the house payment and unable to sell it without Danny's signature. In addition to the hefty mortgage, I had the burden of Danny's truck payment because I was co-financer on the loan. Those two obligations alone consumed almost my entire monthly income with very little money to spare. Since I was not residing in the house, I reduced some of my expenses by decreasing the utilities to a bare minimum, cancelling all unnecessary services and turning off all nonessential appliances. However, those adjustments caused a whole new array of problems. Most of the services were in Danny's name instead of mine. Repeatedly, I had to explain why he was unable to call them himself. Usually, the reason (he's in jail) would gain me their cooperation, but there were instances when that did not even work.

During those days, it seemed that everything I tried to do was met with resistance. That held especially true concerning my pending divorce. My divorce lawyer had said on the first day that we met that after the papers were served on Danny, he would have thirty days to respond. If he did not answer within the thirty day time limit, I could request a divorce by default (meaning no answer from the opposing party). After waiting for over thirty days with no reply from Danny's attorney, Mr. Hood, I asked my divorce lawyer to contact him and find out if he was planning to represent Danny in the divorce suit as well as the criminal case. Each time my divorce lawyer called Mr. Hood, he was either "out of town" or had some other excuse to avoid speaking with my divorce lawyer. I waited for over sixty days with no response. I finally persuaded my lawyer to file for a divorce by default on July 10, 2001. The very next day, he received an answer from Mr. Hood about the divorce dated July 10, 2001.

The letter stated that Danny's criminal trial and the divorce proceedings had both been assigned to Judge Strong's docket; thus creating a serious conflict of interest. If Danny admitted to harming Bryanna in the divorce proceedings, it could compromise his right to a fair criminal trial. Mr. Hood further asserted that the divorce was not a primary concern for Danny because he was facing the death penalty. Then he had the audacity to add that since Danny was incarcerated that I was free to enjoy all of the marital assets anyway. Enjoy them! How could I derive any pleasure from our house knowing that Danny had brutally murdered Bryanna there!

The papers asked for the divorce proceedings to be delayed until after the criminal trial was over in January 2002. If that was not possible then they wanted an extra sixty days to file an answer to the suit and to try to settle the dispute out of court. However, if we settled out of court, we would basically end up dividing everything evenly, and I would not be granted any alimony. I did not really want to share our property because I was angry at Danny and did not feel like he deserved to be given anything. The truth was that it did not matter if I was more agreeable to a compromise or not. Mr. Hood's main intention was to delay the divorce at all costs. His real goal was for Danny to go to trial still married to me because it would make him look better in front of the jury. My feelings or desires did not matter to Danny or his lawyers because I was not facing "capital murder charges." Keeping me tied to Danny against my will was his family's way of forcing me to "stand behind him" whether I wanted to or not. They expected me to peacefully comply with their plans. I had been quiet all of my life; now it was time for me to be loud.

Mr. Hood had sent a paper for me to sign that would designate Danny's mother and stepdad as the beneficiaries on his retirement accounts instead of me. My lawyer advised me not to sign it, but I would not have anyway. Danny was making nothing easy for me especially financially so why should I do him any favors. The last paragraph of the response inquired as to the whereabouts of Danny's truck. Why did they want his truck? He could not drive it in jail.

My divorce attorney had asked if Danny would be willing to sign the house over to me so that I could sell it, but Danny refused to do that. It would have really helped me out financially to have been able to place the house on the market, but as I have said before, Danny was making nothing easy for me. I am sure that he wanted his share of our home equity to help pay the fifty thousand dollar up-front fee that Mr. Hood had charged just to accept the case; however, none of them ever once compensated me for Danny's share of the house payment.

I was powerless with no control over my life which was governed by the slow court system. Even though Danny was in jail, it seemed he could easily place obstacles in my path. He had already said on two separate occasions for me to take everything, sell his stuff, and go on with my life. It was not that I selfishly wanted all of the marital property. It was the fact that paying the bills consumed my entire income but did not grant me the freedom to sell the home or his truck. He must not have meant what he said because his actions proved otherwise.

After thoroughly reading Danny's response to my divorce suit, I told my attorney that I wanted to take a chance and appear in front of the judge to see if he would grant my divorce. My attorney advised that we could try, but there was a good possibility that Judge Strong would postpone the proceeding until after the criminal trial. He promised to get a court date set for the second or third week of August. It could not be soon enough for me. The worst part of the entire situation was being stuck with the last name of Draper. Each time I went shopping or wrote a check, I was so embarrassed thinking someone would know I was related to him or associate me with his crime. At work, I placed a piece of silk tape over Draper on my badge and wrote my maiden name on it so that patients could not see it. It was almost like a curse to me—bearing that last name. Each day, he somehow reached out from behind those bars to inflict more misery upon me.

An Unpleasant Surprise

A few days after we received the divorce response, Mr. Hood contacted my lawyer again, requesting Danny's clothes which caused me to wonder if his family might be planning to post bond. First they asked for his truck, and then they wanted his clothes. My lawyer advised me to pack Danny's garments and figure out a neutral way to deliver it to his family. I gathered Danny's entire wardrobe and some of his important personal belongings such as his wallet and family pictures and loaded the six cardboard boxes onto the bed of his truck. My paternal grandmother arranged for a mutual friend in the neighborhood where they lived to take them to Danny's family which prevented me from having any contact with his family. Sorting through Danny's personal belongings had caused me to experience tremendous pain. There was no way I could enjoy the marital property as Mr. Hood had so callously told me to do.

※

Around the middle of July, Danny appeared in court regarding his mental evaluation. The examination revealed "he is competent to stand trial and that an insanity defense could not be supported." General Steele presented an affidavit of complaint compiled by the police department about the heinous nature of Danny's crime which was partially read into the record by Judge Strong. Afterwards, Mr. Hood filed a motion to reduce Danny's two hundred and fifty thousand dollar bond, but Judge Strong promptly denied that request, mainly because of the horrible details contained in the report filed by the police department.

⁂

The following week beginning July 22, 2001, I took a couple of days off work and went with my parents to visit my brother who lived out of town. It felt so refreshing to take a short break from all the stress we had endured over the past few months. On the way home, Wednesday, July 25, 2001, my cell phone rang. It was my lawyer with news concerning my divorce.

First, he gave me the only good report that he had. Danny had finally agreed to sell our house with the understanding that any proceeds would be placed into an escrow account to be divided equally when the divorce was final. Secondly, Danny's mom and stepdad wanted me to keep Danny on my health insurance plan indefinitely, stating they would reimburse the premiums to me. If they intended for me to keep him on my policy, then they were certainly planning for us to remain married until after the trial. They also wanted me to give them Danny's truck on the stipulation that they would assume the payments. They did not offer to reimburse me for my share of the equity or for any of the payments I had made since Danny's arrest. Since they were very insistent about receiving their share of the equity on the house, it would only seem fair that I receive my equity in the truck as well. Why did they need his truck anyway? I barely had time to wonder before my lawyer revealed the final devastating news. He had heard a rumor that Danny was released on bond the previous day.

I panicked at the possibility that he was out of jail. Had his family at last posted bond? If they were planning to bail him out, I thought they would have done it right after he was arrested. Furthermore, when the motion to decrease his bond was denied by Judge Strong, I had stopped worrying about it. I had mistakenly assumed their request for a reduction was because they could not afford the fee after paying for his attorney. The motion was denied almost two weeks ago making his release even more unexpected. In shock, I barely spoke a word during the rest of the ride home.

As soon as we walked through the front door, my father contacted Detective Sharp to see if the rumor was true. Detective Sharp was unaware of Danny being released and said that he would have to make some phone calls to find out. Thirty minutes later, when Detective Sharp called back, he confirmed that Danny had been let out of jail the previous day on the two hundred and fifty thousand dollar bond. My chest tightened, and I felt like I was suffocating. The sensations were easily recognizable as a panic attack because I had experienced them several times since Bryanna's death.

General Steele was on vacation that week; thus, no one was present to object to Danny's release. Evidently, Mr. Hood had planned to post bond while General Steele was gone. Detective Sharp called us back the following day and said it was on the record that Danny was not supposed to contact my father or me as a stipulation of his bond.

Danny's release from jail was very frightening for me at first. I did not feel like I knew who he was at all anymore. I wondered if he would try to contact me in spite of the restriction. What would I do if he did?

I alerted my coworkers that Danny was out on bond in case he tried to contact me at work. I also gave the hospital's police department a picture of Danny so that they could surveillance the parking lot for him. I was scared walking to my car for many nights, but as time passed, with no sign of him, my fears gradually diminished. Part of me was terrified of him. Part of me was angry at him. Yet, at other times, a remote piece of me just wanted to hug him. Sometimes the mixture of emotions made me feel insane.

After careful consideration of Danny's multiple requests, I told my lawyer to give him these two messages. First, Danny would be terminated from my insurance plan during the next open season if not sooner. Secondly, I did not want to give him his truck. It would have been a financial relief to not have that payment, but I could not stand the thought him having the freedom to go wherever he pleased while Bryanna was dead in the ground. Actually, he should still be in jail.

Angry at Danny for being released from jail, I wondered why someone charged with first degree murder facing the death penalty would ever have a bond amount set in the first place. The natural thing for someone in that position to do would be flee the country and disappear forever. As I investigated the matter further, I found out that our state was one of the few states that permitted someone charged with first degree murder to have a bond set. However, one thing was for sure. Now that his family had him, they would do everything in their power to keep him as long as they could.

I quickly arranged for a realtor to create a listing agreement on our house and delivered the papers to my lawyer to be forwarded to Mr. Hood. All Danny had to do was sign the forms and the house would be placed on the market. The target price recommended by the realtor was actually a few thousand dollars less than what we had originally paid for the house. The realtor said that we had probably overpaid for our home when we bought it and that if we wanted it to move quickly we would have to be willing to accept less money. I feared that Danny would refuse to sign the papers unless he was assured of obtaining what we had paid for it or more.

The week after Danny was released, I received a postcard at our home address stating that he was having all of his mail forwarded to his mother's residence. That created another unforeseen inconvenience for me. All of the utility bills were still in his name. How was I supposed to pay them if I did not receive them? I wondered if he would pay them and decided that he most likely would not. Water and electricity were still needed until the house was sold. Later that night when I discussed the new development with my pastor and his wife, she said that it was probably only the beginning of things that he would do to me while he was out on bond and that I should "brace" myself. Knowing that she spoke the truth, I dreaded his next move.

I was able to change all of the utilities into my name except the water and sewer bills. I decided to chance letting him get those two bills just to see if he or his family would pay them. I wondered if they would have the nerve to make Mr. Hood forward the bills to my lawyer for me to pay. However, that theory would never be tested because I attended church with the mail carrier. She said that she would make sure that all of the utility bills came to my mailbox instead of being forwarded to him. The whole problem was solved with no effort on my part, but I have to admit that I was slightly disappointed that I did not get to see what he would do if he received the bills.

Some time after I received the mail forwarding postcard, the mutual friend that had delivered Danny's clothes, stopped at my paternal grandmother's house to describe her recent visit with Danny. She told my grandmother that she was very worried about Danny because he seemed so depressed. Of course, he was sad about the shape of his life. What bothered me the most was did he ever think about what he had done to Bryanna? I had been depressed, even suicidal at times and had to take prescription medication just to function. Eleven months of my life were spent in a state of utter anxiety, not knowing what had happened to her while he was playing computer games and thinking of ways to spend our tax refund money. I guess Danny did not feel depressed until he lost his freedom, belongings, and job.

I suspected that Danny wanted his mail forwarded so that he would get his magazines and catalogues about computer gaming, telescoping, and ship modeling. He was out of jail, unemployed, and looking for something to ease his boredom. I wanted him to think about what he had done to Bryanna (especially) and everyone else instead of seeking to entertain himself. In the last few months prior to Danny's arrest, he spent most of his free time playing computer games. He also ran up some credit card debt buying a lot of telescope equipment, modeling supplies, and video games. Looking back, it seemed almost like he knew that he was going to be arrested, and he was really trying to enjoy himself as much as possible before it happened. It made me feel sick to my stomach to think of it.

His refusal to cooperate with the divorce proved that he was being extremely selfish with no remorse for his actions. Danny and his family's complete disregard for my financial situation and indifference to leaving me to pay the bills alone showed that they only cared about getting their money from the house and Danny's welfare. The sole relief they had offered to provide was assuming his truck payment, and Danny only wanted his truck so he could go out and run around wherever he pleased. It did not appear to me that he had ever considered the pain and suffering he had inflicted upon Bryanna. He seemed to be exclusively concerned with his own misery and predicament.

The mutual friend also shared that all of Bryanna's pictures had been removed from Danny's mom and stepdad's house. Sadly, she must have been entirely forgotten by them. That was very disturbing considering she was their granddaughter and part of them, too (the same as Danny). I wondered if Danny's family blamed Bryanna for Danny's dilemma or maybe they held me responsible because I had wanted a child. It was heartbreaking to realize, in the end, after all of those months that we grieved for her together that she meant so very little to them.

Danny's family was probably thinking that we were wrong for taking him to the police department that night. One might be inclined to agree with them—until you read his confession. A close friend of my dad made this very profound comment about Danny's confession. : "Danny would not have signed that statement unless it was true and he actually did those things. If someone put that confession in front of me, held a gun to my head, and said 'sign this or I am going to kill you,' I would have said 'shoot me because I did not do those things and no way am I signing my name to that.'" I think that observation said it all. The only way Danny would have signed that paper was if he really did write it, and it was actually true. No one could have made those things up for him. His mom really needed to read the confession, but everyone protected her from seeing or hearing it. They thought she was too fragile to handle it. In reality, she needed to see it—to know and accept what he did. Instead, it seemed like they wanted to blame everyone else for what Danny did.

⁂

August passed with no hearing in front of the judge concerning my divorce. September arrived with no further communication from Danny's attorneys. I continued to beg my lawyer for an appearance in front of the judge, but I could not get anything confirmed. Mr. Hood was always out of the office and virtually impossible to reach.

Meanwhile, I decided to propose signing the house over to Danny. He could then sell it and keep all of the equity. Of course, he would also have to do all of the maintenance and make the house payment until it was sold. I was losing so much money per month in the house payment that soon my share of any profit would be consumed. If I could get rid of that monthly bill, then I could reclaim my lost equity in no time. I added one further stipulation to my proposal on the house. It was for Danny to sign the divorce papers immediately. My divorce lawyer wrote a letter containing my idea and forwarded it to Mr. Hood. I became so excited thinking I could persuade Danny to exchange the money from the house for a divorce really believing that the idea would work.

At the end of September, Mr. Hood finally responded to my proposal to sign the house over to Danny. The reply stated "Mr. Draper is not interested in taking the house and the responsibility for making the corresponding house payments. As I am sure you can understand Mr. Draper is not in any position financially to meet the house payments."

One extremely unfair concept seemed to persist throughout the entire affair concerning the house. Danny insisted on having his share of the profit but refused to help with the payments. Danny was using his unemployment as an excuse for not contributing to our shared bills. However, his parents were spending thousands of dollars for a pricy attorney and bond but nothing toward our marital obligations. Since I would not willingly "stand behind him," I guess they had discovered a way to force me to support him, at least financially. In order to save my assets, I was actually sustaining him as well. Danny and his family showed no consideration for my struggling financial situation. Their sole concern involved only Danny's welfare and needs.

However, Danny's refusal to take the house was only the beginning of the demands contained in the late September response. My attorney had proposed that the case be split, meaning that Danny would grant me a divorce immediately and that the property would be divided at a later date. Danny was not interested in separating the case and giving me a divorce, but he did want his belongings very badly. He invited me "to make a proposal concerning an *equitable* division of the Parties' marital assets and debts." Danny also claimed that I had only returned one box of summer clothing, and he wanted his winter clothes. That was completely untrue because I distinctly remembered delivering six boxes full of clothing and personal belongings to the mutual friend. They had contained Danny's entire wardrobe. There was nothing left to give him. I had no idea what could be missing.

Furthermore, he submitted a list of his "separate personal property" that he wanted returned to him "as soon as possible" which included:

> three telescopes and associated equipment, including star atlases; the scrapbook of Mr. Draper's childhood; binoculars; golf clubs; completed wooden ship models, completed car models and all modeling equipment; all photographs relating to Mr. Draper's family; lawn mowers; and the bed and dresser given to Mr. Draper by his father.

I had already returned the bed and dresser three months prior. Why were they asking for it again? My father had explained the need to keep the lawn mowers until the house sold personally to Danny's stepdad. Their repeated requests for the lawn mowers to be returned demonstrated their absolute disregard for the money, work, and effort that my family and I were investing into the house. However, a striking common thread can be noted to the items that Danny asked for—they were all related to his hobbies and entertainment. Each letter from Mr. Hood stressed Danny's inability to concentrate on the divorce because he was facing the death penalty. His obsession with all of those leisurely items did not fit the picture of a man concerned for his dismal plight. They actually gave me the opposite impression—that he planned to have some fun before his trial.

In the last half of the response, Danny demanded money. He wanted his final two paychecks from First Street Hospital. By having his mail forwarded to his mom's house, Danny had received the six hundred dollar tax refund check issued by President Bush. Mr. Hood said that if I had kept Danny's final two paychecks, then it was only fair that he keep the entire six hundred dollar tax refund. His last two paychecks had already been spent on joint bills. Basically, I no longer had it to give back, but what bothered me the most was that he was asking for the only money that he had contributed to our financial obligations since his arrest to be returned to him.

The lawyer's inconsiderate response infuriated me. I went through all of my financial records since April when Danny was arrested. I was tired of being responsible for all of the bills while he made all of the demands. Bryanna was the victim, not him, but one would never know that from reading their nasty reply. I compiled the necessary legal documentation proving his obligation for half of the debts. If he did not want to pay them now, then they could be deducted from his share of the house equity after it was sold. He wanted his money from the house, but hopefully, the judge would reduce his share based on what Danny owed to me for his half of the bills. I cannot begin to describe how aggravated I was with his demands for money and property, and delays in granting me a divorce. Why did I have to be the one to always give in? I guess I catered to him so much while we were married that he expected me to continue after our separation.

I calculated all our expenses since April 23, 2001 and divided the sum in half minus Danny's final two paychecks and profit from the sale of the telescopes. That left Danny indebted to me in the amount of $1834.44 with the understanding that the number was subject to increase until the house was sold. My divorce lawyer took the figures and sent them to Mr. Hood on October 3, 2001.

In the letter, my lawyer asked that the six hundred dollar tax refund check be turned over to me to help with the house payment. He also wrote, "The request he made for the bed and dresser seems to be moot, since these items were returned to his father months ago. The lawn mowers need to stay where they are, so the grass can be trimmed if the house is going to be listed for sale." I agreed to pack any remaining winter clothes, pictures, or scrapbooks and return them through the mutual friend.

My divorce lawyer advised me not to sell any more of Danny's separate property. He also encouraged me to be more cooperative about an equitable division of the marital assets, hoping that if I were willing to give Danny his personal belongings, maybe he would grant me my much desired divorce. I was reluctant to give Danny anything but decided to try to be more reasonable on the possibility that I could get a divorce. My lawyer included in the letter a proposal for us to each keep our vehicles, divide the equity on the house equally after it was sold, and to make a list of what furniture and personal property we wanted on the stipulation that Danny would immediately grant me a divorce. The letter was sealed and mailed, but more than a month would pass before I received any type of response.

Bickering

While I anxiously awaited a reply concerning the proposed property division, a suppression hearing was scheduled for October 18, 2001. The suppression hearing was the special court session that General Steele had warned us about in May. It involved Mr. Hood attempting to have Danny's confession statement suppressed, meaning that the jury would not be able to hear or read it during the trial.

My father and I had been subpoenaed to appear as witnesses for the suppression hearing. We would have to testify about the events of the day that Danny was arrested. Mr. Hood planned to prove that Danny had been forced against his will to go to the police station that night, that he was not in a suitable state of mind to confess, and/or that the interrogation was somehow performed inappropriately. Of course, all of those things were false, but nonetheless, the defense did not want a jury to see such a condemning piece of evidence because it would probably insure that Danny received the death penalty.

When October 18 arrived, I was actually more nervous about seeing Danny face to face after all these months than I was about taking the witness stand. That morning my parents and I, unknowingly, parked right across from him. After my dad turned off the engine, as we were exiting the van, I noticed Danny's stepdad's truck across the lot from us. Danny and his stepdad's shadowed forms were visible in the front seat of the truck. I could not discern any details on their faces or their eyes but I am sure they could see us clearly as we got out of the van and rushed into the courthouse away from them.

Seeing him, even remotely like that, traumatized me for a little while. It was even harder than I had imagined it might be. To avoid accidentally running into them again, we quickly climbed the stairs to the second level where we found General Steele and Mrs. Good waiting for us. Mrs. Good placed us in a private conference room away from any passing crowds or news media. After we were comfortably seated and offered coffee, she reminded us that we would probably be there the entire day. Then she left to join General Steele in the courtroom.

At around ten in the morning, after waiting for only an hour, the victim's coordinator entered the private conference room and told us that the suppression hearing had been postponed until November 30. We were allowed to leave. At home, for the rest of the day, I wondered what had happened during court that morning and why the suppression hearing had been delayed. Mrs. Good called us sometime after five in the evening and said that Mr. Hood had presented almost thirty motions to Judge Strong in regard to Danny's trial and the jury selection. She had been tied up in court with them all day long and was just now able to call us.

The first motion that Mr. Hood submitted was to delay the suppression hearing until Danny underwent an extensive psychological examination to determine if an insanity plea was possible. Judge Strong set a deadline of November 19 for Mr. Hood to officially announce if they planned to pursue a mental defense. Other motions involved Mr. Hood demanding that the state surrender all of its evidence against Danny to which General Steele responded that he had already given them everything he had. Mr. Hood also presented several complicated and lengthy motions involving jury selection such as questioning potential candidates about their religious beliefs and feelings concerning the death penalty.

During the session, Judge Strong dismissed one of the three aggravating factors. It was "the defendant knowingly committed the offense." Two other aggravating factors remained: "the killing was committed against a person under age twelve and the defendant is over the age of eighteen" and "the murder was especially heinous, atrocious, or cruel in that it involved torture or serious physical abuse beyond that necessary to produce death." The prosecution only needed two aggravating factors to seek the death penalty so Danny still faced capital punishment. The one dismissal changed nothing.

I thought Mr. Hood was Danny's sole attorney, but that day, I discovered that he was actually being represented by two attorneys. His other counsel was Mr. Hood's close associate and partner, Mr. Petty. Mr. Petty argued, at length, that lethal injection was too harsh a punishment. Lethal injection was the chosen form of execution in our state of residence at that time. Mr. Petty said, "Our argument is in a civilized society, any state-sponsored execution is cruel and unusual punishment. It may be a more sanitized form of bringing death.... (But) it doesn't escape the fact lethal injection is nothing more than killing someone with high-tech battery acid." Judge Strong denied the validity of their allegations, stating that the death penalty was upheld as "constitutional" by the Supreme Court.

As I thought about him arguing that lethal injection was an inhumane punishment, I wondered if Mr. Hood and Mr. Petty considered being slowly beaten to death to be a "cruel and unusual" way to die. Their adamant defense of Danny amazed me knowing that they had read his confession. However, I guess it was what they were being paid very well to do. I hoped that the lengthy hearing was not a foreshadowing of how the court process would progress, but I feared deep inside that it was. Danny's family had hired one of the finest, if not the best criminal defense attorney in the area. Mr. Hood would cleverly try every possible way to either get Danny acquitted or his punishment lessened. We knew from the beginning that he was an excellent lawyer; now, we would find out just how good he really was, and I feared that it was not going to bode well for me.

During the first week of November 2001, I finally received a response to my property division proposal. The reply was written by Mr. Hood's associate, Mr. Petty. Unfortunately, he was even nastier than Mr. Hood. First of all, Danny absolutely refused to agree to a divorce on the stipulated grounds of "inappropriate marital conduct." Proposing an equal division of the marital property had proved useless. Looking back, Danny and his lawyers never intended to consent to any type of divorce or property division. They were arguing back and forth in letters as a way to delay the divorce from happening at all until after the criminal trial.

Secondly, Danny refused to pay any of the utility bills or credit card debts that he accrued in the last few months before his arrest. His lawyers wanted copies of the credit card statements so they could determine "when the charges were incurred and for what." Thirdly, Danny was very upset that I had sold all three of his telescopes "without his consent" for "far less than they were worth." He said that I "basically gave them away" and that they were worth at least eighteen hundred dollars collectively. By exempting Danny from all expenses except the house and truck and recalculating the value of his telescopes at eighteen hundred dollars, his lawyers argued that he only owed me $629.

Mr. Petty included an Annotated Code in the letter and accused me of breaking the law by selling Danny's property without his consent. I guess Danny forgot to tell Mr. Petty that he told me on two separate occasions to sell all of his stuff and use the money to go on with my life. His lawyers were trying to make it look like I had committed a crime. I was the victim in all of this! Yet, the criminal seemed to have all of the rights while I (the victim) was being repeatedly persecuted by the legal system!

Mr. Petty stated that the lawn mowers were Mr. Draper's separate marital property, but that he would "allow" me to use one of the mowers until the marital residence was sold; however, he wanted the other one returned to him immediately. Our property rested on almost an acre lot. We needed both the riding mower and the push mower to maintain the yard. To demand the return of one of the mowers was simply selfish and unreasonable.

Danny also no longer wanted his truck after I had proposed to give it to him because he had no means to make the payment. I had heard through the grapevine that he was borrowing his stepdad's truck if he needed to go somewhere. It was easier for him to just drop the expensive truck payment on me along with everything else.

The only thing that Danny agreed to was that the equity on the marital home be split equally after it was sold. Mr. Petty said that he would have Danny make a list of all our marital property, its respective values, and how he thought it should be divided. What I could not figure out was how Danny (who was unemployed) had not had time to make a list of the marital property that he wanted during the past month. We had passed several letters now; yet, we were no closer to a divorce than when we had started. The letters were merely a delay tactic. In the last paragraph, again, Danny requested the return of his golf clubs, binoculars, models, and modeling equipment, but until he agreed to sign the divorce papers, I refused to return any more of his property.

The very last paragraph of the letter hurt me the most. "It has come to my attention that Ms. Draper also has a porcelain doll collection, many of which were acquired during marriage and therefore subject to division. Please let me know the status of this collection and how many of the dolls she has sold since the parties' separation." I guess it was not enough for Danny to have tortured and destroyed the most beautiful doll I ever had; now, he wanted to take half of my doll collection. Many of those dolls were bought while I was grieving and perhaps, subconsciously trying to replace Bryanna. He demanded half of my doll collection as revenge for selling his telescopes.

I told my lawyer that negotiating through letters was futile. Danny did not want to agree to anything and had no intention of signing the divorce papers. I wanted to go in front of the judge and see if he would grant me a divorce. Furthermore, if Danny wanted any more of his personal belongings, he would have to obtain a court order to get them. At least that way it would cost him something.

Even if I did not get a hearing with the judge, at least, it was November. Danny could only delay the divorce for two more months. After the trial was over, surely nothing else would prevent the inevitable. I told myself to be calm and patient. One way or another, soon Danny's inappropriate marital conduct would be proven in a criminal court. Then he could no longer deny it as grounds for divorce.

On the positive side, the house was finally for sale, but unfortunately, it was not viewed very often. I feared that people would associate the home and address with Danny's crime; thus, destroying the possibility of it ever selling. To prevent that, the realtor suggested that I remove all of Bryanna's baby furnishings from her room. She said that the presence of unused baby items could raise questions and lead to revealing the story of her death. After I removed those objects, I hoped the possibility of our house being associated with Bryanna's murder would no longer be an issue.

⟨⟨⟨

In November 2001, I received the first official reply from the radiologists concerning my civil suit filed in May 2001. The response was long and complicated but basically stated one thing: the radiologists denied any responsibility in Bryanna's death. They reverted the blame back to me, saying that I was negligent and "should have known that the child was being abused by her father or by someone else."

Their lawyers introduced the concept of comparative fault which was a way for them to assign guilt for Bryanna's death among several parties; ultimately decreasing the amount of money that they might be required to pay in restitution. For example, if the jury were to find me 25 percent liable for Bryanna's death, then any money awarded to me would be reduced by 25 percent. Their lawyer's main concern was obviously to pay little or no compensation. However what they did not know was that my primary goal in the lawsuit was never about money. It was about people taking responsibility for their actions, and the radiologists had missed multiple injuries and needed to, at the very least, apologize and admit their guilt.

My lawyer had already warned me that the defense would claim that I should have known that Bryanna was being abused. He also predicted that they would use the fact that I am a nurse against me to support that accusation. Yes, I am a nurse, and for that reason, I know that Bryanna did not have classic signs of child abuse. She had stomach upset, rashes, and fever—all indications of a disease process, not abuse. Those symptoms were why I took her to the doctor over and over and willingly complied with all tests, x-rays, and hospitalizations. I could only see the outside of her body where there were no signs of physical harm. However, she did have many internal injuries detectable only by x-ray films—x-ray films that were misread. The radiologists were educationally prepared to diagnose fractures on x-rays. I could not because I did not possess the expertise and training required to interpret films. Yet, they missed not one fracture, not two fractures, but multiple fractures. Next to Danny, that made them very much at fault in the matter.

To further spread the blame, they cited negligence to the Department of Children's Services (DCS), which was Mrs. Blakely and her employer, the state and Detective Gray, and his employer, the sheriff's department, claiming that those two individuals should have detected that Bryanna was being abused and removed her from the home. How could they have done that? It was after all, the radiologists who failed to provide the DCS with the evidence (fractures and bleeding in the brain) required by the state to remove Bryanna from our home. Mrs. Blakely and

Detective Gray even consulted Dr. Story on May 16, 2000 personally for a second opinion on the x-rays and CAT scan hoping he would provide them with the diagnosis of "child abuse" but according to their reports, Dr. Story refused to state those two vital words. Rather he told them that the abnormality was of little concern and that the arm fracture could have happened on the pediatric ward. When you were as undeniably guilty as the radiologists, I guess the only thing you could do was spread the blame to as many people as you possibly could.

However, the radiologists accusations caused some major revisions in my law suit. My lawyer had to officially include Mrs. Blakely and Detective Gray in the suit. He also dismissed First Street Hospital. I had mixed feelings about the revisions. First of all, I hated to see Mrs. Blakely and Detective Gray forced into the legal litigation because the radiologists refused to take responsibility for their actions. I truly felt the DCS had done the best job possible given the information they were provided by the medical staff. Second, I disagreed with my lawyer about releasing the hospital. They were liable for allowing Danny to actively participate in the performance and transportation of Bryanna's films. I shared my opinion with my lawyer, but he still recommended dismissing them from the suit. Proving Danny's actual involvement in those processes would be time consuming and almost impossible. He advised that since we had unquestionable evidence against the radiologists, we should invest our time and energy into pursuing them.

In the response, the radiologists offered no settlement out of court; instead, they demanded a jury trial. At first, I was intimidated by the possibility of a jury trial, but after reviewing all of the facts, I realized that the radiologists were hoping to frighten me into dropping the lawsuit. It did not take a medically educated person to see all the mistakes that they had made. They needed to be held accountable for their negligence, and I planned to do everything in my power to make them.

On a related note, I was confused and disheartened that Dr. Green, Bryanna's pediatrician, had somehow evaded the entire litigation. In my opinion, she was guiltier than the DCS because she also failed to provide them with the two magic words that they were seeking—"child abuse." Moreover, when the DCS asked her to "make the call" (officially diagnose child abuse) she refused, saying that it was their job to do that, not hers. She summoned the DCS to the scene insinuating our wrongdoing after finding the two fractures; then, she backed down and refused to supply them the vital diagnosis required to safeguard Bryanna. I wanted her included in the suit from the beginning, but after it was filed, she charmed my lawyer by offering her unconditional assistance on the case against the radiologists, even volunteering for a deposition on our behalf. Her cooperation persuaded my lawyer to exclude her from the suit. She could not step forward to protect Bryanna, but she certainly could to save herself.

❦

On November 19, 2001, Danny had brief hearing in front of Judge Strong. His attorney, Mr. Hood, introduced yet another motion requesting that the prosecution be banned from entering expert testimony or other evidence about Battered Child Syndrome or Shaken Baby Syndrome at the trial. Mr. Hood was trying to prevent the prosecution from proving that Bryanna died from a "pattern of abuse." If they could eliminate that fact, then they could possibly get rid of one of the two remaining aggravating factors. If one more aggravating factor was dismissed, then the prosecution could not ask for the death penalty.

Once again as the date for the suppression hearing approached, Mrs. Good called and said that it had been postponed until December 17, 2001. I was nervous about testifying but desperately wanted that part of the judicial process behind me. I secretly feared that all of the small delays were leading up to one big major delay.

Suppression Hearing

Time seemed to drag while I waited for the suppression hearing and trial, but December 17, 2001 did finally arrive. The suppression hearing was scheduled during the afternoon. Once again, the victim's coordinator took us to the private conference room away from Danny's family and the media. As potential witnesses, we were not allowed to sit in the courtroom and listen to the other testimonies. During a short break, Mrs. Good came to the conference room to speak with us briefly. She gave us one simple piece of advice—tell the truth. Since all court proceedings are recorded, she also cautioned us to answer all questions audibly and avoid shaking or nodding our heads.

A few minutes after Mrs. Good spoke with us, the director of the Children's Advocacy Center (CAC) joined us in the conference room to provide emotional support. She had known about Bryanna's murder since the day of her autopsy. My parents were already acquainted with her, but that day was my first opportunity to meet her. She described how she had kept a rose on her desk every day since June 5, 2000 in memory of Bryanna. I felt so touched by that stranger's sentiment in contrast to the coarse disregard Danny and his family had displayed. After we had waited for two long hours, I thought surely the hearing was close to being finished, and we were not going to have to testify after all. Just as I was allowing myself to feel relieved, Detective Sharp entered the conference room and announced that my father was being called to the witness stand and that I would follow him.

I suddenly realized that I had been living in denial. I was sure that Daddy would have to testify due to his contact with the district attorney's office on the day of Danny's arrest, but I mistakenly thought that I would be spared. Weak, dizzy, and faint, I could barely speak. My legs lost all of their strength. My dad was gone for just a few minutes, but it seemed like hours. I prayed to God for courage and asked Bryanna to be with me, and somehow let me know that she was there. I quickly removed my two small photos of Bryanna at age one month from my purse to take with me. As they escorted me out of the conference room to go downstairs and wait, the director of the CAC said that she would slip into the courtroom and sit in the rear to give me a "friendly face to look at."

⥇

The courtroom was rather small, containing about four or five rows of seats. A wooden divider separated the general public from the attorneys and the judge. Judge Strong was seated on a raised podium facing the audience and lawyers. He was an older gentleman probably in his fifties with a graying mustache and well known for taking his time and examining all of the evidence meticulously before rendering his final decision.

On Judge Strong's right-hand side resided the prosecution—General Steele and Mrs. Good. On his left-hand side, the defense—Mr. Hood and Mr. Petty—sat with their accused client, Danny. Mr. Hood was a big, burly looking guy whose presence seemed to overpower those around him. Mr. Petty was a skinny, hyper, younger gentleman. The two of them seated together made quite a contrast. The witness stand was located on the left side of the room adjacent to the defense; therefore, all participants were placed in close proximity to Danny during their questioning. Each witness was required to state their full name and "swear to tell the truth and nothing but the truth" before their testimony began.

The suppression hearing opened with Judge Strong verifying that a Miranda warning was issued and signed prior to Danny's interrogation by Detective Light and Detective Sharp. Afterward, Detective Sharp was questioned by General Steele. General Steele established that Danny, my father, and I arrived to the police department around five in the evening on April 23, 2001. The exact contents of the Miranda Rights were read into the record.

Detective Sharp recounted that after Danny and I signed the Miranda Statements, he asked to speak with Danny "individually" because "with this kind of case it gets confusing if you try to talk to more than one person at a time. So I asked him if he would be willing to talk to me individually, and he indicated that he was willing to do that."

"Did you force him to tell you anything?" General Steele asked.

"No, sir, we did not."

"Did you threaten him in any manner?"

"No, sir," Detective Sharp confirmed.

"Did you abuse him in any manner?"

"No, sir."

According to Detective Sharp's testimony, Danny talked with the officers between the hours of six in the evening and nine at night. After nine, Detective Light began to put Danny's confession into writing. During the interrogation, they provided Danny with sodas to drink and even sent an officer to a local fast food restaurant to bring back dinner. The three of them took a break and ate dinner together in the questioning room. Before nine, Danny made several trips to the bathroom alone, walking right past the exit to the police station each time. No one guarded the door to prevent him from leaving. Danny was free to go at any time until after nine, when Detective Sharp said he "admitted that he had placed his hands over Bryanna's airway causing the suffocation and subsequent death." During the questioning, Detective Sharp read Danny's entire confession verbatim into the record. Mr. Hood adamantly protested to it being read aloud in court, but Judge Strong overruled his objections.

Following the reading of the confession, Mr. Hood cross examined Detective Sharp going straight to the point that he wanted to pursue. "Do you have the capability at the police station to videotape the interrogation of suspects?"

"Yes, we do," Detective Sharp replied.

"Is that an accepted police procedure, or is there some policy that prohibits you from doing that?"

"We have a policy that we do not tape or video tape statements from victims, witnesses, or suspects."

"Can you explain the basis of that policy?" Mr. Hood further inquired.

"In my recollection, that policy is there because we want to be true and correct for everybody involved. We do not want it to appear that we are selecting who we are going to tape and who we are not going to tape. Sometimes, we may have to speak with a suspect where we do not have the capability to video or audio tape. There is also the possibility of equipment failure."

"Wouldn't you agree that a tape recording would be a more accurate explanation of what this man said other than what someone writes down to account for a period of over six hours?"

"It could be if the equipment was working properly," Detective Sharp replied.

"So you did have the capability to video record Danny's confession that evening, if you had so desired. You have taped statements before, have you not?"

"No, Sir."

"Never taped a statement in your life?" Mr. Hood asked with raised eyebrows.

"Sometimes, in narcotics, I have taped statements wearing a body wire in an undercover role. But I have not taped a statement from a suspect in the interrogation room."

Mr. Hood continued, "The reason I am asking about this is: have you ever heard Angie's father say that he heard the tape of Danny's confession?"

"No, sir, I've not heard that."

"If he said that, then it would not be true because there actually was no tape?"

"Correct. There was no tape," Detective Sharp confirmed.

"Was Angie's father allowed to watch the interview?"

"Not that I'm aware of."

"Can you describe, for the record, the interview room where Danny's confession took place? In particular, I'm interested in if it has a one way mirror window?" Mr. Hood inquired.

"Yes, sir, it does."

"Is that window mirror there for people to discreetly observe interrogations from the other side?"

"No, sir. The window was put in there as a process when they built the building. The only time that it is ever used is occasionally for the supervisors to watch. But the office that you look through that window mirror from was locked because it is the captain's office and the captain was not there."

Mr. Hood began to question Detective Sharp about Danny's mental state of mind that night. "The evening you interviewed Danny Draper were you told by Angie or anyone else that he had threatened to kill himself?"

"No. What Angie's father said to me was 'Danny wants to come down and talk to you and I don't know what he'll do.' So I said, 'If he wants to come and talk to me, that will be fine.'"

"The reason I asked you that is because later you learned that they put guns away."

"Yes, they told me that later," Detective Sharp responded.

"When you observed Daniel, can you describe his demeanor and how he appeared to you? Was he anxious? Was he calm?" Mr. Hood pounded out several questions at one time.

"He was not anxious. I would classify him as *calm*."

"Did you deny his family members from having contact with him when they came to the police station?"

"No we did not deny him contact with anybody that he wanted to see," Detective Sharp replied.

"Do you recall Danny's stepfather and aunt making several requests to see him while this interview was in progress?"

"I knew they were outside."

"Do you recall going to the door and telling them on several occasions that they could not see him?" Mr. Hood asked.

"No, we told them that we were interviewing him, and then we went back in and let Mr. Draper know who was out there."

"Well, at that point, you wouldn't have allowed Mr. Draper to leave anyway, would you?"

"It depends on what time they were there. From what I recall when his stepfather was there, no sir, he would not have been able to leave," Detective Sharp confirmed.

"Let's get down to the bottom line here, Detective Sharp," Mr. Hood said sharply, "From the time he came in there, you all were not going to let him leave that police station at all, were you?"

"No. Up until the point that he confessed to killing his child, he was free to leave."

"Did you ever tell him, your family is here wanting to talk to you, do you want to talk to them?"

"Yes, Sir. I told him every time I was aware that someone was there," Detective Sharp replied.

"And did you tell him that his stepfather, whom he calls his father, was requesting to see him?"

"Yes."

"But you wouldn't have allowed him to see anyone, would you?" Mr. Hood accused.

"Actually, Danny did not ask to see them. He did not want to see his mother until the end. He told us that he was not ready to speak to her yet."

"Okay. Who called the meeting at the courthouse on the Morning of April 23, 2001 with Angie's father?"

"I did," Detective Sharp replied.

"Why did you choose to speak to Angie's father? Why would you show him what you had? I mean, he was not related to Danny except as a father-in-law."

"I chose him because during the waiting period for the results of the final autopsy report, he was the only one that was calling and asking for information. So when we received the final autopsy report, I choose to call him and show him what we had."

"Did you feel he was interested in the welfare of his daughter?" Mr. Hood quickly interjected.

"No. We had just reached a point where we were able to release information. We were still not completely sure if the suspect was Danny or Angie, and we were not ready to speak to either one of them yet."

"Why did you choose not to call Daniel's parents and ask them to come?"

"I would have asked them if they had called me and asked for information. I was simply returning a call to Angie's father because he was the only one calling and asking for the results," Detective Sharp explained.

"Had you been instructed by anyone to keep Angie's father informed?" Mr. Hood asked.

"No."

"Did you get the feeling that he was calling because he was concerned about his daughter being charged or that he was protecting her interest?"

"We did not feel that he was protecting anybody's interest. We were just releasing information to him about the case," Detective Sharp simply replied.

"When did you exclude Angie's father as a suspect in this case?"

"When we put together the time frames of the care, who had care, custody, and control of the child at the time the injuries could have occurred, we excluded Angie's father as a suspect."

"But on the actual day of the child's death, Mr. Draper had not been with the child all day long according to your investigation. In fact the child had been taken to the doctor that morning by Angie and Danny's mother, right?" Mr. Hood asked.

"Yes, sir. She was."

"But at the conclusion of that April 23 morning meeting, you told Angie's father that if Angie wanted to talk to you that you would give her the same information that you had given him. So why did you say you would talk to Angie but were not ready to talk to Daniel at that time?"

"That is just the conclusion that I was coming to at that time. I can't really tell you why," Detective Sharp related.

"So at the conclusion of that meeting you intended to charge Daniel Draper with the homicide of his child and not Angie Draper or anyone else, correct?"

"Yes, at that time, I was pretty conclusive that Mr. Draper was the prime suspect and that all other suspects had been excluded," Detective Sharp confirmed.

"At the end of that meeting, Angie's father indicated that he would get Danny to come and see you, didn't he?"

"No, sir, he did not."

"You mean that no one gave any instructions to Angie's father about Danny when that meeting was finished?" Mr. Hood inquired skeptically.

"The only instruction, Angie's father asked, was 'what do you want me to do?' And I told him I really did not want him to do anything. I was just giving him the information that he was asking for at that time. And in my mind, I was not ready to speak Daniel."

"So when they showed up at the police station that evening did you know that was a result of Angie and her father talking to Daniel?"

"Yes they mentioned that they had talked with Danny when they came in and that he had told them what he had done," Detective Sharp affirmed.

"Did Angie sign a Miranda Waiver that day?"

"Yes, she did. They signed them at the same time."

"Can we see that for the purpose of—?" Mr. Hood attempted to ask, but Judge Strong interrupted him saying, "Are you through yet, Mr. Hood?"

"No, Your Honor."

"Well, what's the materiality of getting into Angie? She's not charged, is she?" Judge Strong inquired.

"No, Your Honor, but I would like to see the totality of the circumstances that occurred that day. I have Danny's that is signed, and I just want to compare them time wise. I think it's important."

Judge Strong allowed the introduction of my signed Miranda warning as an exhibit to the hearing. Mr. Hood continued by establishing that both officers were armed during the confession and that Danny could view their weapons at various times. Detective Sharp admitted that he left Danny alone with Detective Light briefly on one occasion.

Mr. Hood attempted to portray the two officers as aggressive and threatening while they interrogated Danny.

"Did Danny's stepfather or mother mention to you that he should have a lawyer?"

"Somebody asked me that. I don't remember who. I told that person that we had Mirandized him, and he understood that he had a right to an attorney," Detective Sharp explained.

"The truth of the matter is though Detective Sharp, as a good part of your police work, you really did not want him to talk to anybody there other than yourself and Detective Light, did you?" Mr. Hood asked sarcastically, driving straight to the point.

"There are a lot of things I don't want but if he had asked to see them, I still have to follow the—"

"I understand," Mr. Hood said before he could finish his response. "Now that you have had time to analyze his confession and compare it to the autopsy and so forth, isn't it true that he actually admitted to injuries which never occurred? I am talking about the scapula fracture and the asphyxiation."

"No, sir, the scapula fracture is part the pediatric radiologist's report."

"Okay, but what about the asphyxiation?"

"Again, if you'll look at the autopsy report, the cause of death can be partly attributed to asphyxiation," Detective Sharp stated.

After pausing to examine the medical reports, Mr. Hood was forced to relent. "Oh, I didn't see those things there before."

Judge Strong again interrupted, "You might bear in mind the issue we have before us, Mr. Hood."

"Well, Your Honor, these questions concern whether or not the confession was voluntary. If he admitted to injuries that did not occur, that might have some bearing on whether it was voluntary or not."

After arguing with Judge Strong, Mr. Hood concluded that he had no further questions for Detective Sharp. General Steele announced that the prosecution would not be calling any other witnesses. Judge Strong told Mr. Hood to proceed with his next witness which was Detective Light.

Mr. Hood began the interrogation as follows, "What I'm going to be focusing on, Detective Light, is Danny's mental status at the time of the confession. When you first saw him that evening, did he appear distraught?"

"He appeared to be upset," Detective Light replied.

"Were you concerned that evening that he might hurt himself?"

"No, sir, I was not."

"Did you know Danny prior to that evening?" Mr. Hood asked.

"Yes, I did. Several years ago we attended the same church."

"Do you recall his family members asking for him to have a lawyer that night and someone saying that he did not need a lawyer?"

"I remember speaking to them outside. I was trying to console them. I do not remember that being said," Detective Light replied, thoughtfully.

"Would it have been important to you if members of his family were there asking to see him and wanting to hire an attorney for him?"

"Due to his age, I mean he's over the age of eighteen, I think he could probably make that decision himself."

"But what I am asking is did you physically deny his family members access to the room he was in that night?" Mr. Hood pursued.

"Oh, I am sure that I did. The reason being he was inside the detective division, which is locked or secured from the general public where they can't flow in and out. I received a call from the secretary saying that there were people outside wanting to see us."

"So he was in a secure area and he could not have left that area if he had wanted to," Mr. Hood retorted, seizing an opportunity to make it look like the two officers testimonies were in conflict.

"Yes he could. Let me clarify that. If you want to exit the police station, you can. It is not locked on the inside, but it is locked on the outside. The general public would have to use the door buzzer for admittance."

"But from the time he entered that station, you did not intend to let him leave, did you?"

"Well, we never told him that he could not leave and we did not guard him from leaving," Detective Light said.

"Did anyone follow him to the restroom?"

"No, there were only two of us so I don't think so."

"But you all knew where he was going and watched him, right?" Mr. Hood accused.

"No, he said he was going to the restroom.I hoped that was where he was going."

"Could you see the restroom from where you were?"

"No, there was a closed door between the interrogation room and the restroom," Detective Light confirmed.

"Was the statement he gave you recorded?"

"No, sir."

"Do you have the capability of recording statements at the police station?"

"Yes, we do, but we have a policy dictated by our department that the statements of witnesses or suspects are never recorded because of the possibility of mechanical failure," Detective Light stated, corroborating Detective Sharp's earlier testimony.

Mr. Hood grabbed some hand-written notes that Detective Light had made in accordance with the night of the confession and used them to further question him. Looking at the notes, Mr. Hood continued, "Now I am going to ask you about a conversation that you had with Danny while Detective Sharp was out of the room. Do you remember telling Danny that you had been observing his actions when he was asked specific questions about the child's death?"

"Yes, sir."

Then Mr. Hood began to read from the report filed by Detective Light as follows: "'I insisted that he was minimizing his actions; easier to solve his savage conscience or just to get out from under any possible legal actions that might be imposed.' Do you remember telling him that?"

"Yes, I could have, sir," Detective Light acknowledged.

"And at that moment, did you say that 'even an animal did not deserve that type of treatment'?"

"Yes, I probably made that statement, too."

Mr. Hood continued to read from Detective Light's report as follows: "'I concluded that this was not going to go away no matter how much he tried to tell me he was innocent of his daughter's death, that I could see the guilt all over him as if he had a sign around his neck stating his guilt. I told Draper that he might as well go ahead and tell me about this or it would become the worst haunting nightmare of his life.' Did you tell him that?"

"Yes, sir, I did," Detective Light said.

"And at that time would you describe Danny as distraught?"

"As far as the definition of distraught, Mr. Draper showed very little emotion."

"You have interviewed many people and some people show more emotion than others, right?" Mr. Hood continued.

"That's correct."

Mr. Hood then read one more time from the report:

"And at that the time, Danny said he wanted to talk. He took a deep breath and said that I was right, he did kill his daughter, that he had not been honest.'"

"That's correct."

"Did you have your coat on or off at that time? What I am asking is, was your gun visible?"

"I don't remember if my jacket was on or off at that time," Detective Light responded thoughtfully.

"Did Danny ever act scared?"

"He did not appear to be. Like I said, we've known one another for several years. I don't know why he'd be afraid of me. I'm sure he'd seen me in even a more police identification attire."

"Was there some reason that you waited for Detective Sharp to leave the room before you told him this could be 'the worst nightmare of his life' if he did not talk?" Mr. Hood inquired.

"Yes, I was not conducting the interview per se. I was originally only a witness. Detective Sharp left the room to answer the door. I just saw an opportunity, sir."

"So while Detective Sharp was fending off his family members, you saw the opportunity to get Danny to talk to you," Mr. Hood concluded sarcastically, trying to put words into Detective Light's mouth.

"That's not exactly true."

After that harsh statement, Mr. Hood stopped questioning Detective Light. General Steele briefly cross examined him
with two final questions: "Until Danny admitted to killing his
daughter, was he free to get up and leave the police station, and
if he had asked for a lawyer, would you have let him have one?"
Detective Light answered "yes" to those last two questions, and
that completed his testimony. Mr. Hood called his second witness which was my father.

Mr. Hood began the interrogation with: "Who called you to
come to the courthouse on April 23, 2001?"

Detective Sharp," my father replied simply.

"Who did you meet with that day?"

"I met with General Steele, Detective Sharp, and Mrs. Good,"
my father answered pointing to the district attorneys, seated as a
group on the left side of the courtroom.

"Did you know any of those people prior to that day?"

"Yes, I knew Detective Sharp. I had talked with him on various occasions."

"Did you know anybody on the attorney general's staff?"

"Yes, I knew Mr. Taylor, as a friend," my father replied, referring to a friend that worked in the district attorney's office but
was not involved in Bryanna's case.

"How did you know him?"

"I have known Mr. Taylor's father for many years. And Mr.
Taylor used to be my father's neighbor."

"Had you been communicating with him about this case?"
Mr. Hood asked.

"I had called him on several occasions to find out if he knew
anything about Bryanna's autopsy report, and he never told me
anything. He said he was not assigned to her case, but he was sure
that everyone was doing their job."

"When you came down to the courthouse that day, was it your intention to see that your daughter was not implicated in the death of her child?"

"No, sir," my father stated firmly.

"Have you heard a tape recording of the interview with Mr. Draper?"

"No, sir."

"Did you ever tell anyone that you had heard a tape recording of the interview and confession of Mr. Draper?" Mr. Hood further inquired.

"No, sir."

"Specifically, did you tell Danny's father that you had heard the tape and you've got him and he'll never get out of it?"

"No, sir."

"Did you talk with Danny's father on April 23, the day of Danny's confession?" Mr. Hood asked.

"That night, I believe he called my home, or I returned his call. I don't remember exactly which one, but we did speak."

"Was that after the confession?"

"I am pretty sure it was after the confession," my father confirmed.

"Do you recall what you told him?"

"He asked me what had happened, and I told him that Danny had told me that he hurt Bryanna. That he had done it. I think that was my exact words."

"How did you know that? Did anyone tell you what Danny said that night at the police station?" Mr. Hood asked.

"Before we went to the police station, Danny told me that he had hurt Bryanna."

"Did you ever ask Detective Sharp or Detective Light what Danny had told them?"

"I believe I did," my father replied.

"Did they tell you?"

"No sir, they did not."

"So all you knew when you left that evening before you talked to Danny's father was that Danny had been arrested for the murder of his daughter?" Mr. Hood asked.

"No, all I knew was that Danny had told me that he had hurt Bryanna."

"That's all you knew?" Mr. Hood asked with a hint of disbelief in his voice.

"That's basically all I knew."

"Did you observe Danny's statement being given?"

"No, sir, I did not," my father attested.

"Did you have access to seeing into the interrogation room from where you were sitting in the detective office?"

"No, sir, I did not."

"Were you ever in a room that you could look through a two way mirror and observe the confession?" Mr. Hood continued.

"No, sir, I was not."

"Now, following the meeting that morning with General Steele and his staff, did Detective Sharp tell you that they were going to charge Danny with murder?"

"Yes, sir, he did," my father verified.

"And you knew that your daughter was not a suspect any longer?"

"Yes, sir, I did."

"Where did you go after that meeting?" Mr. Hood demanded to know.

"I went into the parking lot and told my wife and daughter, who were waiting, what had happened to the baby."

"As a result of that meeting, what did you do insofar as Danny was concerned?"

"I told my wife and daughter the evidence that the district attorneys and Detective Sharp had presented to me. My daughter asked me if I believed them, and I told her that I did. Then Angie called Danny and he came to my home where they talked," my father explained.

"Were you concerned at that time as to what Danny might do to himself?"

"Yes, I was."

"You even took precautions to take the guns out of their house, right?" Mr. Hood asked.

"Right. So that he would not hurt himself."

"And from what you saw, Danny became very distraught at the house?"

"Correct," my father confirmed.

"So after you got to the police station, was Danny's state of mind emotionally upset?

"I would say—we were all upset. That's just all I can tell you, you know. I don't know Danny's state of mind."

"Well you have known him for how many years?" Mr. Hood continued.

"Twelve years."

"At that time, in the state of mind that Danny was in, if he were going to buy a house or make a really important decision, would you have advised him to do it or calm down before he did anything?"

"He was not in that state of mind. We were talking *calmly*. Let's put it that way. Even though we were upset we were talking *calmly*," my father stated, unknowingly confirming the testimonies of Detective Sharp and Detective Light that Danny was composed that day.

"Did you tell Danny at the police station in the presence of Detective Sharp and your daughter, that he was among friends, and he did not need an attorney?"

"No, sir, I did not," my father responded, puzzled as to where that question had originated.

"You never made that statement?" Mr. Hood asked again.

"No sir, I did not," my father confirmed for the second time.

"I just have one last question. You had been told by Detective Sharp that they believed that Danny was the perpetrator of the crime?"

"That is correct," my father acknowledged.

"And that they were going to talk to him and see if they could get a statement from him?"

"No, sir, they did not tell me that. As a matter of fact they indicated to me that they would like to talk to Angie, but they said that they did not need to talk to Danny," my father stated confirming Detective Sharp's earlier testimony.

Mr. Hood then indicated that he was finished questioning my father, and he was allowed to step down from the witness stand. General Steele declined the opportunity to cross examine him. It was now my turn to testify.

Accompanied by the bailiff, I entered the courtroom with trembling legs, clutching my photos of Bryanna hoping the tiny pictures would enable me to feel her presence and remind me that I had to testify for her sake. Stepping up onto the witness stand, I took a deep breath and prepared for the interrogation.

"I am going to be questioning you about the written statement that you previously gave to Detective Sharp concerning the events of April 23, 2001. After your dad came out of the courthouse that morning, the three of you decided to contact Danny, right?" Mr. Hood began.

"Yes, I felt like I needed to talk to him after what my dad told me he had learned from Detective Sharp and the district attorneys."

"What I am wondering about is from this statement that you gave, were you very concerned about what Danny might do to himself?"

"Yes," I answered.

"You even made sure that the room that you talked to him in could be observed by your mother?"

"Yes."

"During the time you talked to Danny, did he threaten to commit suicide?" Mr. Hood asked.

"He said that his life was over," I explained.

"So from this statement that you gave, the state of mind that Danny was in that day could be classified as very distraught?"

"I guess so," I said rather unsure. Danny had actually appeared relatively calm that day considering the circumstances, I thought afterwards.

"You'd been married to him how long?"

"Over five years."

"Had you ever seen him threaten suicide before?" Mr. Hood continued.

"No."

"Had you ever seen him that upset before?"

"No," I affirmed after reflecting back through our many years together.

"And going over there in the car Danny continued to be extremely upset and distraught?"

"I am trying to remember," I said in exasperation. *The best that I could recall, Danny was not overly upset or crying,* I thought. I glanced at Danny through the corner of my eye because it was too disturbing for me to look at him directly. He shook his head and blew like I was lying or something. At that time, the director of the CAC slipped into the back of the courtroom. I focused my eyes toward her to avoid visual contact with Danny.

Mr. Hood's interrogation continued: "About how long a ride is it to the police station?"

"Seven minutes maybe," I replied becoming increasingly addled and confused.

"So what did you all talk about on the way there?"

He was hammering me relentlessly with questions. I was trying to remember, but my mind was blurry due to being so upset myself that day. I could not recollect the details he was requesting or I was not answering him satisfactorily because he continued to pound me with questions. I could not stand it anymore. I just wanted it all to stop.

Finally, at my wit's end, I burst into tears and exclaimed, "You know I was in such shock after he told me that he had hurt that little baby that I don't remember a whole lot of what we talked about on the way over there." The Bailiff kindly handed me a box of tissue.

"You take a moment there…" was Mr. Hood's response to my outburst.

The judge then asked me, "Do you need a break? If you need to rest we can let you step off for a minute." I had so hoped that my explosion would make the interrogation end. I did not want to pause; I wanted them to dismiss me from the witness stand and let me return to the room where my family waited, but when Judge Strong asked me if I needed a recess, I realized that I was not leaving that confining box until Mr. Hood was absolutely finished with me. I decided a break would only delay matters. I looked down at Bryanna's pictures for strength and courage to finish the formidable task.

My quiet reflection on her two pictures was abruptly interrupted by Mr. Hood hatefully shouting, "What do you have in your hand? Are you looking at notes to help you remember about that day?"

"No," I replied solemnly, startled.

"Oh, it is a pic—well, I could not see what it was from here," Mr. Hood said as he approached me and saw the picture grasped between my thumb and index finger. "I did not know what it was. So, it is not notes that you brought with you?"

"No, it is not notes."

"Okay. I don't, I, ,I, I don't know. I saw you looking at something and I just had to ask you," Mr. Hood responded, stuttering very badly.

Judge Strong then interjected, "You have a right to know what she has in her hand. It looks like a photograph to me."

"Well I could not see that from here, Judge," Mr. Hood replied harshly, looking flustered.

"Is it a photograph?" Judge Strong asked, looking directly at me.

"Okay, that's fine," Mr. Hood said quickly, waving his hands like he did not want me to answer the judge. I looked at both of them unsure of what to do next.

"Do you want to inspect it?" Judge Strong asked, looking intently at Mr. Hood.

"No, Your Honor, I do not. As long as it's not notes…" Mr. Hood murmured.

"Mrs. Draper," Judge Strong said, turning to face me again, "Just so we'll be assured of having a correct record for the court, is the item you have in your hand a photograph?"

"Yes, it is," I replied.

"And who is it a photograph of?"

"Bryanna," I replied firmly. I wanted to speak her name aloud in the courtroom and not refer her as "the child." I was tired of hearing everyone on the defense side call her "the child." She was a living, breathing human being with a real name.

"Was that your daughter?" Judge Strong asked.

Choking back a flood of tears, I could only nod my head even though I knew that I was supposed to speak all responses aloud for the court recorder.

Now turning again to Mr. Hood, Judge Strong asked one more time, "Are you sure you do not want to inspect the photograph? You have a right to see anything that she has brought with her into this courtroom."

"I only wanted to know if it was notes. I do not need to see it," Mr. Hood replied hastily with obvious discomfort, waving his arms in the air.

A long pause of silence followed the interaction. Mr. Hood appeared extremely flustered. It was like he needed a few seconds to collect himself. He sorted through a stack of paperwork with a great degree of concentration. I don't know for sure, but I had a peculiar feeling that Judge Strong was actually enjoying Mr. Hood's distress. Mr. Hood finally composed himself enough to continue the interview. "Okay, I know you were upset and I know you are upset today, but what I would really like to know is when you got to the police station, did Danny continue to be upset?"

"Like I said, I was in such shock that day, it's hard to remember," I said exasperated. It's truly amazing how just a few minutes can totally exhaust a person. To avoid visual contact with Danny or his family, I focused my eyes toward the district attorneys seated on the left side of the room. Their friendly faces provided me with a source of strength to get through the rest of the proceedings.

"Okay, but is it fair to say that in five years you had been married to Danny you had never seen him this upset or threaten to kill himself?"

"Yes," I said, drawing strength from Mr. Hood's remaining agitation.

"Did you hear your father tell Danny that he was among friends and that he did not need a lawyer?

"I don't remember Daddy saying anything like that."

"Did you see his mother, stepfather, and aunt at the police station that night?" Mr. Hood asked; his discomposure now almost completely gone.

"Later, when we returned around midnight, I did."

"Did you hear them talking about that they were refused the right to see Danny?"

"I don't remember that," I answered honestly.

"Did you hear them say that they wanted to get Danny an attorney?"

"I don't remember."

"Okay. That's all, Your Honor," Mr. Hood concluded.

General Steele said that he had a few questions for me to answer. He began with, "Mrs. Draper, you did not force your husband to go down to the police station and tell them what he had told you, did you?"

"No, sir."

"Your father did not force him to go down there, did he?"

"No, sir," I replied. I was more relaxed answering General Steele as opposed to Mr. Hood.

"Did your husband tell your father that he was willing to go down there and tell them what had happened?"

"Yes."

"Mr. Draper knew where he was and where he was going when you went to the police station, did he not?" General Steele asked.

"Yes, he did."

"He was able to answer the questions that you put to him about what he had done to your child in a rational manner, wasn't he?"

"Yes, he was," I answered truthfully.

"Did you ever see anyone threaten to do anything to him in order to get him to confess to having killed his baby?"

"No, nobody."

"When you were allowed to see him briefly after he had signed the confession, did he complain to you about having been mistreated, threatened, or falsely promised anything by the police?"

"No, he said that he had been treated well. Because I asked him," I responded remembering seeing him that night after he had signed the confession.

"After the confession was signed at that time, did he give all the appearance of knowing where he was and what he was doing and what was going on?"

"Yes."

"That's all, Your Honor," General Steele concluded. Judge Strong then looked to Mr. Hood and asked him if he had any further questions for me. I so prayed that he would not, but of course, he did.

"In response to one or two of those questions, Mrs. Draper, is it fair to say that you were very upset that night?" Mr. Hood asked me.

"Yes."

"And Danny was upset. Would you have trusted Danny to make a decision under that kind of stress if you all had been trying to make an important decision about something?"

I was completely disgusted with the entire hearing. What kind of question was that? What did that have to do with Danny murdering Bryanna? I couldn't stand any more inquiries. I blurted out a very harsh response without carefully considering my words. "He was upset, I felt like, in the sense that he was caught at what he was doing, but I feel like I was more upset about all of it than he was. In some senses, he was *calm* about everything." Now, unbeknownst to me, I had just confirmed three other testimonies regarding Danny's actual emotional state that night.

I do not know where those words came from but they must have been something that Mr. Hood really did not want to hear because suddenly the Bailiff removed me from the witness stand and escorted me back to the conference room with my family. The judge instructed me, as he did all the other witnesses, not to discuss my testimony with anyone else because there was a possibility of being recalled for further questioning before the end of the hearing. My legs were still weak and shaky but somehow they carried me away from that dreadful interrogation. I honestly do not know how I walked in and out of the courtroom that day. There must have been an angel holding each side of my body just to keep me upright.

After my interrogation, Judge Strong issued a short break. Mrs. Good came upstairs at that time to tell me that I had given an excellent testimony. It was nice of her to commend me, but I felt like I had done a terrible job. However, after the stress of the event was over, I had to admit that I enjoyed the way Mr. Hood was completely flustered over Bryanna's pictures in my hands.

My family and I decided that Bryanna had reached down from heaven and made her presence known in the courtroom by rendering a fancy, hot shot lawyer speechless. I wondered why Mr. Hood refused to look at Bryanna's pictures and finally concluded that it was probably easier to defend Danny without being able to put a mental image to his victim.

After the brief recess, three other witnesses were called by the defense. The next person questioned was Danny's father.

Cutting straight to the point, Mr. Hood asked Danny's father to describe the phone call with my father the night Danny was arrested. Danny's father had only seen Bryanna once while she was alive. He did not even come to visit her when she was ill and in the hospital two times. The day Daddy met with Detective Sharp and the district attorneys concerning Bryanna's autopsy report, he was not even concerned enough to be present. The only thing he could testify about was their brief conversation on April 23, 2001.

Danny's father stated, "I received a phone call from Angie's father between ten and eleven that night central time which is one hour behind the time here so it was probably about midnight your time. I had been trying to reach my son all day. Angie's father called me and said 'we've got him. He can't get out of it. I've heard the tapes. Danny is guilty of Bryanna's murder. He's suicidal; he needs help; we love him; we're going to stick right with him.' So I asked 'Does he have an attorney?', and her father replied, 'No he did not need an attorney, he was among friends.'"

After Danny's father made his untruthful statement concerning that phone conversation, Mr. Hood said that was all the questions he had for him. Judge Strong turned to General Steele and asked him if he would like to cross examine him. General Steele nonchalantly responded, "Judge, I don't have any questions. I don't know of anything that this would be relevant to."

Next Mr. Hood called Danny's aunt to the witness stand. He began by asking her about the events of the evening of April 23, 2001. "Why did you go to the police station?"

Danny's aunt responded, "Danny's mother called me and asked me to go because she was sick and could not go. She said 'he'll need a lawyer, you know.' So I went to the station with Danny's stepdad."

"Why did you think he needed a lawyer?"

"Well, with what he was accused of I guess," she replied.

"Do you recall what time you went to the police station?"

"It was sometime between five and six in the evening. I know it was before six."

"Did you speak with anyone at the police station?" Mr. Hood continued.

"No, when we got there the doors were locked. We could not get in. I rang the bell. Someone answered the door and said, 'It'll be a few minutes.' We waited for what seemed like forever but was probably only about a forty-five minutes to an hour. Then Detective Light came out and said 'Well it's all over. He has confessed to everything.' Then he led us outside and talked to us some more because I was just in shock. I could not believe it."

"So at the time you rang the buzzer you could not go any further in the police station?"

"No, the doors were locked. But we could see through the doors. I saw Angie, her father, and their preacher sitting back in there, but I did not see Danny. They got in, but yet we could not, and we were family too," Danny's aunt declared.

"Did you ever see him that evening before you left?"

"No. Detective Light told us that we should go home and check back in a couple of hours. He said Danny would spend the night in the county jail. So we left and went home at a little after six in the evening," Danny's aunt concluded.

Next, she was cross examined by General Steele. "So you were able to see Angie and her father sitting in the police station through that frosted door?"

"It's not frosted over that I remember. Maybe part of it was, but it was plain clear glass," Danny's aunt protested.

"Plain clear glass?"

"Well I'm not sure about the glass, but I could definitely see people back there. I saw you in there. You came in while we were waiting outside."

"So what time did you leave from the police station? Was it six-thirty or seven in the evening?" General Steele asked.

"It was more like six-thirty," Danny's aunt responded thoughtfully.

"Would it surprise you to know that it was eight at night or later when I showed up down there?"

"I don't know. I don't know about that, but you were there. I don't think it was that late."

"You say you went down there because you knew that Danny needed a lawyer?" General Steele inquired.

"Right."

"Did you call a lawyer to come there for him?"

"No, I, I didn't. But I was going to let him know, you know, I wanted him to know that—I was just going to tell him, you know, you need a lawyer before they question you," Danny's aunt replied, stuttering.

"Would it surprise you to know that the police told him he could have a lawyer if he wanted one?"

"Well, I suppose he should have been told that."

"Would it surprise you to know that he chose not to have a lawyer," General Steele continued.

"Yes, it would surprise me if he said no."

"Okay, I don't have any other questions."

Danny's aunt was dismissed from the witness stand. Next, Mr. Hood called Danny's stepdad and began with, "Okay, please tell the court what occurred when you and Danny's aunt went to the police station to try to see Danny."

"We rang the bell and a voice came over the speaker and told us it would be a while before we could see Danny. Later on, Detective Light came out and told us that it was all over with, that Danny had confessed," Danny's stepdad stated.

"All right. Do you know about what time he came out and told you all that?"

"It was probably about six-thirty or six-forty."

"Did you all have a discussion with Detective Light?" Mr. Hood asked.

"Yes, he told us that we could probably come back in a couple of hours and find out what the situation was and when we could see him."

"What was your intention of wanting to see your stepson?"

"Well, I wanted to find out if he had an attorney to represent him. I felt like he needed one if he was being questioned," Danny's stepdad replied.

"And were you in a position to obtain those services for him if he wanted them?"

"Yes, sir."

"Did you see General Steele there that evening?" Mr. Hood asked.

"I saw him going into the police station after we were there."

"How many trips did you make to the police station that evening?"

"Two. We went home after talking to Detective Light. My wife came back with me around nine at night," Danny's stepdad answered.

"And what did you all do then?"

"We rang the bell again. We told them we were there to see Danny and a voice came on and told us it would be a little while. After waiting for about an hour, around ten at night, we saw Detective Sharp standing behind the door and my wife pecked on the door. He opened the door and she asked him if Danny needed a lawyer and he told her 'no he does not need one.'"

"What did you all do after that conversation with Detective Sharp?" Mr. Hood continued.

"We sat there until around one in the morning."

"What happened then?"

"Well, then Angie and her family came back to the police station," Danny's stepdad responded.

"Had you seen any of Angie's family there earlier that evening?"

"I saw Angie, her father, and their preacher all standing inside the police station when we were there earlier that evening."

"Could you have yelled at them?" Mr. Hood inquired.

"Probably not till they could have heard me. I was looking through the tinted glass door and everybody just ignored me like I wasn't there. The door was locked and we could not go in."

"When you saw Angie's father later that evening, did you talk to him?"

"Yes, I did that night at about one in the morning when they came back," Danny's stepdad stated.

"That's all I have, Your Honor," Mr. Hood concluded.

General Steele then cross examined Danny's stepdad as follows: "When exactly was it that Detective Light came out and said that your stepson had confessed?"

"The best I remember it would have been about 6:35 or six-forty," Danny's stepdad replied.

"Did Detective Light come out and tell you that after you saw me go in the police station or before?"

"It was afterwards."

"Let's get right down to it. You're not at all sure about the times you are talking about, are you?" General Steele continued, about to make a very valid point.

"No, sir."

"It could have been nine or nine-thirty when Detective Light came out and told you that Danny had confessed and it was all over with, couldn't it?"

"No, no sir," Danny's stepdad insisted.

"How do you know?"

"Because he told me that on the first trip I was there and I didn't go back down there until nine at night on the next trip."

"Did you see me walk into the office that you all were trying to get into?" General Steele asked.

"Yes, I saw you go through the tinted glass door."

"Okay. Now would it surprise you to know that it was sometime after seven that night before I ever came down to the police station because I was being videotaped giving a talk to an accreditation group for the city police department?"

"Well, like I say, I wasn't sure about the time," Danny's stepdad finally relented.

"That's why I asked you these questions, because it probably would have been around eight o'clock before I ever arrived to the police station. And it was probably close to nine when I left. And I remember seeing you down there. So you are not at all sure about the times, are you?" General Steele stated, cornering Danny's stepdad.

"No, sir, I'm just telling it the best I remember it."

"And you wanted to see if your stepson had an attorney?"

"Yes," Danny's stepdad responded.

"Did you call an attorney to go down there and check on him?"

"No."

"Did you take an attorney with you?"

"No, sir."

"And the officers treated you all politely, didn't they?"

"Yes," Danny's stepdad conceded.

"And it turns out that there were only two officers in that entire detective division which was why they could not come to the door every time you knocked," General Steele finished, basically discrediting both Danny's aunt and stepdad's testimonies because they really did not know what time they were at the police station.

Afterwards, both the defense and prosecution rested. The case was submitted to Judge Strong to examine all of the testimonies and determine if probable cause to suppress the confession statement had been presented. Meanwhile, we waited upstairs in the conference room for the verdict. We had to remain at the court house until the hearing was officially completed in case we were recalled for further questioning.

At around six in the evening, the district attorneys, General Steele and Mrs. Good, came to the conference room to let us know that Judge Strong had decided not to suppress the confession statement. The jury would view it as evidence during Danny's trial. The verdict was a victory for the prosecution. All major tasks were now completed. We were ready to proceed with the trial on January 23, 2002.

⫷⫸

Later that night at home, my chest felt sore. I looked in the mirror wondering what could be wrong and noticed a bruise on my left clavicle. Bryanna's left clavicle was the one that was fractured. Since I could not recall any injury that would have caused a bruise in that area, I concluded that it was Bryanna's mysterious way of assuring me that she was indeed present in the courtroom that day.

⫷⫸

Later that week, I discovered through the grapevine that one of Danny's uncles was in the courtroom during the proceedings. His uncle stated that hearing Danny's confession read aloud caused "the hair on the back of my neck to stand up." He left the court-room and told Danny's aunt (the one who testified), "Danny deserves whatever they do to him. What I just heard made me sick!" Danny's aunt's response was to plead with him: "But I do care what happens to Danny because I love him."

Divorce?

The week before Christmas, I received an offer on the house for a few thousand dollars less than our asking price. I feared that Danny would decline the bid and expect me to continue making the house payment alone. However, to my pleasant surprise, he accepted the contract. I was so relieved at the possibility of getting rid of that tremendous financial burden. Also, at the end of the year, I deleted Danny from my health insurance premium, providing additional financial relief for me. With the trial now only about one month away, I hoped for some peace in the near future. I needed to put the tragedy behind me, get a divorce, and try to move on with my life. That was the only way I could prevent him from completely destroying me.

Christmas and New Year's Day passed with very little enthusiasm from me. It was my first holiday season in thirteen years without Danny. It should have been Bryanna's second Christmas. We should have all been having a wonderful time, but thanks to Danny, we were all actually quite miserable. I regressed into a deep depression dwelling on the "what ifs" and "whys," and finding no satisfaction. It was the worst holiday season of my life.

Around January 9, 2002, I discovered that Mr. Hood was planning to appear in front of Judge Strong to ask for Danny's trial to be postponed because Danny was being evaluated by a forensic psychiatrist. The new doctor claimed that he needed at least four months to do a detailed review of Danny's entire work, family, and social history. Mr. Hood was also conferring with a nationally recognized sleep disorder expert in California. Last year, Danny's lawyers did not file an official motion stating they would seek an insanity defense; now, suddenly, they were going to say that Danny was mentally ill. I was beyond angry at the new unexpected attempt to delay the trial. I just prayed that Judge

Strong would rule that they had already been granted sufficient time to plead insanity and order the trial to proceed as scheduled.

In a state of panic, I called Mrs. Good, the assistant district attorney, and asked her opinion of what might happen. She said that Danny was scheduled to appear before the judge on Friday January 11, 2002 and that there was a good possibility that the trial would be postponed mainly because Danny was facing the death penalty. She promised to oppose all arguments for a delay and to let us know Judge Strong's decision as soon as the hearing was completed on Friday.

On January 11, I anxiously waited all day long to hear from the district attorney's office. At three-thirty, I reported to work as scheduled. At about five in the evening, I called my dad, but he said the district attorney's office had not notified him of Judge Strong's decision yet. Desperate for some information, at around seven, I looked at the local newspaper on the internet because their articles were kept very up-to-date.

The first article on the screen was about Danny's trial being postponed. I was upset but not really surprised because I was expecting Judge Strong to grant them a few months for the mental evaluation. As I read further into the article, I noted that the date was reset for September 23, 2002. The site of that date caused me to become completely hysterical. September 23 was over nine months away! That was almost another year of my life with no closure and no divorce!

I immediately called my parents and told them the dreadful news. They tried to console me over the phone but I was too upset. I wanted to throw things and scream until my lungs were sore, but being at work in a hospital, I had to control myself. There was no feasible way to vent my anger and disappointment. The worst part of the delay for me was the high probability that I would have to remain married to Danny for nine more months.

I called Mrs. Good at home to ask her if the trial was really postponed. She confirmed that the article was correct and apologized that I had found out by reading it on the internet. I was so distraught that my coworkers made me lie on a stretcher while they checked my blood pressure. Since they could not calm me down on the phone, my parents came to the hospital to check on me. They were finally able to console me after a while. In the end, there was nothing I could do but wait. To me, it was an open and shut case because he had already confessed. The delays and psychiatric evaluations seemed meaningless, especially when you read the details of his confession, but, as I have already said, the court system was set up for the criminal, not the victims. My rights and concerns seemed of little consequence in comparison to providing Danny with every opportunity to prove his innocence and avoid the death penalty. What about Bryanna's right to justice? Did that even matter to the court system? I was sure that since Danny had tasted six months of freedom, neither he nor his family would ever want him returned to prison. I quietly prayed for strength to wait nine more months for justice and that Judge Strong would grant me my greatly desired divorce much sooner than that.

The newspaper article further explained that Mr. Hood did not file an insanity plea last November because the new forensic psychiatrist was "not on the scene" at that time. Mr. Hood claimed that he had only first talked to the doctor that very week (convenient of them to wait until the trial was about to start to consult him). After reading the physician's affidavit supporting further psychiatric examination of Danny, Judge Strong had agreed that it was a "strong" case. Mr. Hood stated in court, "It's a matter of stress and what happens when people are put under stress." Judge Strong rescheduled the trial so far out to give the defense and prosecution adequate time to complete "all" mental evaluations and set April 1, 2002 as the deadline for Mr. Hood to officially file a motion of the intent to plead insanity. *Another meaningless deadline*, I thought, annoyed. They seemed to hold little significance in Danny's legal world, but it would have been another matter entirely had I failed to make the house payment on time.

I went to see my lawyer early Monday morning and told him that since the trial was delayed for nine months that I wanted a divorce right away. I stressed how I had been waiting patiently for the January trial date, but there was absolutely no way that I could tolerate being married to him until after September. He pacified me by promising to arrange for a hearing in front of the judge as soon as he could.

While at his office, I signed the legal documents completing the sale of our home. My lawyer said if I endorsed them in advance, he would attend the closing on January 16, 2002 in my place. After lunch on January 16, my lawyer informed me that the house was officially sold, and he was placing the profit in an escrow account to be divided at a later date. I also learned that Danny had appeared in person at the closing session, accompanied by his two lawyers and stepdad. I was shocked that he had the audacity to appear in front of the people purchasing our house. They knew about Bryanna's murder! If I were him, I would have been way too ashamed to face those people. My own embarrassment about being married to him and the reasons for selling the house were why I did not attend myself. Now I was relieved that I had chosen to stay away. I would have found myself face to face with him, something I did not yet feel ready to do. Why did he go anyway? Was he hoping to see me? Maybe I should have gone after all. A stipulation of his bond was not to have contact with me. Coming to our house closing could have been construed as intentional contact with me; thus, revoking his bond.

The following week, my lawyer scheduled an appearance in front of Judge Strong for February 15, 2002. He planned to request a divorce be granted immediately because the criminal trial was postponed until September 23. In the paperwork, my lawyer proposed that the divorce case be divided from the criminal trial and that marriage dissolution be based on mutually stipulated grounds so that I would not have to wait more than seventeen months from the original filing date for the divorce. Danny would not be required to testify or cause any harm to his criminal proceeding.

I remained extremely angry about the trial delay for weeks. I mostly blamed Danny's family for wasting all of their inheritance money on an expensive attorney. Now that they had Danny at home with them, they would never want his trial to take place. My family and I debated on several occasions how everything would eventually end. Would his family give him enough money to skip the country so that he would never go to prison? Would Danny commit suicide, as he had threatened on the day of his arrest? If Danny had been appointed a public defender instead of his family hiring him the most expensive, dirty lawyer in town, would the trial have proceeded differently? The worst part of all was that I envied his mother because she could hold her child in her arms, but I could not.

After much contemplation, I concluded that the main reason for the postponement was Danny being free on bond. What if September came and they found yet another reason to delay the proceedings? With a top notch lawyer, who could create an unknown number of excuses, the whole process could literally go on indefinitely. I decided that maybe if I could get Danny's bond revoked, the affair would proceed more smoothly.

Not knowing anything else to do, I began to write letters to all state and national congressmen asking that Danny's bond be revoked. I even wrote a letter to the president, George W. Bush. The correspondences explained my fear that Danny would skip the country and never be seen again. I hoped that maybe if he was incarcerated again, his family would have no further reason to delay the trial. Although I made an admirable effort with my numerous letters, in the end, I received only one response. It was from the senator that my father had called to instigate a state investigation while we were waiting for the autopsy results. He replied that he knew my family and was very sorry for our loss and circumstances, but unfortunately, there was no way to revoke Danny's bond. Those long hours of writing ultimately changed nothing. The trial was still delayed until the end of September, and Danny remained free on bond while the victims of his crime suffered every day.

During the winter months of January, February, and March, I dwelt in a very troubled state of mind. On a subconscious level, I think I sought ways to avoid facing the reality of what Danny had done to Bryanna and our lives. In a deep despair, I passed most days not caring if I lived or died. My thoughts were filled with anger at him and his family, thus preventing me from fully comprehending the pain and misery that he had inflicted upon my baby.

Before February 15 arrived, my hearing in front of Judge Strong was cancelled due to him being out of town. The appearance was rescheduled for March 15, 2002. Another month would have to pass before I had a chance to plead for my freedom.

During the month of March, I was asked for a date by one of the police officers (Bill) that worked nightshift at the government hospital. Even though my divorce was not yet final, I was divorced from Danny in my heart the day that he told me he had hurt Bryanna. Feeling that way, I decided to accept the police officer's invitation for dinner. Afterward, we began to see each other on a regular basis. I felt comfortable being with a person of the law because it was such a contrast to Danny. I desperately needed some type of pleasurable distraction to get my mind off of everything that Danny had done, and Bill seemed to provide that to me very well.

I became increasingly preoccupied with my new social life. I stopped writing down my thoughts and feelings in my personal journal, and I decreased the frequency of my appointments with my counselor. For a short while, I stopped thinking all the time about what Danny had done to Bryanna. Anyway, his actions were almost more than my mind could comprehend most days. I tried to put some of it aside for few months while I waited for the trial and my divorce, but doing that may not have been the right thing for my emotional healing. Perhaps I should have dealt with my unresolved pain before I tried to move on and start a new relationship with another person. However, Danny's crime was so overwhelming that it was actually a great relief to not think about it every moment for a little while.

One thing that I was battling during those long months after Danny's arrest was loneliness. Danny and I had been together for thirteen years. Suddenly, I found myself incredibly alone, in spite of being surrounded by family and friends. It was not the same. I missed our marital relationship and having my own home. When Bill came along, I was actually very vulnerable, whether I realized it or not, and he seemed to fill the empty void in my life.

Since he was a police officer, Bill had a decent understanding of the legal system and judicial process. I was always able to vent my frustrations about the court system to his sympathetic ears. He appeared to understand what I was going through much better than a lot of other people. That played a big role in my attraction to him. He already knew what Danny had done before he ever asked me out. That made it so much easier for me to talk to him about my thoughts, feelings, and struggles. I began to share a lot of my frustrations with him which was probably one of the reasons that I decreased the frequency of visits to my therapist.

Bill had an eight-year-old son from a previous marriage. All I could see was a chance to step in and be a mother again which was, of course, another great distraction from my current problems. A lot of people warned me to stop dating Bill. They felt we were getting too serious way too soon. Some people were critical of our relationship because legally I was still married to Danny. Others said that he knew about my lawsuit against the radiologists and that he might be a gold digger, but to me, he just seemed like a good hearted gentlemen so I blocked out their advice and followed my heart, continuing to pursue our relationship during the upcoming months before the trial. I was not sure it was the right thing to do, but in so many ways, he filled a huge vacuum in my life at that time.

Finally, March 15 arrived, the morning that my hearing was scheduled in front of Judge Strong. I reported to the courthouse at nine in the morning to find my divorce lawyer waiting outside anxiously for me. He said that Judge Strong was not presiding that day, and he was unsure if the substituting judge would involve himself with my complicated case. My lawyer left my mom and me waiting outside the courtroom while he went to the judge's private chambers to try to persuade him to hear my divorce that morning. He returned a few minutes later with a grim look on his face. The presiding judge refused to hear my divorce because he was unfamiliar with it, and it was on Judge Strong's docket. The hearing would have to be reset for April. My mom and I left the courthouse defeated. I felt hopeless that I would be granted a divorce before September. We were constantly confronted with obstacles, and there was no way to get around them.

My divorce case was rescheduled for April 4, 2002. My grandmother accompanied me that day so that I would not have to go alone. On the way there, we debated on what excuse his lawyers would concoct to stop the proceeding. Disheartened, I was sure I would be leaving within a few short minutes of our arrival still as Mrs. Draper. My lawyer was waiting for me outside the courtroom. I anticipated the dismal news as we approached him.

"Now when you take the witness stand, I want you to say that Danny was mean to you," my lawyer quickly counseled me before court convened.

"So, we are really appearing in front of the judge today?" I asked excited.

"Yes, we are," my lawyer answered.

"How can I say that Danny was mean to me? I can't lie. He never physically hurt me," I asked puzzled.

"You want a divorce, don't you?"

"Oh, yes, yes," I exclaimed.

"Then just do what I tell you so we can get this over with. Say he was mean to you, mentally abused you, whatever you want but that is the way we have to do this today in order to get the divorce. They don't want his criminal charges mentioned in this proceeding," my lawyer advised.

"Okay, okay," I agreed, perplexed by his instructions, but actually Danny was very mean to me so I guess I could use that excuse.

Upon entering the courtroom at around nine in the morning, I quickly scanned the chamber for any sign of Danny, but he was not there. However, I spotted Mr. Petty, his lawyer, sitting on the front row. A few other cases were presented before Judge Strong called Draper vs. Draper. I slowly approached the witness stand. Remembering what I had been advised to say, I raised my right hand and swore to tell "the whole truth and nothing but the truth."

"Why are you seeking a divorce?" Judge Strong directed at me, after I was comfortably seated in the witness stand.

"My husband was mean to me," I recited as instructed.

"How was he mean to you?"

Not wanting to lie under oath, I responded, "He was just mean to me."

Mr. Petty interjected, "Your Honor, we have already agreed upon the grounds for a divorce." He looked toward my lawyer who nodded in agreement.

Ignoring them, Judge Strong looked at me, "Did he beat you?"

"No," I replied truthfully.

"Was he unfaithful to you?"

"No." I could not force myself to lie which was not helping to plead my cause.

"Did he abuse alcohol or drugs?"

"No, but he abandoned me," I quickly added because I remembered that desertion was a valid reason to grant divorce.

"Well, I need to know exactly what he did to you," Judge Strong said, not accepting my answer.

My lawyer stood up and stated, "We have already mutually agreed upon the grounds for the divorce."

Judge Strong surprised everyone and said, "Did he abuse your child?"

"Yes, he hurt my baby," I confirmed.

Judge Strong slammed the gavel thunderously loud down on his podium and announced forcefully, "Divorce granted upon the grounds of inappropriate marital conduct!"

Immediately, a terrible commotion erupted from the right side of the courtroom. Mr. Petty stood up and began repeatedly shouting, "This is not what we agreed upon! This is not what was supposed to happen today! This is not how this was supposed to have gone! This is not what we agreed upon!" His face was quickly turning a brilliant shade of fire red. He was pivoting in rapid circles glaring at the Judge, then my lawyer, and then me. The bailiff removed me from the witness stand, and I exited the courtroom as his angry shouts continued behind me. As I passed through the exit doors, the last thing I heard was, "This is not what we agreed upon!" I turned around to look at him one last time. He appeared almost breathless yet even more agitated than at first. He was shouting at Judge Strong who sat quietly, unruffled by Mr. Petty's outburst, signing the official copy of the divorce papers. Even his ranting fit could not dampen my spirits. I dared not speak it aloud, but I silently wondered what it was that "they had agreed upon." Was it not to mention Danny's criminal actions, or was it not to grant me a divorce at all?

I waited outside for my divorce attorney to bring me my official copy of the divorce papers. When he handed them to me, I gave him a big hug for finally accomplishing the seemingly impossible. Before leaving, I quickly reviewed the document, looking for the single most important element. There it was in writing—my maiden name restored. I would never have to feel embarrassed by the last name of Draper again. The divorce was granted on the grounds of inappropriate marital conduct and failure to respond within the time frame required by law, but the best part of all was that Judge Strong had charged Danny with all of the court expenses. I know that it was not nice, but I had a good laugh when I read that part. Danny certainly did not have a job to pay for them, but perhaps his family would have to pay them with some of their inheritance money instead of giving it all to Mr. Hood and associates. I often wondered if Danny's step-dad's father (who was not even a blood relative to Danny) "rolled over in his grave" knowing how his hard earned lifetime savings was being spent.

❦

The deadline of April 15 arrived for the defense to determine if they planned to seek an insanity plea. Mr. Hood submitted a claim written by the forensic psychiatrist stating that Danny was mentally ill when he murdered Bryanna. The prosecution now had to decide if they wanted to have their personal psychiatrist re-examine Danny. General Steele told us privately that their mental illness claim was invalid and would easily be proven false in court. He would probably not even need to have Danny re-evaluated. How much more money had his family wasted on fruitless specialized psychological assessments?

❦

One day that spring, I visited the cemetery and found some unfamiliar flowers on Bryanna's grave. I questioned all of my family members about them and no one knew who had put the arrangement there. They resembled a bouquet placed on her grave by Danny's aunt shortly after Bryanna's death. I assumed that she or his family must have done it, and I became livid. After removing all of her pictures from their walls, none of them had a right to come near her resting place.

The flower incident rekindled the fact that it was killing my family and me every time we looked at "mommy and daddy's little angel" on her permanent marker. Even though markers were very expensive, my dad decided to replace it with his own money. Another irritating thing on the stone was the last name of "Draper." I was rid of that embarrassing name, and I wanted her to be as well.

The new marker simply said:

> Bryanna Faith
> Daughter of Angela K. Wills
> Feb. 11, 2000—June 2, 2000

The new marker was decorated with an etched angel and some roses. We were still able to use the original concrete mount. My dad only had to purchase a new bronze insertion piece, costing about five hundred dollars. In order to save the cemetery service fee of two hundred dollars, one morning late in April, my dad did the actual extraction of the old marker and implantation of the new one himself. I had already lost a fortune in house and truck payments, so who could blame us for doing it in a cost effective manner?

❦

Time passed slowly as I waited for the trial to start. I dreaded the actual proceeding and wanted it over at the same time. General Steele told us that we would definitely be testifying at some point during the trial. If we were not questioned during the official litigation, we would certainly be called during "the character witness stage." The "character witness stage" would occur after the verdict was issued to assist the jury in deciding whether or not to impose the death penalty. The defense would be provided the opportunity to call witnesses during that stage as well, including Danny's mother, to testify that he was a good person and did not deserve to die. On the other side, the prosecution would use us to certify the intentional overt cruelty of his crime, our irreplaceable loss, and the irreparable damage that he had caused.

My main concern was when Danny would be returned to jail. I worried that he would remain free while the jury determined his punishment. General Steele said Danny would be taken into custody "immediately after the guilty verdict was issued." Danny's undeserved freedom had been a source of a lot of problems for me, and I wanted him back where he could cause much less trouble. I asked General Steele again if he could go back to jail any sooner, but the answer remained the same; as long as Danny did not violate the restrictions of his bond by engaging in criminal activities, leaving the state, or showing intention of elopement, unfortunately, there was still no way to revoke his bond.

❦

During that summer, I heard a couple of disturbing rumors about Danny through the grapevine. First of all, I discovered that he was playing with his cousin's one-year-old daughter at their July family reunion picnic. The very thought of him with a small child seized my heart with terror. How could his cousin allow her baby daughter to have contact with Danny after what he had confessed to doing? Was his whole family in denial? Maybe his insanity defense was not so irrational after all.

I also found out that Danny was hospitalized sometime that summer with endocarditis (a bacterial infection in the heart valves). Supposedly, he was alternating between staying with his mom and his dad who lived out of town. He was probably able to move about more freely when he stayed with his dad in another city. There would be less possibility of running into someone that he knew. After all those years, was his heart finally causing the problems that the doctors had predicted it would? I did not know the answer, but I often wondered just how weak his heart really was considering what he did to Bryanna.

≪≪≪

Late in August, with the trial a mere month away, I found myself in the most precarious situation; I was pregnant. Ashamed and thrilled at the same time, I knew one thing for sure—I wanted that baby more than anything in the world. For months, my life had no purpose; now, suddenly, I had a reason to live again. Since Bill and I were not married yet, I kept the baby a secret, sharing my joy with only a few close friends. When I told my mom, she could not be angry at me for long. She smiled with glassy tear filled eyes and said chokingly, "Now we will have a baby to love again."

My main concern centered on how the tension during the estimated three week trial would affect my unborn child. I asked my obstetrician if stress experienced by the mother could harm the baby. He said that they could not feel our emotions so there should be no adverse effects. My counselor advised me to tell the district attorneys about my pregnancy. I called Mrs. Good and told her my news and asked her to share it with General Steele if she felt he needed to know. She confirmed that it would be wise to apprise him of my condition and promised that she would take care of telling him about it sometime before the trial started.

Bill and I decided to wait until after the trial was over to get married. Now I had small piece of joy growing inside of me to ease some of my pain. I could no longer live recklessly. I would have to take care of myself for the sake of my child. It was scary to be pregnant during the trial, but God knows what we need. My baby was created for a special purpose. I just knew it! I put my faith and trust in God that in the end everything would be okay.

The Trial Begins

In the early weeks of September 2002, my family and I received a long list of potential jurors. We had to review it so the prosecution could remove any of our relatives or personal acquaintances that may have accidentally appeared on the list. I was not familiar with any of the names, but a couple of people were deleted because my parents knew them.

The defense planned to argue that Danny suffered from a sleep disorder that made him unaccountable for his criminal actions. Danny's consultation with the forensic psychiatrist and the sleep disorder specialist supposedly supported those findings. On two prior occasions, Danny had been evaluated by the state psychiatrist and was found to be mentally sane. The two new evaluations should prove very interesting during the trial.

Monday, Sept 23, 2002 marked the beginning of Danny's long-awaited trial. Judge Strong had estimated it would last about two weeks. The proceedings would start with jury selection. General Steele requested that my family and I be present for the jury selection phase. Early that September morning, my parents, paternal grandparents, Bill, one of my aunts, and I all reported to the courthouse anxious for the process to commence. The director of the Children's Advocacy Center (CAC) met us in the lobby to offer emotional support during the trial. I was grateful for Bill's presence on that trying day. It was very sweet of him to take time off from work to be at my side. My stomach was filled with butterflies. My worst fear rested in the guarantee that I would now have to face Danny after all this time.

The court process began very slowly that morning. Several other cases were reviewed before they reached the State vs. Daniel Draper. That seemed to take a long time, but I am sure it was really only a few minutes. I could only see the back of

Danny's head, but his hair did seem to have more grey in it than I remembered. Preparing for the trial had probably aged him quite a bit. Just seeing him from behind was enough to cause me severe distress. Danny was seated on the right hand side of the courtroom between his two lawyers, Mr. Hood and Mr. Petty. The prosecution, General Steele and Mrs. Good, were on the left hand side of the courtroom. My family and I sat a few rows behind the prosecution. Detective Sharp occupied the front bench directly behind General Steele. I looked at all the seats behind the defense, searching for the presence of any of Danny's family to support him. His stepdad was the only person that I saw. He and Danny exhibited the same forlorn posture—shoulders hunched and faces looking down at the floor. I felt a pang of sympathy for Danny because his stepdad was the only family member that accompanied him to his trial for murder. Where was his mother at? She suffered from poor health, but one would think that she could have put her own problems aside on a day such as this and made an effort to "stand by" her son.

The atmosphere was extremely serious as the two opponents prepared to submit their arguments. Danny, the perpetrator, was physically present in the room, but Bryanna, the victim, could only attend in spirit. When all of the other business was finished, Judge Strong announced that jury selection for the State vs. Daniel Draper would begin. The words were just leaving his mouth as Mr. Petty stepped up to the podium positioned between the prosecution and defense tables. After clearing his throat, he tapped on the microphone to test the sound and stated, "Representing the defense, I would like to respectfully request a delay in the jury selection today."

"Why are you requesting a delay?" Judge Strong asked.

Mr. Petty explained, "The Drapers are experiencing a serious family emergency. Danny's stepmom was rushed to the hospital early this morning with chest pain. She is at this very moment undergoing a heart catheterization. The family is very upset because she may be having a heart attack, and it does not look good. Danny's father was not able to drive here for the trial because he is at his sick wife's side. Danny's father's presence at this trial is of the upmost importance. He has played a key role in the preparation of our defense during the past several months."

Completely furious, I balled my hands tight into fists and gritted my teeth to keep from screaming at the outrage. I so wanted the trial over, and it appeared like there would be yet another delay. I should have mentally prepared myself better for that possibility. Now I knew why Danny's mom did not come. They had planned all along to delay the trial.

As I sat there listening to Mr. Petty's pathetic argument to postpone the jury selection, my anger quickly escalated. Why had Danny's stepmom suddenly developed chest pain only hours before the trial was set to begin. I could not help but be suspicious of her faking an illness to postpone the proceeding. If the trial was delayed Danny could remain free on bond several more months. How could Danny's father be a key witness in the case? He only visited Bryanna on one occasion while she was alive. He was not even present during her illnesses or hospitalizations. I tried to take deep breaths (as instructed on many occasions by my counselor) to calm down. I feared being too upset would be unhealthy for my unborn baby.

Judge Strong requested that a family member obtain more information on Danny's stepmom's condition. Meanwhile, Mr. Petty began to present a list of pretrial motions. Considering Danny's stepmom's health status and the multiple motions, Judge Strong sent the potential jurors home for the rest of the day with instructions to return at nine the following morning. I had arrived thinking that we would be choosing a jury panel, but unfortunately, the selection process would not begin until the next day or later.

The first motion that Mr. Petty introduced was for the trial to be moved to another location. Mr. Hood began to cite current similar news reports involving negative publicity about child abuse as the reason for the requested change of venue. Those cases included an infant that was left locked in a hot car and suffocated to death and a toddler that was thrown into a wall by the mother's boyfriend. He even went as far as to use the lady in Texas who drowned all of her children as an example. That incident did not even occur anywhere near our area. Mr. Hood also said that Danny's case had appeared twice in the newspapers over the past week. He asked for the news media to be banned from the courtroom during the jury selection. Judge Strong listened patiently to all of Mr. Hood's arguments but did not make an immediate ruling on any of them.

Then, Mr. Hood stated that he did not want the jury to see the diagnosis of multiple trauma/battered child syndrome. General Steele quickly disputed that it was part of the coroner's report and essential evidence. To resolve the argument, Judge Strong issued an immediate subpoena for the pathologist to testify about her medical findings. An officer was dispatched with the official papers summoning her appearance in court with instructions to return with her as soon as possible.

Mr. Hood did not want the jury to hear the terminology battered child syndrome because it proved that the abuse was repeated over an extended period of time; thus confirming that Bryanna's death was very non-accidental. Furthermore, the diagnosis justified one of the two remaining aggravating factors: "the murder was especially heinous, atrocious, or cruel in that it involved torture or serious physical abuse beyond that necessary to produce death." Battered Child Syndrome substantiated that Danny was engaging in a crime (child abuse) when he committed the crime (murder) (that was the definition of felony murder). The felony murder charge and the two remaining aggravating factors warranted the prosecution's request for the death penalty. The other aggravating factor could not be eliminated: Danny was over the age of eighteen and Bryanna was under the age of twelve when the crime was committed, but if the "cruel, heinous" aggravating factor or the felony murder charge could be dismissed, then the possibility of getting rid of the death penalty existed.

The next motion Mr. Hood presented was for the jury not to know the fact that Danny was fired from First Street Hospital after his arrest. I failed to see the importance of that request other than it was wasting court time that should be used for jury selection. Danny's lawyers had already produced numerous motions before the suppression hearing. As a matter of fact, those motions had actually caused the postponement of the suppression hearing. I wondered how many more they could concoct, and more importantly how many more would be allowed before the nonsense was stopped. Meanwhile, someone reported back that Danny's stepmom was still in the heart catheterization lab in serious condition, but no other details were available at that time.

After the update on Danny's stepmom's condition, Mr. Hood stated that on several occasions, he had requested the full disclosure of the department of children's services (DCS) records maintained by Mrs. Blakely during the ongoing investigation for child abuse. General Steele and Mr. Hood compared the documents that each had in their possession and determined that they were identical. Mr. Hood claimed that there were additional unreleased hand-written notes and that was what he wanted. An argument ensued concerning the entirety of the DCS report. Mr. Hood continued to insist that there were other records that he had been unable to obtain while they prepared for trial. To settle the dispute, Judge Strong signed an affidavit stating that the complete DCS record was to be surrendered to the court before the end of the day.

While the affidavit was being taken to the DCS department, Judge Strong issued a brief recess. During the break, my family, Bill, and I were escorted to a private room down the hall so we would not accidentally bump into any of Danny's family or the news media. While we were in that room, I vented my frustration to everyone about Danny's stepmom's mysterious illness. Since I had known her, she had always suffered from some kind of new health problem. I decided that it was just too fishy for her to become conveniently ill right before the trial was scheduled to start. I made no secret of my belief that she was faking the whole incident to delay the trial. During my outburst, the director of the CAC commented that she had even seen lawyers pretend to be sick to postpone trials for their clients. I could not believe that an attorney would resort to such deceitful measures to merely delay a trial. Furthermore, it was unimaginable that the court system would condone such actions, and yet, after what I had witnessed during the past year, it was actually quite believable. In many ways, I was far too naïve to comprehend just what a lawyer could be paid to do.

When we returned to the courtroom, no news regarding Danny's stepmom's condition was even mentioned. The pathologist had arrived during the break and was seated next to Detective Sharp on the front row. Judge Strong reopened the proceedings by calling the pathologist to the witness stand. The first thing that I noticed about her as she walked across the room was her stomach. She was visibly pregnant. It was distressing to watch her testify about my infant's cruel death with a baby inside her. Yet, I felt connected to her in a strange way because we shared the same sweet condition.

The hearing started with General Steele verifying her credentials for the record. She had been a doctor for thirteen years and had performed over eight hundred autopsies. Those qualifications established her as an expert witness in the field of forensic pathology. Her autopsy report and the letter from the pediatric radiologist were added as exhibits to the hearing. Those two documents supported the medical definition of Battered Child Syndrome: "a finding of multiple injuries that occur over recurrent episodes to different areas of the body." General Steele stressed that all of that information was very relevant to the final diagnosis in Bryanna's particular case.

When General Steele was finished, Mr. Hood interrogated her relentlessly. He wanted to know if any of the individual injuries alone could have caused Bryanna's death. She replied that no single injury or fracture sustained prior to June 2 by itself was fatal. Mr. Hood hounded her until she finally relented that the acute bleed in Bryanna's head and the anoxic brain changes that she suffered on June 2, 2000 could have possibly caused her death without the other injuries. However, before she was dismissed from the witness stand, she reiterated the importance of looking at all of the injuries and their occurrence over a period of time.

Mr. Hood was very harsh with the pathologist, pounding her with questions, but she held up extremely well under the pressure. She was definitely professional and knowledgeable in her field of expertise. Mr. Hood tried multiple times to manipulate her, but she stayed firm in her stance—Bryanna died from multiple trauma/Battered Child Syndrome.

It was unbearable to sit in that room listening to each one of Bryanna's injuries described in detail. It was even worse to see how lightly they were viewed by the defense. What she suffered did not seem to matter to them. They had one and only one purpose—-to clear Danny of the charges. Listening to the pathologist's testimony left me teary eyed and exhausted.

In the end, I was not sure which side had benefited from the brief hearing. It seemed to end in a draw and basically did not change anything. I think it was conducted mainly to consume more time and delay the start of the trial. As long as the defense could prevent the trial from officially beginning, it could still feasibly be postponed to a later date all together.

After the pathologist's testimony, Judge Strong ordered another short break. When we returned to the courtroom, Mr. Petty approached the podium to speak. "Your Honor, I am not feeling well at all," he lamented. "It has been all I can do just to get through this morning's proceedings. I have an ear infection and severe vertigo. Right now, I feel like the room is spinning. If you could at all just consider continuing today's proceedings tomorrow, I would deeply appreciate it. I feel just too dizzy to stand up any longer."

I could not believe my ears! Could what the director of the CAC was talking about during our first break, attorneys faking illnesses, be what was happening? They were obviously trying everything to delay the trial, but would they go that far? Only God knew the answer to those questions and the intentions of their hearts. While Mr. Petty was talking, a man entered the courtroom carrying a large package, wrapped in brown paper. He handed it to Judge Strong stating that it contained the full disclosure of the DCS records. Judge Strong slowly opened it to reveal a very bulky notebook. I was amazed at how thick the report was because I thought Mrs. Blakely only covered the case until Bryanna's death. That appeared to be a lot of notes for a one month investigation.

At that time, it was about eleven-thirty in the morning. Mr. Hood asked for some time to review the records. Judge Strong stated considering Danny's stepmom and Mr. Petty's illnesses that court would recess for the day, but he wanted a full report on the seriousness of Danny's stepmom's condition the following morning, especially her prognosis. He further told Mr. Petty to rest and recuperate and be prepared to reconvene at nine the following morning for jury selection. Did I detect a sly grin on Judge Strong's face hidden beneath his graying mustache as he told him that?

My family, Bill, and I left the courtroom with heavy hearts. We traveled down the street just a few blocks to a local restaurant for lunch. I had to force myself to eat a few bites for the baby because in reality, I was too upset to be hungry. We were dismissed so early in the day that I could have easily gone to work, but I was far too anxious to concentrate on any important tasks.

I decided to stay home and rest. Although very little progress was made in the trial, I was absolutely exhausted. Listening to the pathologist's testimony and the hassle of events not going as planned was extremely stressful for me. Worst of all, I feared the possibility that the trial would again be postponed for several months. Resolution seemed like a dream that would never come true.

⁂

The next day, we (my parents, paternal grandparents, aunt, and Bill) returned to the courthouse at nine in the morning. The director of the CAC met us again to provide emotional support. We seated ourselves on the left side of the courtroom a few rows behind the prosecution and Detective Sharp.

The first issue opened for discussion was, of course, Danny's stepmom's condition. Amazingly, she was doing much better and had not suffered a heart attack. However, Danny's father was not able to leave her side yet, and Danny's mom was not present either. Again, he was accompanied by only his stepdad and two lawyers. Surprisingly, Mr. Petty was also feeling quite better. To be honest, considering his hyper temperament, I would be at a loss to determine if he was well or ill. I sat quietly listening to all of the good announcements thinking it was time to start jury selection. Unfortunately, however, that was not what was about to happen. All of the wonderful news was, in fact, too good to be true.

Mr. Hood told Judge Strong that they had discovered some questionable statements contained within the DCS records surrendered yesterday. He claimed there were remarks requiring further exploration before jury selection could begin. *What were they trying to do now?* I wondered exasperated.

Judge Strong consented to opening a discussion about the contents of the DCS record. Mr. Hood stood up and turned to face my family and me in an accusatory fashion and said, "There are potential witnesses in the courtroom that should not hear this conversation." Judge Strong asked him to name who needed to leave the proceeding. He said my parents, my grandparents, and then he stared directly at me and said "Angela Draper." I was already angry at their outrageous attempts to delay to trial, but when he called me by that name, I became completely furious. After all my hard work to be rid of that name, for him to use it was an unforgivable insult. Even though it was probably against the rules, I spoke aloud in front of the entire courtroom. "It is Angela Wills now please!"

He replied nonchalantly, "Wills or Draper, whatever," waving his hands at me, like I was being silly, like he had done nothing wrong. I wanted to scream at him, "How dare you call me that!" I think my dad sensed that my fury was escalating because he grabbed my arm and quickly removed me from the courtroom before I could say anything else. His lack of respect for me and their elaborate tactics to delay the trial had infuriated me. The shy girl that I was in high school would have never spoken out like that. It made me realize how my tragic experience had really changed me. Bill and my aunt were allowed to remain in the courtroom because they were not potential witnesses. The director of the CAC followed us out.

When we stepped into the foyer, we found ourselves completely surrounded by over fifty potential jurors waiting in the lobby. We could barely move through the crowd to the private room where we stayed during the breaks on the previous day. It seemed like their discussion lasted for hours, but I know it was only a few minutes. I anxiously waited for Bill and my aunt to find us during a break. I certainly hoped they could provide some enlightenment on what was found in those records. Supposedly, all reports had been surrendered months ago. While we waited, my family and I debated on what it could be, and finally decided that it was probably nothing at all. In all likelihood, his lawyers were just trying something else to delay the trial.

My anger intensified while we were left to wait in that room without a clue as to what was happening. I wanted to do something but was helpless to stop any of this nonsense. I decided to call my lawyer and let him know what the defense was doing; however that proved futile as well. He could not do anything to stop them. He could only reassure me like everyone else was doing. I really don't know why I bothered him. I had just somehow hoped that he could prevent them from postponing the trial again, but naturally, he had no influence over it. Desperately, I wanted closure. Danny needed to be back behind bars, but that was not happening. In reality, there was really no reason to be so upset or surprised because nothing for the past two years had went as planned. Why should that one single day have been any different?

During a brief break, Bill and my aunt found us in the private waiting room. I quickly asked them what was happening in the courtroom. The complicated nature of the case combined with their lack of knowledge concerning the intricate details made it hard for them to understand and explain a lot of what had occurred. Bill said that they were discussing reopening the subject of suppressing the confession statement during the trial because of some remark in Mrs. Blakely's records. Bill did not know what the comment was because it had not been read aloud in the courtroom yet. He then told us how one of the potential jurors was requesting to be dismissed. Judge Strong placed her on the witness stand and asked her how she felt about the case. She replied, "He deserves the death penalty for his crime, and it will take an act of God to change my mind." After she said that, Judge Strong released her from the obligation and sent her home. That was all they had time to tell us. They rushed back to the courtroom as not to miss any of the proceedings. I sat silently after they left thinking about the potential juror's statement. It really proved how difficult it was going to be to find a jury panel for the trial. Most people in our area had probably heard about the case and already developed an opinion. That incident actually gave the defense a valid reason to move the trial to another location.

Bill and my aunt returned in a few minutes and said that Judge Strong had once again stopped proceedings for the day and sent all of the potential jurors home. General Steele followed them into the room to explain everything to us. Evidently, there was a statement written by Mrs. Blakely in the DCS file that indicated that Danny's confession had been tape recorded. General Steele thought he had reviewed the entire DCS file, but unfortunately, there were several notes handed over yesterday in the complete file that he had not ever seen. Mr. Hood claimed that the interviews with the doctors and radiologists in the complete handwritten notes contained vital evidence for the defense to use in changing their entire litigation strategy. Mr. Petty stated that the notes "filled in the blanks" of the typed transcripts, creating a whole different scenario for the case. Mr. Hood further alleged if a tape existed of Danny's confession, it could prove that it was performed inappropriately.

The decisive statement written by Mrs. Blakely that changed everything was on the last page. In April 2001, Detective Sharp had called Mrs. Blakely to let her know about Danny's confession. She was not actually working on the case, but he knew that she was very concerned about it and would want to know the outcome. She was, in fact, so emotionally involved that she was still keeping a record of the events. Mrs. Blakely wanted to know how Detective Sharp could be sure that I (the mother) did not know about Danny abusing Bryanna. That was when Detective Sharp told her that he and Detective Light had watched Danny and me from another room via the camera to observe my reaction when we spoke after the confession was signed. He recounted to her how I screamed and fainted when Danny told me he had twisted Bryanna's arms. To him, my reaction confirmed that I did not know what Danny was doing to Bryanna. In reference to that event, Mrs. Blakely wrote, "The whole thing is on tape but the Drapers don't know that." I believe she was referring to when Detective Sharp watched us talking afterward, not the entire confession. Nonetheless, the way she wrote it was vague and easily misinterpreted especially by a defense looking for a loophole.

General Steele assured us that the confession had not been tape recorded, and he did not know why Mrs. Blakely had written that inaccurate statement into a legal document. Recording confessions was against General Steele's police interrogation practice as confirmed by the testimonies of Detective Sharp and Detective Light during the suppression hearing. Even so, the existence of her statement created a reason to reopen the suppression hearing on Thursday morning at nine. Judge Strong was allowing a day for attorneys to prepare for the hearing but promised to provide additional time if necessary. General Steele warned us that Mrs. Blakely's statement would probably cause the trial to be postponed again. I immediately asked him when it might occur if delayed. He replied probably sometime in April 2003. That news filled my heart with dread because it was the same month that my baby was due to arrive. I feared the trial would be postponed yet again because I would be the one unable to attend at that time. I wanted the trial over so I could have a normal healthy pregnancy. The new development was more than I could bear. The perpetrator was once again winning while the victims suffered.

A secretary entered the room while we were talking. She handed us subpoenas for all of our phone records (home and cell phone) from the time period when Bryanna had died on June 2, 2003 until after Danny was arrested the following April 24, 2001. The defense had requested the phone records so they could claim that my father had engaged in an ongoing relationship with the district attorney's office and the police department from the time Bryanna died until the day Danny confessed. They planned to allege that my father was acting under the police department's instructions as a temporary agent to bring Danny into custody. A thorough review of our complete phone records would show how many times my father had called Detective Sharp throughout the investigation. Furthermore, the defense was looking for the exact time of the phone conversation between my father and Danny's father the night Danny was arrested when Danny's father claimed that my father told him he "heard the tapes." (That statement was taken out of context by the defense. My father was actually talking about the 911 phone call made by Danny the day Bryanna died.) They also wanted to know how many times Danny's father had tried to contact Danny that day so they could say that we were intentionally not informing him about what was happening. Using the phone records, they intended to make it appear like the police department, the district attorney's office, and my father had plotted a huge conspiracy to make Danny "take the rap for everything."

General Steele told us to contact the phone companies as soon as possible and ask for the records. Exasperated, I felt that the demand would be impossible to accommodate. I did not even know how long they kept such records. General Steele instructed us to do the best we could and plan to return to court on Thursday morning at nine for the reopening of the suppression hearing.

When we left the court house that morning, I did not know if I was more angry, depressed, or disappointed. The reality that the entire process would not be over any time soon was starting to register. With that thought in mind, I decided to work that afternoon hoping to preoccupy my mind with something else, but in reality, it was hard to concentrate on anything. Being so disturbed about my lack of control over what was happening, I really should not have tried to work in that state of mind, but fortunately, I did not make any terrible mistakes.

The next morning shortly after I woke up, my dad came to tell me that General Steele had called and asked us to come to the court house right away. He wanted to discuss with us the possibility of the prosecution accepting a plea bargain from the defense. If General Steele agreed to a plea bargain, then it would happen the next day instead of reopening the suppression hearing. There would be no trial. I dressed in a hurry so we could go to the district attorney's office. My mom was at work so we decided not to bother her until we knew more details.

Upon our arrival to the court house, the victim's coordinator took us immediately to General Steele and Mrs. Good in the conference room. It seemed like we had spent a lot of time in that old familiar room during the past year. General Steele began by explaining that the plea bargain was being considered based on the remark in the DCS records about Danny's confession being on tape. General Steele again assured us that Danny's confession had not been videotaped; however, he was positive if Danny was found guilty and sentenced to death, the verdict would be automatically appealed based on that single inaccurate statement.

His case would become entangled in an appeals process that would last for years. In the end, the death penalty would most likely be overturned; however, during the ongoing appeals process, Danny's case would repeatedly appear in the news, preventing us from having peace and closure for a long time. For those reasons, General Steele believed it would be in everyone's best interest to accept the plea bargain and end the matter the next day. If Danny did not plead guilty the following day, the trial would definitely be postponed until April 2003 to grant the defense more time to review the contents of the complete DCS record.

General Steele admitted that Mr. Hood had approached him several times during the past year and a half, asking to plea bargain for his client's life. General Steele had refused to agree to one until now because he felt that Danny's crime deserved the maximum punishment by law, but the new findings in the DCS record had changed his mind. The terms of the plea bargain would be that Danny received life in prison with the possibility of parole which meant that he would have to serve fifty-four years before being eligible for release. The life sentence would begin as soon as Judge Strong accepted the guilty verdict. At that time, Danny would be handcuffed and taken to the State Prison. Finally, he would be returned to confinement.

General Steele wanted to know our feelings about Danny receiving a lesser degree of punishment than expected. We told him that so far he had done a wonderful job, and we would trust whatever his decision was on the matter. To me, the penalty was satisfactory. I had never really wanted to see Danny put to death anyway. Fifty-four years was a long time. He would probably never live long enough to see his parole date. The most important thing was to have all of it behind us so maybe we could finally heal.

While we were talking, someone pecked on the door to inform General Steele that Mrs. Blakely had arrived. He quickly excused himself from us. From the grim look on his face when he left, I suspected that she was in a lot of trouble. I would not want to be reprimanded by General Steele. I had always been glad that we were on the same side. Perhaps, I should have pitied Danny more during the past year and a half than I had. To be honest, no one would want General Steele prosecuting them. He was tough against wrong doers taking his not-so-easy job very seriously. I did not envy him for what he had to face every day, but I did admire his dedication.

We left the courthouse, immediately going to the school cafeteria where my mom worked. We wanted to tell her the good news in person. She became very anxious when she saw us enter the back door. I know that she was thinking the very worst because she had received too many bad phone calls during the time that Bryanna was ill. We quickly told her that we did not have bad news, but we did not want to tell her about the meeting with General Steele on the phone. After Daddy told her that Danny would plead guilty the next day, and there would be no trial, she grabbed us and hugged us both with joy. I could actually see the load being lifted from her shoulders. I recognized it because it was the same relief that I felt in my heart. The trial was a long stressful process that we had all dreaded. Even worse was the possibility of a postponement. Now, we would not have to endure either one.

When I went to work that afternoon, I felt a lot less weary than the previous day. It was a consolation to know that all of the stress would end in one day. However, one tiny bothersome thought intruded into my mind. What if he reneged at the last minute and decided not to plead guilty? All I could do was hope for the best. I wanted the burden gone for my own sake, but more importantly for the health of my unborn child.

Guilty

On Thursday September 26, 2002, I reported back to the courthouse at nine in the morning accompanied by my parents, paternal grandparents, aunt, sister, brother and Bill. My parents allowed my sister to miss school that day to attend the court session. I think it was important for both of my siblings to have resolution on the matter. Prior to entering the courtroom, we had to empty our pockets and open our purses for a thorough inspection. The foyer was packed with a crowd of people including the press and various members of Danny's family. I quickly spotted Danny's mother, father, stepdad, aunt, and a couple of uncles. His mother was red faced and clutching a wad of tissue in her fist. It was obvious that she had been crying a lot. The press knew ahead of time that Danny would be pleading guilty that day. Several cameras were positioned around the courtroom to capture the entire session on film. I did not know if I should weep for Danny, the living, or for Bryanna, the dead. They were both filled with absolute sorrow.

We quietly took a seat on the left side of the courtroom behind the prosecution. Again, I could only see the back of Danny's head. He was sitting between his two lawyers. Actually, I was glad that I could not see his face. I sat between my brother and Bill so that I would have a strong man on each side of me. My lawyer had wanted to be present, but due to a previously scheduled engagement, he could not come. My other lawyer that was helping him with the civil suit attended in his place. I had never met him and did not even know what he looked like, but he came to greet me and let me know that he was there. It was rather uncanny that our first introduction occurred on that dark occasion.

Everyone stood up respectfully as the Honorable Judge Strong entered the courtroom. After he was seated at his huge desk, court was called to order. Judge Strong announced that the State vs. Daniel Draper would resume. He summarized that at closing on Tuesday, jury selection had not commenced, and the defense was granted a day to prepare for the reopening of the suppression hearing. He began by asking the prosecution to call their first witness.

General Steele stood up and addressed Judge Strong directly. "It is my understanding that the defendant is going to enter a guilty plea to the charge of first degree murder today." Judge Strong then determined that the suppression hearing would not be reopened as planned. Mr. Hood handed him the signed guilty plea form. Judge Strong took a few minutes to review the form. After a long stretch of silence, he asked Danny to stand up and raise his right hand, "Mr. Daniel Draper, do you solemnly swear that the testimony you are about to give in this cause will be the truth, the whole truth, nothing but the truth, so help you God."

Danny replied, clearing his throat, "Yes, sir." His voice sounded hoarse. I was sure that he had been crying even though I could not see his face.

After taking the oath, Danny was allowed to sit back down at the table with his two lawyers. Judge Strong told Danny that he was required by law to answer a series of questions before the guilty plea could be officially accepted. The judge further explained that Danny had the right against self-incrimination meaning that he could still consult with his attorneys before answering any questions or not respond to them at all.

Danny's charges of first degree murder and felony murder were reviewed, and the three potential punishments available for those offenses were listed as follows: "Death by lethal injection, life without the possibility of parole, and life with the possibility of parole." Life with the possibility of parole required the incarcerated person to serve eighty-five percent of a sixty year sentence before being eligible for release. That calculated to about fifty-one years. Danny was also charged with Aggravated Child

Abuse, categorized as a Class A felony. The punishment for that crime was a prison sentence of fifteen to twenty-five years and a hefty fine. Judge Strong informed Danny that he could potentially be convicted of a lesser offense if he chose to have a jury trial, such as second degree murder, voluntary manslaughter, reckless homicide, or negligent homicide. Those verdicts carried lighter punishments than first degree murder; however, that possibility rested in how the facts developed during the jury trial.

After that information was presented, Judge Strong began to ask Danny a series of legal questions. "Are you knowingly and voluntarily changing your plea from not guilty to guilty?"

Danny replied, "Yes, sir."

"And are you knowingly and voluntarily giving up your right to a jury trial?"

"Yes, sir."

Judge Strong advised Danny that he was entitled to legal representation at every stage of the proceedings. If at any time, Danny could not afford an attorney, the court would appoint him one. Furthermore, if Danny was convicted of first degree murder by a jury of his peers, he would have the right to appeal the verdict. If he could not afford a lawyer to handle the appeals process, the court would provide him with one. By pleading guilty, Danny was "giving up all appellate rights, because the plea agreement encompassed all sentencing issues."

Judge Strong described in detail all of the rights that Danny was relinquishing by pleading guilty that day. Danny was forfeiting his "right of confrontation" which was "the right to be present in an open public courtroom when any witness testifies against you," and "the right of your attorney to confront and cross examine any witnesses appearing against you for the purpose of testing that witness's credibility and believability in court." Danny was surrendering his "right of compulsory process for witnesses." That right involved compelling witnesses under penalty of law to testify on Danny's behalf. Danny was sacrificing his right against self incrimination, meaning he was not required to present any evidence against himself. The full responsibility of proving his guilt "beyond a reasonable doubt and to a moral certainty" resided with the state (or the district attorney's office).

Judge Strong concluded, "Now, Mr. Draper, do you understand that by pleading guilty today that you'll be giving up all of these rights?"

Danny replied, "Yes, sir."

I listened quietly as all of the forfeited rights were explained to Danny. Judge Strong was obligated by law to advise Danny of what he was forsaking by pleading guilty. Assuring that Danny fully understood his actions locked his sentence forever. He would not be allowed to appeal at a later date.

After Danny officially gave up all of his rights, Judge Strong asked General Steele to present the evidence that the State had intended to use in the case. The proof had to be entered into the record to substantiate a basis for the guilty plea.

General Steele began to read a statement aloud to the entire courtroom that summarized all of the events leading to Danny's arrest as follows:

> "If Your Honor please, the evidence that the State would have to produce in this trial would be that the defendant was the natural father of Bryanna Faith Draper, who died on June 2, 2000. A telephone call was received by the 911 dispatcher sometime around five o'clock on June 2, 2000 from the defendant stating that his daughter had stopped breathing. Emergency personnel were immediately dispatched to his home. They found the defendant with the baby, not breathing. She was taken to the emergency room at a local hospital where medical personnel attempted to resuscitate her for some period of time before she was pronounced dead. The department of children's services and the police department were summoned to the hospital. A previously instigated investigation by

the department of children's services was continued. An autopsy was ordered and performed on the baby.

"The pathologist, completing the autopsy, reported three separate bleeds in her brain, bleeding into her eyes, a clavicle fracture, arm fracture, and seven broken ribs. All of the injuries had occurred at different times over the months before her death, thus causing:

"The ultimate conclusion that Bryanna Faith Draper died of multiple trauma. The final autopsy report was not filed with the state medical examiner or furnished to my office until March 2001. Following that time, the defendant was interviewed at the police department and provided an intricate statement explaining what he had done, in great detail, to account for each and every one of the injuries.

"As the court is well aware from the ruling of the suppression hearing, that statement was allowed to be introduced as evidence. Part of the defense inquiry at that time was whether or not there was a recording, either audio or visual, made of that interview. The testimony concluded that no tape was made. However, as we discovered Tuesday morning in this courtroom, an official department of children's service's (DCS) record reflects that there was a tape recording made. The statement contained in that record is the basis for my acceptance of a guilty plea in this case and converting the punishment to a life sentence, as opposed to the original recommendation of the death penalty.

"I am positive if we proceeded with a trial right now in this county, that Daniel would be convicted of first degree murder and sentenced to death. However, I am equally persuaded that the DCS statement concerning a tape recording being made would not allow the death penalty to survive.

Listening to General Steele's speech that day was extremely difficult for me. It was like instantly reliving the entire nightmare of the past three years in a few brief moments. The enormity of her various injuries was overwhelming. The pain she must have endured—unbearable. I wanted to cry out loud for her, but instead, I sniffed and sobbed as quietly as I could. I wondered what his family, especially his mother, thought as they heard her injuries named one by one and described in vivid detail. The rumor was that his mother had been sheltered from much of the evidence due to her fragile condition. That day could very well have been the first time that she was confronted with the horrid details about what he had done. I listened for any sounds from the other side of the room during General Steele's long speech, but I do not recall detecting even a sigh. My family was sniffing and sobbing out loud, but not even a whisper came from Danny's family. I was left to sadly wonder what Bryanna had meant to them.

Following General Steele's presentation, the defense attorneys confirmed that they had been given ample opportunity to study all of the State's evidence against Danny. Furthermore, they had shared all of that data with Danny on multiple occasions. Danny verified that he was not under the influence of any mind-altering medications that morning and that he fully understood his choice to plead guilty. Next, Judge Strong asked Danny if he was completely satisfied with the job that his attorneys had performed in representing him, and he confirmed that he was. Danny verified that he was the sole person making the decision to plead guilty and that no one had coerced him into doing it.

After Danny substantiated all of those points, General Steele said, "I think the record should reflect that Mr. Hood has met with me on at least three occasions to discuss the possibility of his client pleading guilty to something other than capital punishment. He has actively sought, on behalf of his client, something other than the death penalty, but I would not agree to it. In fact, we met as recently as last week."

Judge Strong asked Danny to rise. "Mr. Daniel L. Draper, to count two of the indictment, charging you with first degree murder, felony murder, how do you plead to that charge?"

Daniel replied, "Guilty, Your Honor."

"Mr. Draper, upon your plea of guilty to felony murder, in count two, it's the judgment of this court that you are guilty, and I sentence you to serve life in prison with the possibility of parole. No fine will be imposed. You will be rendered infamous and disqualified from holding an office of public trust because this is a felony. Mr. Draper, as to count three of the indictment, charging you will class A Felony Aggravated Child Abuse, how do you plead to that charge?"

"Guilty, Your Honor, " Danny said with his head hung down.

"Mr. Draper, upon your plea of guilty to class A felony Aggravated Child Abuse, it's the judgment of the court that you are guilty, and I sentence you to serve twenty-five years as a range I, standard offender. Count two and count three will run concurrently with each other, giving you a total sentence of life with the possibility of parole. Concurrently means that the two separate sentences will in effect be served at the same time. I think you did serve some time in the Sullivan County Jail prior to making bond. You will be given credit for all of that time."

After pronouncing Danny's sentence, Judge Strong asked both sides if there were any other issues that needed to be explored. At that time, Danny was still standing up. All I could see was the back of his head. He tremulously spoke, "I just want to say that I'm sorry that I failed everybody so much, and if I could take it back, I would." He sobbed out loud as he continued to talk. "I'd take every bit of it back. Though it looks really awful, it was just too much . . . getting ready for Bryanna's arrival. I just could not handle it. And if I could have understood that I was doing something wrong, I would have gotten help. I'm sorry. I'm so sorry."

He was crying intensely and seemed to want to say more, but Judge Strong interrupted him and said, "All right. All right, anything further, Mr. Hood?" I am not sure why Judge Strong stopped him. I did not know if Danny really was not supposed to have spoken aloud without permission, or if Judge Strong feared that Danny would ramble on indefinitely.

The bailiff took the plea bargain papers from Judge Strong and removed Danny from the courtroom. He did not place him in handcuffs. He merely took him by the arm and led him out the back door. Danny was gone. At his disappearance, finally, an audible cry erupted from his side of the courtroom. Danny's stepdad grabbed Danny's mother as she swooned into a faint still clutching a wad of toilet paper in her fist. A police car was supposed to be outside waiting to transport Danny to the closest state prison. There, the intake process would begin with registering him into the system, classifying him, and assigning him an identification number. Afterward, they would decide his actual placement for the duration of his prison term.

Judge Strong completed the proceedings by announcing that the case was "closed." It was finally over! As we exited the courtroom, the victim's coordinator was waiting for us at the door. She took us upstairs to the old familiar conference room. Detective Sharp, General Steele, and Mrs. Good wanted to meet with us after the plea bargain was completed. We had to wait a few minutes for them to finish downstairs and join us. When they entered the room, the atmosphere was somber. Few words were spoken, but many tears were shed that day, and not all of the tears were from my family. I distinctly remember Mrs. Good crying with us. She hugged my mother and me several times. Somehow throughout the months of preparation we had formed an attachment to one another that I can't quite explain. We had been brought together by the most terrible of circumstances, but through that, we would be bonded in friendship forever. Mrs. Good promised to get Danny's prison identification number for me so I could look on the internet and know where he was held at all times. I believe my mom was more upset than anyone else in the room. Her entire body was shaking with sobs. That day we truly absorbed the full weight of everything that had happened to us.

I had mistakenly thought for a long time that I would be glad when Danny was sent to prison. When that day finally arrived, there was no joy to be found in it. I was relieved that the trial was over, but not happy to see him taken into custody as I had anticipated I would be. It was actually all very sad. He had destroyed not only Bryanna's life but his own life as well. Danny was an intelligent person, loved by so many people. He had a wonderful life and almost anything that he wanted. We were so happy and blessed. I still could not understand why he did it. I guess I had hoped that the trial would provide some answers, but even what he said in the courtroom did not explain anything. It was like he was making excuses and saying things that his lawyers and psychiatrists had programmed into his brain for months. The trial would have developed with claims that he suffered from sleep deprivation and that taking care of Bryanna was too stressful for him causing him to "crack," but those explanations did not account for his actions by any means.

Danny receiving his punishment did not give me the closure that I had hoped it would. Left with a hundred unanswered questions, I feared that no adequate explanation for his actions existed. After months of psychological manipulation, did Danny now really know why he did it? If there was any truth to be found, it was probably buried months prior.

When we returned home, I was overcome with a deep depression. It was a gloomy, rainy fall day. All I did was lie on the couch. I did not want to talk to anyone about it. The television news station replayed the story of his guilty plea about every hour throughout the day. Each time it was aired they showed him in the courtroom crying and saying he was "so sorry." I hated watching it. I felt like the news media was mocking our lives by playing that tape over and over again. When Danny said that he was sorry that morning, was he truly remorseful for killing her, or did he just regret that he had destroyed his own life in the process? I would probably never know the answer to that haunting question. There was no peace in my heart, just a huge empty space that belonged to two lost souls—Bryanna and Danny. Another piece of me grieved for the lost relationships with his family members. Since Danny's arrest, we had barely spoken. Once I had loved his mom, dad, stepdad, aunts, and uncles; now I felt so much bitterness toward them for making everything more difficult than it should have been. It was truly a day of loss; nothing was gained.

My family shared my melancholy spirit. I know that it was particularly devastating for my little sister. She was only two-years-old when Danny entered our lives, and she could not remember a time when he was not around. My parents had loved Danny like a son. I know that in spite of his horrible actions, a small piece of them still loved the old Danny. The old Danny was what I could remember before his confession. If I could put his offense completely out of my mind, I still loved him. There was no joy for me in the fact that he had ruined his life and would be in prison until he died. Thoughts of him suffering abuse and violation in prison filled my mind. Danny was always so meek. How would he survive in that harsh environment? Some people might have wanted him to have broken bones so that he would know exactly how Bryanna had felt, but I could not share those feelings against one that I had once loved so dearly. For me, love was not an emotion to be turned off and on like a light switch. It was much more complicated than that.

I had to take several days off work after his sentencing to sort out my conflicting thoughts and emotions. I finally had to reach way down once again and pick myself up by the boot strings. I could not wallow in misery forever. My questions were left unanswered, but I did have one thing: a tiny spark of new life growing inside me. Looking to the future, not the past, I would concentrate on what I have, not what I have lost and hope to eventually be happy again.

Resigned that I might never know the answers to my questions on this side of eternity, I had the hope that one day, Bryanna and I would be united forever. Until then, I am surrounded by love from God and my family. I have faith that God will see me through the trials of life. Maybe when we reach heaven, the questions will not even matter any more.

A Time To Sow, A Time To Reap

A few weeks after the trial, using Danny's prison identification number, I logged onto the felony offender's website to check on his whereabouts. Surprisingly, he was no longer at the intake prison. He had been moved to a prison close to where his father lived. Later, through the grapevine, I learned that the facility was located on his father's way to work allowing him to visit Danny frequently.

⁂

Bill and I were married on October 19, 2002. It was a cool, fall day. Our pastor performed the small, conservative ceremony, outside on my parent's patio. It was strange because he was the same pastor that had married Danny and me in 1995. In spite of that dismal association, I tried to maintain a positive outlook and truly hope for happiness at last. Besides, I really did not want anyone else marrying us.

Before the wedding, the four-year old daughter of some close friends slipped upstairs to visit me. She approached me shyly and asked, "Are you hiding a baby in your stomach?" I was speechless. How could she know? Shocked, I replied, "Why do you ask that?" She innocently said, "Because when my mommy and daddy got married, my mommy was hiding a baby in her stomach, and it was me." She ended her explanation with a graceful gesture of pointing to herself. She was so adorable and so accurate that I had to laugh. It was actually a consolation to realize that others had shared my predicament and not only lived, but flourished.

After a quiet reception at my parent's house, Bill and I enjoyed a brief honeymoon at the beach. On our way back home, I called my mom to tell her we would be arriving soon. That was when she informed me of a dreadful incident that had occurred while we were away.

The previous day, my paternal grandmother had gone to place fresh flowers on Bryanna's grave. While there, she discovered that her entire marker had been removed, leaving only a huge empty hole in the ground. Terribly upset, my grandmother marched straight to the cemetery office to find out why the monument was missing. The director informed her that the marker had been removed because it was "illegal." The original headstone, bearing the last name of Draper, had been reported as stolen. Being an honest person, my grandmother truthfully explained that her son (my dad) had replaced the marker himself several months ago. The director told her that her son was guilty of fraud and theft. Evidently, Danny's family had visited Bryanna's grave and saw the new memorial and then went to the cemetery office and demanded to know the whereabouts of the original piece that they had purchased. When the cemetery office investigated the matter further, no records indicated an official replacement of the monument because my father had done it himself to save the administrative charge. With no formal account in their records indicating an exchange of the headstone, the director automatically filed it as illegal. Under those conditions, he had to remove the new headstone, leaving her grave unmarked until the matter could be resolved.

In tears, my grandmother went straight to my dad to tell him about Bryanna's grave. My dad asked Detective Sharp to accompany him to the cemetery office to further investigate the matter. Upon their arrival, the director informed my dad that his actions were unlawful and that he was in a lot of trouble. My dad explained to him the circumstances surrounding Bryanna's death, how she was brutally murdered by her father. Then, he described in detail our agony at seeing the hypocritical phrase, "mommy and daddy's little angel," carved on her monument each time we visited her final resting place. The director was familiar with our story from news articles, but unfortunately, he had not made the connection until my dad told him about it. My dad showed the director the legal papers granting him sole ownership of Bryanna's plot (my grandmother originally possessed the property but had signed it over to my father shortly after Bryanna was buried there). The director was sympathetic toward us but unsure of how to resolve the situation since Danny's family was pushing the criminal charges. He promised to investigate the issue and determine a solution as soon as possible. I believe that Danny's family had seized the opportunity to spitefully accuse my father of illegal activities as revenge because they blamed us for Danny's arrest. They still failed to accept that Danny was responsible for the actions that had placed him in prison.

The next day, the director called my dad with a possible solution to the problem. If my dad was willing to repay Danny's family the thirteen hundred dollars that they had spent on the original marker, then they would drop all criminal charges. My father returned to the cemetery office that same day with the requested amount of money plus an additional one hundred dollars to replace the new marker to the grave. The director said that the one hundred dollar replacement fee was unnecessary, but my father insisted on paying it because it was not their fault that her headstone had been removed.

While at the cemetery office, my father stated that since he had paid Danny's family for the marker he now had sole ownership of the cemetery plot and everything on it. The director agreed with him that it was now his property alone. With that confirmed, my father stated, "Since everything there is now mine, I want you to give Danny's family a message for me. They are not to step foot on her gravesite ever again. If they do, I will sue them for trespassing."

The director concurred, "If they take this payment, then they are giving up their rights to come near the property." Later that day, Danny's family accepted the money and agreed to the "no trespassing" stipulation. I couldn't believe that all of that had happened while we were on our honeymoon. My mom had not told me about any of it because she did not want to ruin our vacation or upset us while we traveled. I could not comprehend how they could so easily sacrifice their rights to Bryanna's final resting place; yet, upon further reflections, their actions were actually so typical of their other behavior since Danny's arrest that it was almost scary.

❧

A few weeks after the cemetery incident, my lawyer issued a check to me for my half of the proceeds from the earlier sale of my house. Danny's half would unfortunately have to remain in the escrow account until we obtained judgment against him in the civil suit. It seemed crazy not to give me all of the money, but I learned during the past two years that the law rarely makes any sense. My lawyer assured me that I would eventually be awarded Danny's share, but for now it was untouchable.

During that time, my pregnancy progressed at a normal healthy rate. As each and every family member became aware of it, no one was upset. I think everyone knew that I needed a baby, and they all equally shared my joy. I suffered some of the same ailments as with Bryanna such as morning sickness and heartburn, but all in all, I knew that it would be worth it in the end when I held a baby in my empty arms again.

❧

In late November 2002, I checked the felony offender's website to see if Danny was still near his father. To my great surprise, he had been moved to the opposite side of the state to a facility in a little town that was situated several miles from the main high-way. I had heard that his family hoped he would be placed in the prison only about an hour away from where we lived. Instead, he had been moved as far away from them as physically pos-sible. Later, I discovered that his family was very unhappy about his placement. I wondered why the officials had chosen such a distant location, and I finally concluded that maybe it was to separate him from the publicity of his crime. If his fellow inmates knew what he had done, no doubt, he would quickly become a target of violence. Maybe they had transferred him to control the level of crime inside the prison system. On the other hand, his family may have been demanding special treatment for him because of his "heart condition". He may have been moved to separate him from his family.

In early December 2002, my lawyer summoned me to his office. I had no clue why he wanted to see me, but I sincerely hoped that it concerned an out-of-court settlement with the radiologists. My dad accompanied me to the meeting where we found both of my lawyers waiting for us. They escorted us to a conference room and closed the door.

My lawyer then revealed that last week he was approached with a settlement proposal to my lawsuit. The sherriff's depart-ment had offered twenty-five thousand dollars to be dismissed from the litigation. My lawyers advised that even though it was not a large sum of money, it would provide us with funds for depositions and expert witnesses to continue pursuing the radi-ologists. On the negative side, by accepting the money now, if at a later date significant fault was found with the sherriff's depart-ment, I would be unable to recover any further compensation from them.

The decision was basically mine, but both of my lawyers advised me to accept the settlement from the county. After giving it considerable thought and discussing it with my family, I chose to follow their advice. Looking at the civil suit from an objective perspective, the true fault mainly rested with Danny and the radiologists. In a sense, it was a gamble to eliminate the sheriff's department, but in reality, the whole entire lawsuit held no guarantees. We could walk away from a jury trial with nothing. At least by taking the money now, it would not be a complete loss. My lawyers would also receive a small compensation for the significant amount of work that they had already invested in the project. If at some point the entire lawsuit folded, maybe I would still have some of the money from the county left.

On December 19, 2002, I met with my lawyer at the county courthouse. Together, we ascended the stairs to a meeting room where I signed the official papers releasing the sheriff's department and Detective Gray from my civil suit. Afterward, I received a check that already had my lawyer's one-third share of the proceeds and the physical expenses incurred by the case so far subtracted from it, leaving me with around fifteen thousand dollars. I had the money; however, it was not really mine to spend. I placed the funds in a separate bank account to cover all future expenses involving the civil law suit.

After the settlement was finalized, I heard that Detective Gray was released from employment at the sheriff's department. Personally, I still questioned his accountability in the entire process in light of the fact that Dr. Story failed to provide him with the needed evidence to remove Bryanna from our home. Yet, it was over now. The county had basically admitted their guilt, and I had accepted it. Again, I was being drawn down an unpredictable path with no turning back.

Before my lawyers told me that the sheriff's department wanted to settle, I was secretly hoping that the radiologists were planning to finally do the right thing and propose a resolution to the lawsuit. I began to realize just how far we really were from reaching an agreement with them. My lawyers warned me to prepare for a long, hard, unpleasant journey. Civil suits, in general, can take many years to be resolved. That fact held even truer for one as complicated as mine. The radiologists would deny their guilt until the bitter end. They wanted to defer the most blame to Danny and all remaining accountability to my family and me. They hoped that the threat of defiling my name with implications that I should have known about the abuse would intimidate me into dropping the lawsuit altogether. Furthermore, my lawyers predicted that the radiologists would use my profession as a nurse against me. They would attempt to say that as a nurse, I should have been educated in the signs of abuse. Since Danny's trial was over, the civil suit was really just beginning. The sheriff's department probably made a smart move by opting to admit their responsibility early in the proceedings and avoid any future negative publicity.

The Sheriff"s department's decision was based on the interrogatories that were completed over the past year since the suit was filed. Interrogatories are series of written questions that each side submits to specific individuals of their choice named in the suit. Since all of those were finished, the next step would involve discovery depositions from various people named in the suit.

My lawyers anticipated that I would be asked to give a discovery deposition sometime in the early months of 2003. A discovery deposition is a verbal interrogation performed outside of the courtroom at an informal setting such as a lawyer's office. A court reporter administers the "oath" for sworn testimony and tape records the entire process. The attorney that ordered the deposition generally begins the questioning of the witness. After he/she is finished, the other attorneys present are allowed to cross-examine the witness. The first lawyer is then allowed to finish with any follow-up inquiries. The purpose of depositions is to allow all parties involved an opportunity to gather information in preparation for a jury trial.

I dreaded the possibility that I might have to do that task while I was pregnant. I still worried that the stress I experienced might have a detrimental effect on my unborn baby, and reliving the nightmare of the past two years would definitely be a trying ordeal. I did not really want to do the deposition in my condition, but I feared that I might have no choice. Even though it would be very difficult for me, my pregnancy did not provide an adequate reason to drop the lawsuit and allow the radiologists to walk away unpunished. They had committed malpractice, and I was one of the only living relatives left to stand up for Bryanna's rights. Danny's family had completely deserted her. Furthermore, judgment against Danny was imperative to prevent him from making money associated with his crime. I had already witnessed his family's greed concerning Bryanna's marker. It would not surprise me to see Danny, one day, trying to sell his story as a way to repay his family for funding his criminal defense. For him to do that would be beyond reproach. I simply could not allow it. I was caught in a dilemma of seeking justice for my first child and protecting the health of my unborn second child. All I could do was pray that God would take care of it.

In March 2003, I received the first response to the civil suit from Danny's lawyers, Mr. Hood and Mr. Petty. It had taken them almost two years to reply. The response was so upsetting that I could not finish reading it while I was pregnant. Mr. Hood and Mr. Petty repeatedly named my mother, father, and me as perpetrators of Bryanna's abuse accusing us of concealing her injuries and even causing them instead of Danny! The response stated that she had visible damage that we should have reported. However, she had no apparent outward signs of abuse other than the fractured clavicle and right arm. His lawyers asked for my mom, dad, and me to be assigned liability in her death which would in effect reduce Danny's collective fault in the matter.

If they were trying to lessen Danny's responsibility so he would not have to pay me money, then that was ridiculous. In prison, he really had nothing to surrender to me. Writing such an ugly, hateful response was actually quite pointless. Danny had already admitted his guilt and was in prison. I felt like the response was an unnecessary spiteful stab at us. Several months later, Mr. Hood and Mr. Petty filed a motion to withdraw as Danny's counsel. It's just too bad that they did not abandon him before they wrote that really long, nasty answer to the civil suit complaint.

No Remorse

Early in the year 2003, Danny filed a "Motion to Correct and/
or Motion for Reduction of his Sentence." *He had served a mere
four months in prison and wasted no time in asking for his term to
be reduced,* I thought, bitterly. Although it appeared to be a very
quick request, I discovered later that by law, a defendant actually
has only one hundred and twenty days to file the petition. The
document was several pages long and contained many untruths
and exaggerations.

First, Danny claimed that he was entitled to a sentence reduction because his confession was recorded, and the tapes had been
"withheld" from him. He insisted that the recordings would
prove that he never said the statements written in his confession.
He named four people alluding to the existence of the tapes: my
dad, Mrs. Blakely, Det. Sharp, and finally, me.

To support his claim, Danny misused the quote from the
DCS worker, Mrs. Blakely's record, "We have the whole thing
on tape, and the Drapers don't know it." Actually, that statement
was referring to Detective Sharp and Detective Light secretly
watching Danny and I interact after Danny signed the confession. Since she wrote the entry based on her conversation with
Detective Sharp, Danny cited him as the third person acknowl-
edging the presence of a taped confession.

The final person he accused of mentioning a recording was
me. I cannot account 100 percent for the other three people, but
I can certainly say that I do not know about the existence of any
tapes. Danny claimed that when I entered the interrogation room
after his confession that I asked him, "Why did you tell them all
of those things? Were you trying to protect me?" In the motion,
he wrote, "The question has to be asked, where had she heard 'all
of those things?' One would have to conclude she heard them on

the same tapes that her dad told my dad that he had heard. After all, they were in the same place, together, the whole time the questioning was going on."

First of all, I don't remember asking him those two particular questions. Secondly, he was the one to pose the question of where I had heard "all those things" insinuating that I had listened to the entire confession from another location. If he had not truly said "all those things," why would he even be asking where I had heard them? In a feeble attempt to exonerate himself, he actually incriminated himself by confirming that he did admit to abusing her as written in the confession.

Yet, to give the devil his due, I will say the fact that Mrs. Blakely wrote in her record, "We have the whole thing on tape, and the Drapers don't know it" could be enough to question the existence of a recorded confession. I do not know why she documented that statement in an official record, but I do know that I never listened to any tapes. In the motion, Danny insinuated that my father and I were in another room observing his interrogation the whole entire time, but in reality we were not even present at the police station for a majority of the evening.

The second argument that Danny posed to have his sentence reduced was that the officers "used mental threats and mental torture over and above extreme measures to force me to believe I had to sign the confession before I could get relief. I was in such a state of mind I would have signed anything and my actions prove it. The interrogation was so intimidating that it frightened me to no end. The officers would get in my face, yell, call me names, curse me, told me I was going to die and then end up in hell. I, a grown man, felt so threatened and was so afraid, I would have signed anything or done anything to get them to stop their torture."

If the two officers did indeed tell Danny that night he was going to "die and end up in hell," regrettably, they were probably right. The two gentlemen that interrogated Danny were both professed Christians. Afterward, Detective Sharp revealed to us that listening to the chilling account of what Danny did to Bryanna was so disturbing that he and Detective Light had to take frequent brief breaks in the hallway to compose themselves. That proved Danny's confession was so horrible that the only way he would have signed it was if he had actually done it.

Danny argued that he should not have signed the confession because it was incorrect. One of the delays in completing the process that night was allowing Danny time to proofread the confession and make corrections. There are actual markings on the type written copy where he did that. If it was inaccurate, Danny should not have signed it. He was a "grown man" as he said and capable of deciding on his own what he should and should not sign. On the contrary, I believe that the confession was the first time that he told the truth in a year, and perhaps the last time he will tell the truth ever.

The third reason that Danny presented for a sentence reduction was that his lawyers did not provide him with adequate legal representation. "It is given that my counsel Mr. Hood and Mr. Petty could have gone further in bargaining for a lesser sentence, because of the discovery of possible false testimony concerning the tapes. My council on TV stated that the discrepancies concerning the tapes would be thoroughly investigated. I am disappointed that the investigation has never happened. While I appreciate their assistance in overcoming the death penalty threats made by the prosecution, I now believe much more could have been done to get a more reasonable result. I was led to believe the plea accepted was the best that could be obtained." Judge Strong asked Danny if he felt he had been given sufficient legal counsel exactly for that reason—to prevent Danny from being granted a sentence reduction or new trial at a later date.

The fourth element that Danny mentioned in his motion was the outrageous accusation that my dad was acting as an "armed" police agent to bring him into custody. My dad had a handgun carry permit and Danny used that knowledge to imply that my dad practically took him to the police station at gun point. In truth, my dad did not even have a gun with him that day. Danny further accused my father of making a bargain with the police and district attorney's office to bring Danny in for questioning in exchange for no charges being placed against his wife and daughter.

Danny stated, "According to the DCS report, the DA was responsible for working it out so I would be the one to take the rap for murder. I trusted my father-in-law and his judgment. I never ever thought he would double-cross me or lie to me. However, he must have been offered a deal that he could not refuse for his acting as a police agent—he was even armed. If he got me in for questioning, it appears police agreed to leave my wife and mother-in-law alone by not pursuing any questioning or investigation of their role in caring for the baby and their activities."

No such agreement was ever even discussed. Actually, my innocence remained questionable until the officers witnessed me speaking with Danny after he had signed the confession. Now that I know General Steele better, I know if he thought any guilt resided with my family or me, he would not have hesitated to prosecute us to the full extent of the law, the same as he did Danny.

The final accusation in the motion was probably the most frightening. Danny alleged that since the mother had cared for the baby during the majority of her life, she "had every opportunity to inflict and or cover up wounds. In fact the medical examiner's testimony from September 23, 2002, states that the subdural hematoma present at the time of Bryanna's death was 'as much as several hours old,' effectively taking me out of the picture as the perpetrator of this injury. The medical examiner also said that the subdural hematoma was the only injury in and of itself that was traumatic enough to cause death. These facts cast an unfavorable light on any arrangements made to keep Angela or other members of her family from being questioned about any and all injuries."

There was a valid reason that General Steele did not question both of us. In a previous similar case, both parents were interrogated about abusing their child, and the stories they told gave each other an alibi; thus the district attorney was unable to charge either parent with the abuse and the case was dismissed. General Steele did not want that to happen with Bryanna so he chose to question Danny alone because all of their evidence pointed to him perpetrating the injuries. Danny further stated that the numerous internal injuries mentioned in the autopsy report should have produced bruises and swelling and accused me of not reporting them or of the autopsy report being exaggerated. I took Bryanna to the doctor's office sixteen times during the sixteen weeks of her life. No physician ever documented swelling or bruising other than her arm fracture and rashes. The fact that I had her examined by health professionals sixteen times and admitted to the hospital twice does not constitute a failure to report her illnesses and injuries on my part.

Furthermore, what would it benefit the pathologist to exaggerate on the autopsy? I can think of nothing. However, the true perpetrator of the injuries was a health care professional with extensive experience and medical training in fractures and human anatomy. Could that educated person have inflicted injuries with the intention of leaving no marks or swelling? He also actively participated in the taking and processing of many of her x-rays; thus, giving him occasion to manipulate her position on the exam table to disguise injuries. He was the one who said we had enough pictures of her during the bone survey, and the x-ray process was stopped. Did he purposefully not want any side views taken of her ribs just in case he had fractured one of them? Those were very important questions to consider in the argument over who precisely had the capability to cover up her injuries.

If we had actually had a trial, I dare to think about what accusations Danny would have made to be cleared of his crime. He might have implicated my mom, my dad, or me of abusing Bryanna—anyone but himself. After all the grief we had already suffered in losing her, I cannot imagine the pain that such hurtful allegations would have caused. In the final sentence of the motion, he wrote, "these things should be grounds for a reduction of sentence at the least, if not much more."

Sometimes I contemplated if it would be beneficial to talk with Danny about why he did it, but decided at that time, it probably would not be. In my own quest for closure, I have discussed him with several family members, friends, and my counselor. From those conversations, a common theory seemed to arise. Maybe Danny loved me so much that he did not know how to share me with another human being. In many aspects, I cared for him more like a parent than a partner. He relied on me to meet most of his day-to-day needs. I also managed our financial situation, reminding and reprimanding him about our monetary limitations. He was able to enjoy himself for years in a basically care-free environment. It was I who shouldered the worry of making our ends meet. Then suddenly, I had to care for another human entirely dependent upon me for her existence. Instead of showering all my affections on Danny, I desperately needed his help. I believe that deep down inside, he begrudged her intrusion upon his way of life and became extremely resentful of her. Furthermore, he may have envied his mother's relationship with Bryanna. On a subconscious level, he simply refused to share his two main caregivers with Bryanna. Eventually, that led to him detesting her as evidenced by the hateful abuse he inflicted upon her. Selfishly, he refused to accept the changes that she imposed on his lifestyle so he finally just eliminated her in a fit of rage, hoping that everything would quickly return to "normal," but instead, after she was gone, our lives would never be "normal" again. If one asked Danny why he killed her, he would not verbalize that sequence of events, but I believe it to be the closest that I will ever come to figuring out a reason for his actions.

Looking back at how events progressed, it is easy to see God hard at work protecting me. If even one incident had changed or happened out of sequence, imagine how differently the results could have been. What if Danny had not confessed at the police station that night? His motion proved that he would have accused anyone and everyone except himself of murdering Bryanna. What if he had a lawyer present at the police station? Any decent attorney would have advised him to say nothing. The night of his confession, he told me that he "loved" me and to "go on" with my life, but merely days would pass before he completely changed his mind. I think it is possible that in the end, he would have accused me of killing Bryanna to avoid imprisonment. I could have been punished for a crime that I did not even know was happening! Therefore, I must praise God for watching over me. I faithfully told the truth throughout the entire incident even when it was painful, or I thought afterwards that I had made a mistake. In my heart, I believe that God honors the truth and maybe that was why he chose to protect me.

There will always be those people who question, "How could the mother not have known what he was doing to that baby?" My only answer is—love. Love blinded me to the point that I could not conceive of him harming his own child. I trusted him with all my heart, and I mistakenly assumed that he cared for Bryanna in the same way I did. I had known Danny for eleven years and never seen him do anything remotely violent. There was no reason to be suspicious; yet, still I asked him at the pediatrician's office if he had ever done anything to hurt Bryanna even accidentally. He looked me straight in the eye and said, "No." He was my husband, and I believed him. As everyone in our family blamed the medical professionals for Bryanna's injuries, he went along with us entirely. During that whole time, he was the only person who knew the truth, and he lied to all of us. Unfortunately we were all fooled by him, including his own mother and father.

I am grateful to God because I know it could be so much worse. I could be in prison right now instead of Danny! It is not for me to question God's divine plan. Yes, He took my daughter, but He must have had a very good reason. I may never know it on this side of eternity, but I cling to the hope that it will be revealed to me in the afterlife. At least I know she is not suffering. He has given me another child to love. Perhaps the answer to why all of this happened rests within this new life. I only know that I do trust God. His grace has always been and ever will be sufficient.

> And he said unto me, My grace is sufficient for thee: for my strength is made perfect in weakness. Most gladly therefore will I rather glory in my infirmities, that the power of Christ may rest upon me.
>
> Therefore I take pleasure in my infirmities, in reproaches, in necessities, in persecutions, in distresses for Christ's sake: for when I am weak, then I am strong. (2 Corinthians 12: 9, 10)

Depositions

On February 25, 2003, Mrs. Blakely was the first person to give a discovery deposition concerning the civil suit. Next, Dr. Story's (the physician that wrote the CAT scan addendum on the day of Bryanna's autopsy) interrogation was recorded on March 21, 2003. Many discrepancies existed between Mrs. Blakely's and Dr. Story's testimonies. One astonishing point from Mrs. Blakely's notes was a statement that she made about Danny during the first interview at the pediatrician's office where she wrote, "No noted signs of deception ... maintained eye contact and open posture nor did he back away when Detective Gray moved in closer." It was very interesting that people who were trained in detecting deceit were fooled by him. He was good at lying to everyone—even skilled, educated individuals.

During her deposition, Mrs. Blakely indicated that she wanted to remove Bryanna from our care, but neither the pediatrician, Dr. Green, nor the radiologist, Dr. Story, would commit to the two words—"child abuse." A later deposition from Detective Gray confirmed her testimony. However, Dr. Story claimed that he told them on May 16, 2000 that the fractures and the head injury were "significant" findings. Furthermore, he insisted that he used the words "child abuse and Battered Child Syndrome" during the meeting to describe his opinion of the films. However if he was convinced that Bryanna was a classic case of child abuse, why did he wait over three weeks after the May 16, 2000 meeting to make the official addendum of his findings? Not to mention, he only made the addendum because Detective Sharp called him from the autopsy room and insisted that he do it. I believe that if Dr. Story had really used the words "child abuse" on May 16, 2000 that Detective Gray and Mrs. Blakely would have removed Bryanna from our home and she might be alive today.

I can only speculate about the differences between Mrs. Blakely's and Dr. Story's testimonies, but there was one point during Dr. Story's deposition that I was absolutely sure he was being untruthful. He claimed that he met with Danny and me two times in his office and accused us openly of child abuse. We did go to his office on one occasion, June 28, 2000, to ask him about the addendum to Bryanna's CAT scan in the computer. That was the one and only time that I went to his office. He testified, under oath, that we came to his office on May 18, 2000 in the evening and asked him what he had told Detective Gray and Mrs. Blakely during their meeting on May 16, 2000. Several years later during my deposition, I set the record straight by saying that I never went to see Dr. Story on May 18, and as a matter of fact, I knew nothing about the May 16 meeting between Dr. Story and the DCS until months after Danny's arrest.

After the two depositions were completed that spring, on June 6, 2003, the county court system granted Dr. Story summary judgment. A summary judgment means the court decides a verdict without a trial based on evidence that no material facts are left to be disputed in the case. Material facts are details that would influence the outcome of a trial. A summary judgment may resolve the entire case or settle only a portion of the case as it did in my instance. Basically, what it meant for me was that Dr. Story was dismissed from the proceedings.

The summary judgment was granted based on two inaccurate allegations from the defense. First, Dr. Story claimed that he should be granted immunity because he was reporting abuse. In reality, he was charged with not reporting the abuse. Secondly, the defense alleged that Dr. Story should be exempt from malpractice because he never received payment for his services; thus, no physician-patient relationship was ever established between Dr. Story and Bryanna. Based on those two erroneous arguments, the defense asserted that no material facts were left to be disputed causing the county court system to grant Dr. Story summary judgment. My two lawyers immediately contested the decision with the state supreme court system. Thus, the entire matter became engaged in an appeals process that lasted for over two years. No further progress was made in the case until October 2005. At that time, one of my lawyers notified me that the state supreme court had overturned the summary judgment ruling because it had been made erroneously without a complete review of all the pertinent facts. Dr. Story would remain in the lawsuit after all, and finally, the litigation resumed.

The state supreme court based their decision on two important points. First of all, the immunity for reporting abuse only granted protection to individuals that actually notified the authorities. Mrs. Blakely's sworn testimony plainly stated that Dr. Story did not report child abuse findings to her; thus causing disputed material facts to arise that could only be resolved during a jury trial. Secondly, the state supreme court determined that when Dr. Story agreed to review Bryanna's CAT scan and x-rays on May 16, 2000 that he engaged in a physician-patient relationship with her.

After over two years of the case being pretty much completely dormant, my life had really changed. I had remarried, had a baby, and moved onto different obligations. Bryanna was, of course, always somewhere in my thoughts, but as far as the lawsuit, I had long ago decided that it was a lost cause. I figured that the radiologists would find some way to avoid admitting any responsibility related to the death of Bryanna. Now, with Dr. Story's summary judgment reversed, my hope was revitalized.

My deposition had been delayed because of the appeals process. Since the law suit was active again, my interrogation was scheduled for the following year on May 26, 2006. It was a long hard day filled with difficult questions and painful memories. At the end, the defense attorneys, of course, asked me if my law suit was all about money or "is there something that you hope to gain?" To which I replied, "I am not here because of money. I am here because my baby died and some people need to take respon-sibility—whether that is the radiologists that missed things on scans or Danny in the prison. Her—it's for her justice! And I know I don't want to see it happen to any other baby!" I was glad for the opportunity to declare that the intentions of my law suit ran much deeper than money. Sharing my story would hopefully prevent another child from dying.

⁂

Although my deposition was completed in May 2006, due to the slow court system, another two years passed before the the case was finally settled. I am not legally allowed to say anything fur-ther on the matter. In the spring of 2008, I signed the papers to end the law suit forever.

With the malpractice suit behind me, only one item remained on the agenda for resolution—damages against Danny. The judge had signed a summary judgment against him concern-ing my civil case in March 2003, based on his conviction and confession; however it stated that damages concerning Danny's fault would be determined at a later date. At that point in time, Danny's proceeds from the sale of the house were locked away in an escrow account awaiting the final decision in my civil suit. In March 2003, the "later date" was presumed to be during a jury trial when comparative fault would be dispersed among all the guilty parties. That changed when I settled the other portion of the law suit. Only Danny was left to face the panel of twelve of his peers.

My lawyer guessed it would probably take about one day in court to obtain a final judgment against Danny. Only two wit-nesses would be required to present evidence, Detective Sharp and me. Afterward, my lawyer assumed, most likely, the jury would rule in my favor. I really did not care about the money. I just wanted all of the court proceedings over. Plus, the judgment against Danny was important so that he would never be able to profit from his crime. I wondered if Danny would be allowed to come home for the trial phase of the proceeding. My lawyer doubted that the judge would permit Danny to travel because his presence was really not required. However, knowing Danny, I was positive that he would want to come back home and be close to his family for a few days. Not to mention, he would want to voice his opinion on the matter. The one thing I had discovered for sure in the past few years was he had no shame in pleading his cause.

Several years ago, my lawyer had advised me to have no contact with Danny. At that time, it was not a problem because I did not want to speak to him. Now years later, I slowly found myself thinking about talking with him. I wanted to hear from his mouth why he had murdered her even though the possibility existed that he would not be able to tell me anything. With a final judgment rendered on my civil suit, I should be able to speak with him safely without any restrictions. Perhaps what I had been waiting for all along was the freedom to ask him "why."

The summer of 2008 passed and was followed by fall with no court date against Danny ever scheduled. The following February 2009, Danny filed "A Motion to Reconsider and Demand for Jury Trial." The court system reviewed it and determined that certain matters needed to be clarified for the defendant's benefit. The new order created an impossible dilemma because it meant that Danny had the right to appear in person for the civil trial, but the state would not pay any transportation expenses for him. Evidently, Danny had multiple criminal appeals pending in state and federal court to have his life sentence overturned. The judge wanted to wait and see if Danny was sent home for a hearing concerning any of those petitions, and the trial on my civil suit could take place at the same time. Unfortunately until that time, my civil suit would be postponed while we waited for Danny to exhaust all of his appeals.

I mistakenly thought that part of the process of accepting a plea bargain meant that he would have to serve his entire sentence without relief. However, my lawyer clarified that an appeal was not exactly the correct term for what Danny was doing. He was filing habeas corpus petitions which are requests to be released for unlawful imprisonment. Danny claimed that he was wrongfully detained due to poor representation from his lawyers and an improperly performed confession.

Danny lived a very solitary existence in prison, locked in protective custody separated from the other detainees due to multiple death threats from fellow inmates. The only activity that he had to pass the time was studying law books and filing habeas corpus petitions one right after the other indefinitely. At one point, Danny had even demanded a new proceeding, but that was quickly retracted when General Steele informed him that he would gladly grant a new trial, but Danny would probably receive the death penalty. The last argument that Danny filed in 2008 was based on my deposition from 2006 and claimed that the state was hiding the tapes of his confession and that the entire investigation of Bryanna's death was "null, void, unconstitutional, and illegal" because the mother was never questioned.

The judge's new motion created an unfeasible predicament by saying that Danny had to be present for the civil trial, yet left no possible way to get him there. Danny was being extremely uncooperative about the matter to even demand a jury trial. He had refused to sign a waiver to be present in court on multiple occasions. Danny was simply not going to agree to anything that would make it easier for me. According to my lawyer, he had fought the entire civil suit "tooth and nail" from the start.

I waited for another year to pass into 2010. No mention was ever made of transporting Danny for any criminal proceedings. I called every few months to check on the progress, but the answer was always the same. It was a decade since Bryanna's birth. While waiting for the hearing to occur, my divorce lawyer passed away.

Although our relationship had only been professional during the past decade, sadly, it felt more like I had lost a good friend. I did not know what would happen to my law suit without him available to oversee it. However, as it worked out, my lawyer's stepson assumed his practice and became my new representation in the matter. He told me the same story that I had heard for the past two years: the order that the judge had signed prohibited my case from moving forward until Danny had exhausted all of his habeas corpus petitions, and he had no idea when that would be. In desperation, I even contacted the judge's office to express my need for closure, but the judge would not speak to me concerning the case at all. The secretary said she would relay my concerns to him, but legally he could not talk to me. She described the case as "very complicated."

I asked my new lawyer if I still should abstain from contacting Danny in light of the summary judgment against him. He could not forbid me to have contact with him, but he recommended that I did not. Furthermore, he seriously doubted that Danny would talk to me due to his pending habeas corpus petitions. Any good lawyer would warn Danny not to speak to me as I am a potential witness and could testify to anything that he said.

I listened to the warning carefully, but it did not discourage me from wanting to question Danny. If the restrictions placed by my first lawyer so many years ago were finally lifted, then I was prepared to seek the difficult answers that I had pondered for so long. While waiting, I had been able to grow in strength and courage to face Danny again. Rather than waste a trip to see him when he might refuse to admit me, I wrote Danny a very simple and direct letter. It merely stated that I had a lot of questions. I wanted to know if he would either be willing to see me in person or write to me. I asked him to please respond and let me know one way or the other. A rented P.O. Box provided a safe way to correspond with him without revealing my actual physical address. Six months seemed to be a reasonable amount of time to see if he would communicate with me. Postage stamp in place, I dropped the letter in the mailbox, and resigned yet again to wait.

After six weeks passed with no response, I wrote Danny another letter, and that time, I was not as restrained. Years of my feelings were vented on two pieces of paper. First, I told him that he may not want to talk to me, but that I had some things that I needed to say to him. Furthermore, I was tired of only hearing him appeal to get out of prison. The letter ended with, "All this time has passed, ten years, and I have yet to hear 'I am sorry for what I did to you—to her—our flesh and blood.'" Again, the envelope was dropped in the mail, and I resigned to wait for a response. Before sending it, I double checked at least three times to make sure that I had used the correct address and prisoner number.

Two more months passed as I anxiously checked my P.O. Box every few days. My angry outburst was an attempt to elicit a response from him, but it did not. Knowing that the P.O. Box would expire at the end of November 2010 compelled me to contact him one more time. The final letter was very brief and explained to him that he would have until the end of November to answer me. Two more months should be enough time for him to make a decision. I did not want to leave the line of communication open indefinitely waiting for a response. If he did not write me within six months, he probably had no intention of contacting me ever.

The end of November arrived with no word from Danny. The mailbox was checked every few days only to be repeatedly empty. I decided that I would have to accept the fact that Danny had no intention of ever explaining his actions to me. After the unanswered letters, and many calls to my lawyer, I basically determined that the civil suit against Danny would never be settled. A proposal from my lawyers for a trial via a televised monitor so that Danny would not have to be transported across the state gave me fleeting hope that the case could be resolved, but nothing ever came of it.

As more time passed, I gradually forgot about the civil suit against Danny. The circumstances set by the judge made it practically impossible to be settled. I concentrated on raising my son and performing well at my job. I stopped contacting my lawyer to ask about it. The ruling was important to me mainly for the assurance that Danny could never profit from his crime, but as the year 2012 approached, even that seemed to fade from my thoughts.

Resolution

On February 9, 2012, I received a surprise call from my new lawyer. Evidently, the judge had finally ordered for the civil trial to move forward. Danny was to be transported to our county jail for the proceeding scheduled on March 5, 2012. The news completely caught me off guard. The case had not even crossed my mind in months. Mistakenly, I had assumed it would never be resolved; now, there was less than a month to prepare. Panic coursed through my veins at the thought that I would have to see him again after all that time.

My lawyer began to slowly prepare me for the hearing. He described how the process would progress that day. Four witnesses would take the stand on Bryanna's behalf—the current district attorney (General Steele had retired about a year prior), Detective Light, a nurse practitioner (to explain the autopsy results), and finally me. I would have my one opportunity to tell my story. Facing him again after all those years made me feel extremely anxious. To prepare for the hearing, I reviewed my diary, refreshing my memory concerning the events surrounding Bryanna's sickness and Danny's deceitful actions. I could not find any of my medical bills for the psychiatric treatment that I received after his arrest. My testimony would be the only proof of the misery that he had subjected me to throughout the years.

My lawyer was unsure if Danny would have legal representation during the proceeding. His family had tried to hire an attorney for him, but probably no one would take his case. Basically, Danny was already a condemned man representing very little interest to any law firm. Still, I was shocked that his family would pay money for his counsel when he was already labeled guilty from the previous summary judgment.

The county jail considered Danny to be a major flight risk. The officers were not very pleased at the prospect of housing him for the civil suit. Danny would be strapped into an electric shock belt during the court proceedings, and if he stepped out of line at all, the guards would not hesitate to push the button on the remote. The device contained enough juice to knock him to the floor. Based on that information, my lawyer assured me that Danny would not harass me in any way. My main fear was that he would badger me with questions concerning his habeas corpus petitions to spread the blame away from himself. Everything that I had read from him since his arrest pointed to him seeking an opportunity to point his accusatory finger at me. However, the judge had already decreed that was not going to be permitted. The session was for the purpose of awarding damages on the pre-existing summary judgment. It was not going to be a day where Danny pled his case for being released from prison.

⫸⫷

On March 5, 2012, my parents and I arrived at the courthouse around nine in the morning. We could not help but reminisce about the long terrible days that we had already spent there. A little while later other family members joined us to provide emotional support including my sister, brother, sister-in-law, aunt, and two uncles. After completing the search process at the door, I frantically scanned the lobby for my two lawyers. Neither one of them were present, but I quickly spotted Danny's family on the other side of the room—his mother, stepfather, dad, and aunt. Wanting to see if we could be put in a room away from them, I tried to call my lawyer's cell phone but there was no answer. Unable to find isolation from them, we moved to the opposite side of the lobby. It was undeniably uncomfortable to be in close proximity to them. I occupied myself by mentally preparing to face Danny in a few short minutes. He could casually disregard the letters that I sent him prison, but for one day he would not be able to ignore me.

While I waited impatiently for my lawyers to appear, Danny's dad walked close by me to go to the bathroom. My posture stiffened instinctively fearing what he might say. The last I had heard, they blamed us for everything, and I anticipated no kind words coming from his mouth. Glancing at me quickly, he mumbled a barely audible "hi," and that was all he said. Stunned, I muttered an almost incoherent greeting in return. He had definitely appeared to approach me with some unknown intention, but I told him with my eyes and stance that I had nothing to say to him. It was not the time or place for him to hurl accusations at me.

After the confrontation with Danny's dad and several trips to the bathroom, I glimpsed my lawyers approaching from the other side of the lobby. Taking me aside to a private witness room, they explained that Danny now wanted to settle out of court. Evidently, the judge had informed him that he would not be permitted to argue his criminal case at the proceeding. Danny's main purpose in postponing my civil suit for so long was that he mistakenly thought he would be allowed to question my dad and I concerning the night he was arrested. When the judge advised him that would not be tolerated, Danny suddenly wanted to settle without a trial and give me the seven thousand dollars held in escrow. The decision rested in my hands as to whether or not we would proceed with a jury trial. For ten years he could have ended the suit by signing the escrow to me, but he had repeatedly refused. It was Danny that had insisted on a jury trial. Should I let him off so easily? My mind raced attempting to decide on a course of action in such a brief time period. I never imagined that he would change his mind after he arrived.

My lawyers left me alone with my family for a few minutes to make my decision. I looked at each of them and asked the same question, "If you were me, what would you do?" They all gave the same answer, "It's your decision. We are behind you whatever you choose." My heart knew what I needed to do, but I hated to be selfish and put them through yet another miserable day on my behalf. I asked them, "If I chose to do this, are you all strong enough to go with me." My main concern was my mother, but she replied, "I am here for you. Do whatever you need to do." The easy way out was so tempting—just collect the escrow account and never have to see Danny again, but I knew in my heart that it was never about the money. The trial was about justice, and my one and only chance to share with the world—what he put us all through. All of those years filled with slighting remarks and accusations from his family could end with the record being set straight. With God's help, I felt strong enough to tackle the challenge.

My lawyers returned to the room stating that the judge needed my decision immediately. "Let's do the trial," I announced and followed them to the courtroom. The rows were filled with potential jurors. I slid a note to my lawyer beside me that asked, "When can my family come in?"

"After jury selection is complete," he whispered to me. Just two rows behind the defense table, Danny's four family members were perched on their seats. I distinctly remember my lawyer telling me for impartiality reasons, both the supporting families would be asked to sit in the back two rows because the judge did not want Danny's family close to him. It definitely seemed unfair that his family was present only two rows back while my relatives waited outside. However, I really should have realized by then that the defense generally has all of the rights.

Interrupting my thoughts, the door at the front of the courtroom snapped open to reveal Danny escorted between two armed guards. He was clad in a black and white striped county jumpsuit and appeared to have lost a significant amount of weight, but it was really hard to determine in that baggy outfit. His shoulders seemed permanently slumped forward giving him the look of a very old man. The thick black rimmed glasses that covered his eyes looked extremely odd and out of place on his face. Danny had always worn his hair long, not long over the ears or neck, but thick. Now it was shaven down in a GI style, and the few sprigs left sticking up were almost completely grey. Danny never once glanced my way.

The armed guards led Danny to his seat at the defense table on the right side of the courtroom and then situated themselves at arm's length behind him. No lawyer was seated beside him. Everyone stood up as the honorable judge entered the courtroom and called the session to order. Jury selection commenced with the judge calling sixteen distinct names as people filed to the front of the room and took seats in the jury box. My lawyer opened with a brief statement to prepare the audience for the emotional content of the trial. He warned that it would be difficult to hear the details of Bryanna's abuse especially if they had children. Afterward, each potential jury member stated their name, where they worked, and if they had children or grandchildren. The pool represented a variety of occupations from a foreman, call center staff, home-makers, and a nurse. The judge offered Danny the opportunity to question the jurors, but he said "I don't know what to ask. I feel like a sitting duck." The selection process continued as my lawyers and Danny passed a paper back and forth to the judge requesting dismissal of certain candidates. Each time one of the individuals was rejected, an alternate took their place until both sides agreed upon twelve members.

The judge counseled the chosen group on how the trial would be conducted, providing specific instructions and definitions of legal terminology. Basically, Danny's guilt in Bryanna's death had already been determined in a summary judgment from March 2003. The only task left to complete was to place a monetary fig-ure on my deceased daughter's life.

When the judge finished briefing the jury, my new lawyer pre-sented an official opening statement. I looked behind me to make sure that my family was present as he began. They all sat on the back row with solemn looks on their faces. "I am here today as the voice of Bryanna. Her suffering and agony is going to speak to you from the grave. I am going to ask you to do the unthinkable—place a monetary value on the life a child. Most children are afraid of the monster under the bed. For Bryanna the monster was in the room with her; it was her dad. Daniel Draper tortured and beat Bryanna for most of the four short months of her life. Today, you are going to hear from four people—the district attorney's office that prosecuted Daniel, a qualified health professional that will review her autopsy and injuries in detail, Detective Light regarding Daniel Draper's confession statement, and finally, Angela, herself, concerning the pain and suffering that she and Bryanna endured at the hands of Daniel Draper. She will describe the deception perpetrated by him. I ask that you please give her the respect she deserves to speak her story to you here today. There were two deaths in this case, the physical death of Bryanna and the spiritual death of Angela. We are asking for you to do the unspeakable—grant ten million dollars for the pain and suffering that they endured and ten million dollars in punitive damages to set a precedent in this community that Daniel Draper's behavior will not be tolerated."

Afterward, the judge turned to Danny and asked if he would like to make an opening statement. In his position, would he say anything? I wondered and quickly found out, yes, he would. "I am continuing to appeal my case," he began, clearing his throat. "I discovered new information about six years ago that indicated some underhanded things went on concerning my confession. I can't bring this out because it is not permissible. So the case stands as it was when I plead guilty ten years ago. All I can ask for is fair judgment. It is what it is." He ended sharply, with a note of bitterness to his voice.

After the opening statements were completed, the jury and witnesses were sworn in. The judge asked Danny if he wanted the witnesses to leave the courtroom during each other's testimonies and Danny replied yes, he did. All of the witnesses except the district attorney were escorted out the back door. Knowing that I was scheduled to testify, I feared that I would have to leave as well. I whispered to my lawyer sitting next to me, "Do I have to go?" He shook his head no.

The current district attorney took the stand. His main job was to enter Danny's guilty verdict dated September 26, 2002 as an exhibit and confirm that Danny was currently serving a life sentence for first degree murder and aggravated child abuse. The second document produced for exhibit was Bryanna's autopsy performed on June 5, 2000 and received to the district attorney's office on March 25, 2001. In conclusion the district attorney declared, "Our conviction in 2002 against Daniel Draper has prevailed against every attack that he has presented. He pled guilty to first degree murder to avoid the death sentence."

Next, a nurse practitioner testified as an expert witness to explain the autopsy results. Using diagrams of the body and brain via an overhead device, she described each injury in terms that the jury could easily understand. To show why the pathologist had used the diagnosis "Multiple Trauma due to Battered Child Syndrome," she clarified that some fractures were old and others were new as the abuse had occurred over a period of time. She described the force, blunt trauma, and potential mechanisms that could have possibly caused each individual insult. "The ribs are free floating bones meaning that each time Bryanna breathed, cried, moved, or was touched the grating on the nerves and surrounding tissues would cause severe pain. The symptoms, which Bryanna exhibited, were fussiness, decreased appetite, and vomiting—all present with a brain injury. A mother caring for a child with these injuries would be under terrible emotional distress and probably need psychiatric treatment," she concluded.

Following her vividly detailed testimony, Detective Light took the stand. First, my lawyers established that Danny was not coerced or forced to confess. As soon as Detective Light confirmed that, Danny's mother began to speak out loud from her seat behind Danny, "Oh yes, he was." She was ignored so she repeated it a couple of more times, getting louder each time. The bailiff went straight to where she sat and told her she had to leave the courtroom. She replied, "No, I am not leaving," and stayed firmly planted in her seat. "Oh yes you are," he commanded, appearing to be prepared to physically remove her if necessary. Finally when she stood up, he took her by the arm and led her out the back door. My brother would later tell me that he heard the bailiff reprimanding her that she could be charged with contempt of court and go to jail for such outbursts.

After the commotion of removing Danny's mother was over, Detective Light proceeded to read Danny's entire confession verbatim to the jury. I was actually disappointed that his mother had to leave. To my knowledge, she had never seen or heard Danny's confession; I had hoped that finally she would have to face the horror of his crime in full, but it was not meant to be. As Detective Light approached the end of the confession, he lost control of his emotions. His voice was tremulous as tears formed in his eyes. I studied each face in the jury as he read it to determine their reaction. The nurse on the back row was perched on the edge of her seat with a pained look of deep concentration covering her face. A lady on the front row was uncontrollably weeping. A young gentlemen on the end (he appeared to be barely eighteen) looked totally disgusted by what he was hearing.

Danny declined cross examining the detective.

After Detective Light exited the courtroom, the judge asked the jury if they wanted to take a lunch break. The young aggravated gentleman on the end signaled with his hand to "keep going." The general consensus was no lunch even though it was half past noon. Thankfully, the judge issued a short fifteen minute recess because my testimony was scheduled next. As I stood up to leave, I noticed Danny's dad trying to speak to him, but the two guards swiftly ushered Danny out the back door. Evidently, Danny was not going to be permitted to remain in the courtroom during breaks or have any contact with his family during the session.

I utilized the short break to mentally prepare for my upcoming testimony. When court reconvened, my lawyers presented life expectancy charts to the jury based on recent statistics. The diagrams showed averages of how long Bryanna and I should have lived together representing a total loss of around forty-eight years of love and companionship. Those years were what Danny had stolen from us of with his horrid inexcusable actions.

Afterward, I shakily took the witness stand, one more time, hopefully the last. It was my chance to finally tell my story. Danny had gotten off easily when he pled guilty. Now he would finally face a jury of twelve of his peers. Would they condemn him? My voice sounded low and hoarse, but I couldn't seem to clear it. I began by telling the jury how long Danny and I had known each other before Bryanna was born and that Bryanna was a planned pregnancy. I described her difficult delivery and how Danny worked nightshift and volunteered to stay up at night caring for her when he was off so that I could rest.

"She was such a good baby. She hardly cried at all and was almost sleeping through the night by the time she was two-months-old," I stated as my lawyer placed a picture of us together in the hospital shortly after her birth on the overhead for the jury to see. My face looked red, puffy, and exhausted, but at the same time smiling and pleased. "She was beautiful with her dark head of hair," I managed, still holding myself together.

I described her illness, the fussiness, the doctor's visits, and how she vomited up her entire bottle almost daily. "At age two months, after her first set of shots, she was hospitalized with suspected meningitis, taken away from me into two separate treatment rooms where I could hear her screaming. Afterwards, she was returned to me with a broken arm. We suspected the hospital staff because of the way it happened, and Danny fully supported this illusion," I finished as my lawyer introduced a second picture of Bryanna on the overhead with her tiny little arm in a splint.

"The following week, she had the bone survey. Danny knew the technicians and convinced them to do only a minimal number of films on her—no side views that might have shown the rib fractures. Danny was the one to point out the clavicle fracture, and misled me to believe it probably resulted from the traumatic birth process. The following day, we were called back to the pediatrician's office where the department of children's services waited to speak to us. From that point forward, I was terribly afraid that someone was going to take my sick baby away from me. Danny lied to me in the doctor's office that day when I asked him if he had hurt Bryanna in any way. He persuaded me to believe that the injuries had occurred in the treatment room at the hospital."

My story continued with her death, and the long ten month wait for the autopsy results, only to be told there was a "big question" on them. "At that point I again became suspicious and asked Danny one more time if he had ever done anything to Bryanna even accidentally. He denied it and even became angry at me for asking." My voice was still husky, but I had managed not to cry until I reached the day of Danny's confession. My composure was completely lost as I recounted Danny hitting me in the head to demonstrate how forceful he was with Bryanna. I crushed and shredded a piece of tissue in my hands as I struggled to pull myself together and finish my story of how Danny refused to give me a divorce and left me paying all the bills alone.

I shared with the jury how Danny made multiple requests for his various belongings but never once contributed to the bills. Recounting the nasty letters I received from his lawyers asking that his personal property be returned, I finished with meanest comment of all, "He even demanded half of my doll collection after taking the most precious baby doll I ever had." Afterward, the funeral expenses paid by my dad were entered as an exhibit. Although I had no bills to present to the jury, I testified to the extensive psychiatric treatment I had required off and on throughout the years just to cope with what Danny had done to us.

The judge then asked Danny if he wished to cross examine me. Surely he would not; yet he did. Was there was no end to his audacity? I looked directly from the witness stand to where he sat staring down at the papers in front of him on the table.

He muttered, never raising his eyes to me, "And how many weeks were you off for maternity leave?"

I counted them quickly in my head, and replied, "I think maybe fourteen or fifteen weeks."

He responded, "So you were off with her for the majority of her life and never noticed anything other than the clavicle and arm fractures."

"No," I declared firmly.

Eyes still averted downward, he stated, "So Bryanna was in your sole care from Memorial Day until the afternoon of her death when I watched her for only a couple of hours." He was trying to advocate his innocence by implicating me even though the judge had warned him that he was not to mention the criminal part.

Exhausted and a little snippy, I replied, glaring hard at him, "You know, I don't really remember." He had no further questions for me. I felt like I had stared down the devil himself.

He mumbled some excuse that the multiple property requests during our divorce were made without his knowledge. To the best of my memory each time my lawyer responded to his attorneys, it was always per my instructions, and I received a copy of the correspondence. I did not believe for one minute that he was not involved in all of those nasty letters that I had received.

My lawyers introduced a stack of about a half a dozen pictures of Bryanna as exhibits to the case. Some photos were made before she became ill and others after she had the splint on her arm. I sat squirming anxiously while I identified the snapshots because I was not finished. One more thing needed to be said before I stepped down.

The judge dismissed me from the witness stand, but I spoke up and said, "May I say one more thing please?" My lawyer's faces flushed with apprehension, anticipating what I might do.

With an approving nod from the judge, I began, "All of this time, he has been filling appeal after appeal to get out prison, but never once has he shown any remorse for what he did. The worst part of all is that he has never said he was sorry. I would just like to know why he did it. *Why?*" I looked toward him one last time, imploring him to apologize as I stepped down from the witness stand and resumed my seat beside my lawyers. Finally, after all of that time, I had asked the burning question—why?

Danny started rattling about filing his appeals and the case not being final. The judge asked him, "Do you have something that you want to say?" Danny rambled some more about the paperwork. "Do you want to take the witness stand?" the judge proposed. Danny rose and shuffled toward the little podium, still hunched over like an old man. My heart thudded hopefully. Could he actually be going to tell me why he did it? All I wanted to hear was "I'm sorry"—two simple words that would mean so much.

"Well as I have already said, my case is not finalized. I learned new information about six years ago which is what my appeal is based upon. Anyone in prison who can fight their case to get out will do so," he concluded clearing his throat and stepped down from the witness stand. Utter and complete devastation flooded my heart and soul. I had come today to face him and seek answers to my smoldering questions. That was what he gave me! I wanted to scream at him, but I knew that I had to remain silent. My time to speak was over. Feelings of emptiness consumed my heart knowing that he would never apologize, never admit that he did wrong, and never tell me why. Even if I won the suit, in an inexplicable way, I had lost.

Before lunch break, the judge gave the jury some brief instructions about how to award damages assuming that they found fault with Danny. He advised them that punitive damages are issued to punish the wrongdoer for being intentionally reckless and require clear evidence of guilt before they are administered. They should be granted with extreme impartiality.

After a late afternoon one-hour lunch break, court resumed with my lawyer presenting our closing argument. He somberly addressed the jury, "Ladies and gentlemen, why do babies cry? They cry because they want to be fed, changed, and loved, but mostly they cry because they want to be loved. Having a baby changes your life. There is never a good time to have a baby. If you listen to Daniel's confession you will hear that he couldn't cope with her crying. He wanted her to shut up. He knew what he was doing was wrong because he hid it, and he lied about it. He used his friendships with his family and coworkers to misdirect everyone, knowing the whole time that he was guilty. Daniel was the monster in the house. Just think for a minute about how miserable Bryanna's life was. She had multiple broken ribs. Every time she took a breath, moved, coughed, hiccupped, or was even touched, she experienced unimaginable pain. Remember Daniel's description in his confession of how her arms and legs would flail back and forth as he held her out and smothered her." At that point, my lawyer choked on his words as tears formed in his eyes. He had to take his glasses off and rub his face. There was a brief pause as he struggled for composure at the very thought of what hands that should have loved in reality did.

He continued, "Angela took her to the doctor over and over again. She had gastrointestinal studies and spinal taps, but all along her problem was sitting right over there," he said pointing to Danny. "I think that the autopsy and confession speak for themselves. I would like for you to consider compensating Angela for the possible forty-eight years that she and Bryanna did not share. At the very least, we pray that you grant funeral expenses in the amount of one thousand, seven hundred and fifty dollars. I cannot envision anything worse than what Angela has been through."

At the conclusion of his solemn speech, the judge asked Danny if he would like to present a closing argument. He declined. "As I have previously stated, the case is still not resolved, and I cannot speak to anything."

My lawyers presented the jury with an award sheet that broke the damages into seven categories. The judge instructed them on how to fill it out. They took the page and left the room at about three-thirty in the afternoon. I roamed around the lobby area with my family members while we waited. Thankfully, Danny's family stayed in the courtroom. I secretly wondered if they were hoping for just a few seconds to talk to him. After about an hour, the jury reentered with a verdict. The leader announced each single category and the amount allotted as follows.

For the mental and physical suffering of Bryanna Faith Draper as a result of the intentional actions of Daniel Draper, a total of three million dollars was awarded. In regard to the wrongful death allegations, one and a half million dollars were allotted. For the loss of consortium (our time together) another one and a half million dollars was added. Then the funeral expenses were included which brought the total compensatory award to over six million dollars, but they were not finished. A big check mark rested in the box for punitive damages. The jury left again to decide on the exact amount of punitive damages that would be granted. They were gone maybe twenty minutes. While we waited, my lawyers informed me that I had just received the largest monetary amount in a jury settlement in the history of the county. When the jury returned to the courtroom, the leader announced that they were granting me the full ten million dollars in punitive damages. The additional judgment meant that her case by far had exceeded the dollar amount of any other jury case in our county to date. Danny had faced the panel of twelve of his peers and failed dramatically. I knew that I would never collect sixteen million dollars, but I was pleased with the verdict because of the principle of the matter. A huge statement was made that day that people in our county would not tolerate Daniel's behavior at all.

As the two guards prepared to remove Danny from the courtroom, there was some discussion about how they would get him transported back to the prison on the other side of the state. The judge said that he would sign whatever was needed to send him back that very afternoon. Evidently, his presence had caused a lot of commotion in the county jail. Danny's dad stood up reaching out to Danny before he left the courtroom, but the guards would not permit them to speak. On the way out, Danny waved his arm at his dad disgusted and said, "I'll call you! I'll call you!" Only the back of his head was visible, but I could tell that he was aggravated. I did not know if he was mad about the verdict or the fact that he was not allowed to engage his family at all while he was in the courtroom.

As I watched him walk away, a sense of relief washed over me. Finally, I had faced him and no longer had to be afraid. The slamming door meant that I would never have to see him again. A perfect resolution would have been an apology followed by an explanation, but he was obviously too selfish and consumed by the desire to get out of prison for that to ever happen. My thoughts and feelings (and worst of all Bryanna's) clearly never entered his mind. Even though it was hard to accept, I know that day represented all of the closure that I would ever have. Danny's dad sent word through a friend that he "held no grudges." Perhaps earlier that morning, he had approached me with the intention of making amends, but lost his nerve at the last minute. I guess his message was the closest that I would come to receiving an apology from anyone. However, a sincere "I'm sorry" would have meant more to me than any money could have.

The sixteen million dollar judgment was truly a victory for Bryanna and abused children everywhere. Perhaps the punishment heaped upon him by the jury will make some other "monster" out there think twice before he raises his hand to an innocent child. After almost twelve long years of waiting, Bryanna had finally received justice.